GENDERED
STATES

GENDERED STATES

Feminist (Re)Visions of International Relations Theory

edited by
V. Spike Peterson

Lynne Rienner Publishers • Boulder & London

Published in the United States of America in 1992 by
Lynne Rienner Publishers, Inc.
1800 30th Street, Boulder, Colorado 80301

and in the United Kingdom by
Lynne Rienner Publishers, Inc.
3 Henrietta Street, Covent Garden, London WC2E 8LU

Library of Congress Cataloging-in-Publication Data
Gendered states : feminist (re)visions of international relations
  theory / edited by V. Spike Peterson.
  (Gender and political theory)
  Includes bibliographical references and index.
  ISBN 1-55587-298-0 (hc)
  ISBN 1-55587-328-6 (pb)
  1. International relations—Psychological aspects.
2. International relations—Social aspects. 3. Women and peace.
4. Sex role. I. Peterson, V. Spike. II. Series.
JX1391.G464 1992
327'.082—dc20   91-42673
                                                    CIP

British Cataloguing in Publication Data
A Cataloguing in Publication record for this book
is available from the British Library.

Printed and bound in the United States of America

The paper used in this publication meets the requirements
of the American National Standard for Permanence of
Paper for Printed Library Materials Z39.48-1984.

For Paula,

*with love and thanks for introducing me to
politics, enchanted forests, and global vision*

Contents

Foreword

J. Ann Tickner

In the late twentieth century, we are faced with an array of global problems, such as a highly interdependent but increasingly unstable world economy, a deteriorating ecosystem, ethnic identities that conflict with state loyalties, and the temporarily postponed threat of nuclear annihilation, all problems that the nation-state appears increasingly unable to solve, at least through unilateral action. Constructed and adapted to meet conventional military threats, today's sovereign states are not well suited to deal with these broader threats to their institutional security and to the security of their citizens and the natural environment.

Theoretical development in the discipline of international relations has also lagged behind these contemporary realities; for example, neorealist international relations theory begins with the sovereign state as a given. Some recent work in international relations has pointed out that this assumption limits inquiry and observation in at least three ways. It posits the essential similarity of states, which are actually quite different in their constitution; it reifies states as "actors," rather than exploring the politics of "state action"; and it ahistorically projects an image of the present back onto the past. Critics of neorealist theory claim that relations among states can be fully understood only when we ask how states have been constituted historically and how they are currently being sustained or transcended.

While contemporary research on the state is beginning to have an impact on the field of international relations, none of it has devoted much attention to gender. Researchers on the state have not explored the role that gendered divisions of labor and power play in the definition and maintenance of the state and its functions, nor have they examined the implications of the fact that most of the public world of the state and interstate power politics is the domain of men. If we look at gendered divisions of labor and power, we may come to agree that modern states and the contemporary interstate system depend in part on the maintenance of unequal gender relations. Such analysis will also allow us to consider the extent to which international politics would have to undergo a genuinely systemic change if hierarchical gender relations are to be eliminated.

In order to examine questions of gender, the state, and international relations, twenty-four scholars with overlapping interests in feminism, international relations, and comparative politics gathered at the Wellesley College Center for Research on Women in October 1990 for a two-day conference funded by the Ford Foundation. The participants came from fifteen colleges and universities and two research institutions across the United States and Canada.[1] The conference, "Gender and International Relations," was part of a larger project titled "The Gendered Construction of the State-Society Relationship: Its Implications for International Relations."

The central question that the conference participants were asked to consider was whether international relations theory and practice is affected, and if so how, by the gendered construction of the state-society relationship. Participants were challenged to question the implications of the fact that most of the public world of the state and its international politics has been reserved to men. They were also asked to consider the implications of the fact that public understanding of the state's nature and purpose has been shaped by men's analysis and experience.

Each participant was asked to write either a brief discussion paper or a longer paper prior to the conference, responding to these questions in light of their own research. During the conference each participant gave a brief oral presentation of her or his paper, which was then commented on and discussed by the other participants. During the conference there seemed to be an emerging consensus that future research on gender, the state, and international relations must draw more on the lived experiences of women in their various roles in hierarchically gendered societies throughout the world. Traditionally, the field of international relations has been male-centered and abstract, and has relied heavily and unconsciously on assumptions inherent in, and concepts derived from, Western experience. Participants generally felt that research on gender and the state must focus on individual experience as well as on states and the international system. Too often women's voices have been silenced by traditional theory that draws on politically powerful men's understandings as a source for comprehending and managing state behavior.

The papers in this volume were written for the Wellesley conference and revised for this book in light of two days of conference deliberations. They explore some of the themes emerging out of the conference from a variety of disciplinary and theoretical perspectives, and they represent an important step in introducing gender as a category of analysis into research on the behavior of the state in the international system.

Working as project director with the stimulating group of scholars involved in this project since its inception in 1988 has been a very rewarding experience for me. The first planners gave of their ideas and time generously, making the Wellesley conference a successful and important culminating event after a long preparatory process. The initial planning of the conference took place at a meeting of nine scholars from the Boston area at Wellesley College in October 1988.[2] Special thanks are due to Craig Murphy for hosting this planning session and to Robert Keohane and Cynthia Enloe for drafting an early grant proposal. Jean Elshtain played an important consultative role throughout the early planning stages of the project.

Participants in the 1990 conference, whose contributions have made this volume possible, also deserve special thanks. It was especially fortunate that Spike Peterson, one of the consultants for the 1990 conference who had herself organized an earlier conference on gender and international relations at the University of Southern California in 1989, agreed to the demanding task of editing this volume; it was a pleasure working with her on the conference.

I am particularly indebted to Peggy McIntosh, Associate Director of the Wellesley College Center for Research on Women and also a project consultant, who gave generously of her time and ideas throughout the entire three-year process. Her many skills were invaluable in helping to formulate the proposal and in planning and executing the conference.

I am grateful to Enid Schoettle, Stanley Heginbotham, and Alison Bernstein, all of the Ford Foundation, whose interest in the proposal resulted in the foundation's funding the conference. Thanks are due also to the Wellesley College Center for Research on Women, and its Director Susan Bailey, for providing such a congenial and supportive atmosphere. There was a sense among the participants that holding the conference at the Wellesley Center, a place where gender and women are taken seriously, allowed for an environment that permitted honest statements about difficult and challenging issues. I believe that the stimulating papers in this volume are groundbreaking contributions to the important task of incorporating gender analysis into the discipline of international relations.

Notes

1. In addition to the contributors to this volume, conference participants included Hayward Alker, Jr., M.I.T.; Richard Ashley, Arizona State University; Carol Cohn, Bunting Institute, Radcliffe College; Cynthia Enloe, Clark University; Beverley Grier, Clark University; Mary Katzenstein, Cornell University; Robert Keohane, Harvard University; Peggy McIntosh, Wellesley College Center for Research on Women; Craig Murphy, Wellesley College; Ariti Rao, Wellesley College; Theda Skoçpol, Harvard University; Ann Tickner, College of the Holy Cross; Joan Tronto, Hunter College; Celeste Wallander, Harvard University; Lois Wasserspring, Wellesley College.

2. Participants in this initial meeting were Hayward Alker, Jr.; Jean Elshtain; Cynthia Enloe; Mona Harrington; Robert Keohane; Craig Murphy; Susan Okin, then of Brandeis University, now of Stanford University; Ann Tickner; and Peggy McIntosh.

Acknowledgments

This book is possible because many people have struggled against conventional boundaries to open spaces for feminist–international relations conversations. Acknowledged here are those to whom I am personally most indebted.

I owe a special thanks to my emotional and intellectual community in Washington, D.C., where my own work on gender and states began. The continued love, support, and dancing spirit of my D.C. friends (you know who you are!) mean a great deal to me.

I thank the Center for International Studies at the University of Southern California for my year as a visiting scholar and the center's support for the first "gender and international relations" conference. At USC, I am especially grateful for the friendship and encouragement of Thomas Biersteker, Joshua Goldstein, and Steve Lamy.

In Tucson I have benefited from the sisterhood and intellectual strengths of the women's studies community. I am deeply grateful for the welcome this group extended to me and for the possibilities of cross-disciplinary scholarship and activism afforded by a community of feminist scholars.

I thank not only the contributors to this volume but all of the participants in the Wellesley conference and, especially, Ann Tickner, Peggy McIntosh, the Wellesley College Center for Research on Women, and the Ford Foundation, who made the extraordinary quality of the conference possible. I personally thank Jean Elshtain, Cynthia Enloe, Anne Runyan, Chris Sylvester, Mary Ann Tetreault, and Ann Tickner for their many contributions toward a feminist-IR community. The present volume has additionally benefited from the editorial assistance of Lynne Rienner, Judith Grant, and an anonymous reviewer. Those who generously provided feedback on my own essays are acknowledged in the relevant chapters.

I take this opportunity to thank others whose encouragement (at crucial junctures) was invaluable for sustaining my belief in and energy for building bridges between feminist and IR studies: Richard Ashley, Ted Couloumbis,

Robert Cox, Valerie French, John Garcia, Robin Hahnel, Mona Harrington, Sandra Harding, Nancy Hartsock, Marilyn Ivy, Jane Jaquette, Bob Keohane, Steve Marks, Jan Newberry, Nick Onuf, Lester Ruiz, Karen Sacks, Molly Shanley, Kathleen Staudt, Rob Walker, Alex Wendt, and Iris Young.

Finally, my greatest thanks go to family and friends whose love keeps me going. For a model of friendship, feminism, and scholarship that inspires and sustains me, I am deeply grateful to Anne Sisson Runyan. For invaluable intellectual insights and emotional support, I thank Mary Margaret Pignone and Nick Onuf. And with much love, I thank my talking and hiking partners—on several continents—who nurture my spirit and help me keep my attitude adjusted: Barb, Beryl, betts, Bill, Celia, Claudine, Eva, Holly, Jane, Kris, Michelle, Paula, Robin, Rosie, Ross, Sandy, Therese, Tom, and, especially, Mzee Ozone.

V. Spike Peterson

Introduction

V. Spike Peterson

The theory and practice of international relations have always been gendered, and . . . international economic and political institutions contain, affect and are affected by understandings of gender [note deleted].[1]

Twenty years after the emergence of feminism within the social sciences, there has begun to be some awareness within international relations of the relevance of this topic.[2]

As a student of both feminism and international relations (IR), I would amend Halliday's observation as follows: ". . . there has begun to be some awareness within IR of feminism, though little understanding of its relevance to IR." Stated simply, those who do not "see" the field as gendered also cannot "see" the significance of feminist lenses and analyses. Similarly, as long as gender is "invisible," it is unclear what "taking gender seriously" can mean. Clarification is required: What do feminists mean when we claim IR is gendered? What are the practical and theoretical implications of this claim? How do feminist lenses contribute to more accurate understanding of IR? More specifically, how does the gendered construction of the state have implications for IR theory? And how do feminist epistemologies transform IR knowledge claims?[3]

In this volume we take up the challenge of opening spaces for feminist-IR conversations. Reframing traditional constructs—states, sovereignty, political identity, security—through feminist lenses, these essays not only reveal how IR is gendered but also explore the implications of that gendering. Contributors sketch the terrain of gendered states and security, probe the constitution of identity and autonomy, examine the construction and contradictions of sovereignty, and analyze the gender dimensions of states in revolutionary transition. By taking seriously the question, What difference *does* gender make? these essays provide guides to our gendered states—

territorial states and states of mind—as well as pro-visions for traveling beyond them.

In this introductory chapter, I hope to ease our way into the conversation by reviewing and clarifying discourses pertinent to feminist considerations of states and IR. I begin with recent nonfeminist work on "the state," identifying a number of recurring themes in this literature, many aspects of which are viewed through feminist lenses in the chapters that follow. I then look at developments in feminist scholarship of particular relevance to framing the contributions in this volume. Specifically, I review the complementary "projects" of deconstruction (revealing "invisible" gender; identifying and "correcting" falsehoods generated by androcentric bias) and reconstruction (exploring theoretical implications of taking gender seriously). To clarify how feminist studies simultaneously add to and transform contemporary knowledge claims, I identify three conversations and the distinctiveness of the feminist voice in each. Having mapped this conversational background, I briefly summarize and situate the contributors' chapters.

Situating "the State" in Nonfeminist Scholarship[4]

> As economies throughout the world have developed, the public sector— what we call here the State—has grown increasingly important in every society . . . and in every aspect of society. . . . Why this occurs, and how the growing State is shaped, has become for social scientists a crucial issue—perhaps *the* crucial issue—of our times. The State appears to hold the key to economic development, to social security, to individual liberty, and through increasing weapons "sophistication," to life and death itself. To understand politics in today's world economic system, then, is to understand the national State, and to understand the national State *in the context of that system* is to understand a society's fundamental dynamic.[5]

While some bemoan the "irresolvable ambiguities surrounding the term,"[6] most agree that "the state" is "back in." Given its definitive role in constituting the field of IR, the state was never so much "out"—as references to "bringing it back in" imply—as simply taken for granted by IR theorists. As Halliday notes, "It is indeed paradoxical that a concept so central to the whole discipline should escape explication as this one has."[7] Frequently cited reasons for this "neglect" include: disciplinary divisions that naturalize rather than problematize fundamental categories; reductionist methodologies that mask interactive processes and institutions; realist/neorealist reification of the state; and political philosophies positing the state as neutral mediator of competing interest groups (liberal pluralism) or withering instrument of the ruling class (Marxism).[8] In addition, historical-empirical conditions (global economy premised upon Bretton Woods; US political and cultural hegemony) had, in the past, deflected attention from the state as a central focus of investigation.

The state is "back in" due to intellectual reorientations (greater attention to cross-disciplinary research; disillusion with behavioralism; and expansion of critical, institutional, and interpretive approaches), empirical transformations (postcolonial increase in the number and "types" of states and the state's increasing role in macroeconomic management), and political realities (declining US hegemony; the search for powerful steering mechanisms in the face of systemic crises; and the blurring of distinctions between the state and civil society divisions).[9] Neither "neutral" nor "withering," the state looms large not only "as an actor in its own right"[10] but one that is increasingly significant for understanding social relations more generally. As Skoçpol argues, "now that debates about large public sectors have taken political center stage . . . a paradigmatic shift seems to be underway in the macroscopic social sciences, a shift that involves a fundamental rethinking of the role of states in relation to economies and societies."[11]

What is the nature of this shift in thinking? While it has not signaled definitional agreement,[12] recent literature on the state exhibits a number of shared themes. First, the most striking feature of this literature, consonant with realist/neorealist depictions, is simply the "autonomy" accorded the state. Neither simply an instrument nor neutral mediator, the state is characterized as an independent actor that "may legitimately be seen as the initiator of important dynamics and as a place where interests are constituted as well as balanced."[13]

Second, while the state may *act* independently, we are warned not to exaggerate either its unity or coherence: "The various components of the state encounter the same pushes and pulls, blurring of boundaries, and possibility of domination by others that other social organizations face."[14] This depiction resonates with pluralist and decision-making perspectives in IR that acknowledge bureaucratic politics and personal perceptions in generating foreign policy. In seeking to appear unitary, state elites attempt to mask the "actual disunity of political power"[15] by controlling differentiation and rendering it as unity "within" the state. In actuality, domination is met with opposition; tension, resistance, and contradictions are as present as "smooth functioning." Recent institutional approaches illuminate conjunctures and potential disjunctures internal to states; external relations are also illumined.[16]

Thus, the third feature common to recent analyses is attention to the Janus-faced nature of states, which "stand at the intersection between domestic sociopolitical orders and the transnational relations within which they must maneuver for survival and advantage in relation to other states."[17] Current theories renegotiate the traditional disciplinary—and disciplining—dichotomy between states understood primarily in terms of internal dynamics and states understood in terms of external relations. Rather, economics, ideological movements, nationalism, militarism, and geopolitics are increasingly approached as interactive processes that must be analyzed through transdisciplinary lenses.[18]

Consistent with this attention to multiple and interactive variables is a fourth feature: characterization of the state not as a "thing" but an ongoing process. "The state is not a fixed ideological entity. Rather, it embodies an ongoing dynamic, a changing set of aims, as it engages with and disengages from other social forces."[19] Regarded as social processes, states are not static "objects" but continuing projects that must be understood in spatial, temporal, and cultural context.[20] Similarly, Keohane urges IR scholars to contextualize "specific institutions" historically and, particularly in regard to states, to examine how they are embedded in practices of sovereignty.[21]

Commitments to "taking context seriously" and attending to historical specificity surface repeatedly across disciplines.[22] For Krasner, the "historical cure" requires understanding "both how institutions reproduce themselves through time and what historical conditions gave rise to them in the first place."[23] For Keohane, to understand international institutions, "it is necessary to understand not only how specific institutions are formulated, change, and die, but how their evolution is affected by the practice of sovereignty."[24]

The proliferation of historical research on the state highlights the complex and contradictory processes at work in state formation, consolidation, and reproduction. Four related insights emerge from these historical studies. First, historical-empirical work attests to the diversity of states and their institutional structures. Though our very definitions of "stateness" impose patterns on the phenomena under examination, states reveal a range of variation that our theorizing must acknowledge and address.

A particularly striking fact emerging from these historical-empirical studies is the extent and recurrence of resistance to the centralization process. Acknowledging this resistance prompts a second insight: state making is a dialectical—rather than uniform—process.[25] Images of unilineal evolution are supplanted by notions of "open-ended," cyclical processes of force and resistance, centralization and decentralization. As is especially apparent in studies of pristine state formation, the recent scholarship on emerging "civilization" and state structures suggests that states were by no means the ready consequence of evolutionary trends.[26]

Shaped by dialectical processes, states, at whatever point in time, are vulnerable to transformation: further centralizing or decentralizing effects are possible. Thus, our study of states must acknowledge and examine practices of resistance by local, oppositional societal forms as well as take much more seriously the direct and indirect violence by which centralizing forces attempt, often successfully, to impose hierarchical state orders. The state's construction of "security" and "sovereignty" and its mobilization of militarism and nationalist ideologies are particularly significant factors in consolidating and effectively reproducing centralized authority.[27]

One model for taking context seriously can be found in large-scale historical and comparative studies that identify the dynamics of, and situate states in relationship to, larger "systems," or the macrocontext. The third insight yielded by an empirical and historical approach is, then, a recognition that our study of states and state making must attend to the position of states within, and their mutual constitution of, encompassing "systems" of political, economic, technological, and cultural *interaction*. The recent revival and expansion of interdisciplinary "world systems" research exemplifies this embedding of particular states within larger frameworks. This research identifies and investigates center-local, core-periphery relations not only in the modern era but as a dynamic of even ancient state making.[28]

The final insight highlights the importance of culture and ideology in the processes by which societies and/or states are differentiated and in the ways that centralization is legitimated and reproduced. Greater interest in these processes surfaces as economistic approaches fail to explain twentieth-century state practices and as behavioralism more generally is displaced in the study of complex social phenomena. Specifically, neither behavioralist/positivist orientations (typical of liberal pluralist research) nor economistic/productivist orientations (typical of marxist approaches) afford an adequate understanding of processes such as legitimation, hegemony, cultural resistance, or social reproduction.[29]

In contrast, recent literature examines the state's role in cultural and ideological productions that selectively shape our understanding of power and its effects. Crucial to the state's ability to rule effectively is "a *claim* to legitimacy, a means by which politically organized subjection is simultaneously accomplished and concealed."[30] These studies place in the foreground "normalizing practices,"[31] surveillance, "information storage,"[32] and routines and rituals of rule"[33] that mask the state's coercive power by effectuating rule indirectly and rendering social hierarchies "natural."

Of note here is the state's role in (re)configuring individual and collective identities, "new" histories, and "imagined communities."[34] Studies of nationalism particularly reveal these converging practices.[35] This literature examines not only what kinds of choices are made but how numerous options are rendered invisible and/or erased—how alternatives are "forgotten" and legitimations of rule "naturalized" and internalized. From this perspective, states matter "because their organizational configurations, along with their overall patterns of activity, affect political culture, encourage some kinds of group formation and collective political actions (but not others), and make possible the raising of certain political issues (but not others)."[36]

In sum, recent nonfeminist scholarship on the state, especially that of comparativists, is marked by commitments to historical, contextual, processual, interdisciplinary, and interpretive orientations. These commitments also surface repeatedly in feminist scholarship, and are visibly at work in this volume. More specifically, contributors elaborate and reframe themes and insights noted above by examining them through gender-sensitive lenses. By contrast, where neorealist accounts predominate in IR, the state continues to be "taken for granted," yielding less adequate theories of how the world we live in was made and how it is ("in reality") reproduced.

Situating Feminist Scholarship/Feminist Theory

> Most of the knowledge produced in our society has been produced by men; they have usually generated the explanations and the schemata and have then checked with each other and vouched for the accuracy and adequacy of their view of the world. They have created *men's studies* (the academic curriculum), for, by not acknowledging that they are presenting only the explanations of *men*, they have "passed off" this knowledge as human knowledge.[37]

Feminist scholarship is now enormously diverse in range and orientation, thus defying easy summary.[38] For the purposes of this volume, I undertake only a brief introduction to feminist studies. Directed toward readers less familiar with but aware of and curious about feminist claims, my discussion focuses on how feminist lenses reveal gender at work in the world and what the analytic, theoretical implications of gender bias are. In other words, I hope to clarify not only what feminists are claiming but how taking gender seriously is essential for more "accurate" (realistic) knowledge claims and, especially, emancipatory praxis.

Two complementary, interactive, and ongoing "projects" are frequently identified in feminist scholarship: the *deconstruction*[39] of gender-biased knowledge claims (revealing androcentrism in fundamental categories, in empirical studies, and in theoretical perspectives; locating "invisible" women; and incorporating women's activities, experience, and understanding into the study of humankind) and the *reconstruction* of gender-sensitive theory (rethinking fundamental relationships of knowledge, power, and community and the developing of feminist epistemologies).[40] A deconstructive mode dominated the earliest phase of feminist research as the extent and effects of androcentrism were revealed. Across disciplines, feminist scholars exposed the omission of actual women and their activities while documenting mainstream constructions of abstract "woman" as deviant from or deficient in respect to male-as-norm criteria. As Spender notes: "While men have checked only with men, it has been almost inevitable that women should be encoded as an absence or a deficiency."[41]

The assumption of men's (more specifically, elite men's) experience as representative of *human* experience emerged as a systemic bias of codified knowledge and cultural ideologies. Deconstructing the errors of androcentric scholarship revealed—and continues to reveal—patterned distortion of truth claims about "social reality."

> Women's experience systematically differs from the male experience upon which knowledge claims have been grounded. Thus the experience on which the prevailing claims to social and natural knowledge are founded is, first of all, only partial human experience only partially understood: namely, masculine experience as understood by men. However, when this experience is presumed to be gender-free—when the male experience is taken to be the human experience—the resulting theories, concepts, methodologies, inquiry goals and knowledge-claims distort human social life and human thought.[42]

Attempts to rectify this systematic exclusion of women constitute a second "moment" in the deconstructive project: correcting androcentric falsehoods by adding women and their experience to existing frameworks. This inclusion of women significantly expands the range of knowledge by "asking new questions and generating new data."[43] Focusing on women's lives entails considering new sources and re-evaluating the selectivity of traditional ones; diaries, quilt making, caretaking, domestic activities, and everyday practices more generally take on new significance.

Documenting ubiquitous androcentrism and its occlusion of gender hierarchy tends to render women as victims—as relatively powerless within male-dominated systems. In contrast, "adding women" disrupts existing frameworks as the mapping of "female worlds"[44] reveals the significance both of women's experience and of women themselves as actors in accommodation with and resistance to structures of domination. No longer "invisible," everyday practices and women's activities—especially when differentiated by class, ethnicity, nationality, age, sexual orientation, or physical ability—illuminate the complexity and contradictions attending gender and other social hierarchies.

In particular, feminist scholarship has documented gender coding in a recurring litany of Western dualisms.[45] Asymmetrical dichotomies—such as public-private, culture-nature, rational-irrational, order-anarchy, mind-body, and objective-subjective—implicitly, and sometimes explicitly, map on to or are derived from a fundamental Western construction of masculine over feminine. Re-cognizing these foundational dualisms as both gendered and hierarchical raises new questions about how power, knowledge, politics, and gender are related: What is "significant" about male-female differences? How did gender hierarchy originate? Is the public-private dichotomy universal? To what does it refer? How are the politics of identity and difference related to the politics of knowledge? What is the nature of dichotomies and how do they shape social relations of domination? How does recognizing women's diversity affect feminism(s)? How do hierarchies of "difference" (e.g., gender, race, class, sexual orientation) interact?

In general, the deconstructive project documents the extent and tenacity of androcentric bias and the cultural codification of men as "knowers." It reveals women's exclusion from or trivialization within masculinist accounts and, especially, women's "absence" there as agents of social change. But even more significant, "adding women" to existing frameworks exposes taken-for-granted assumptions embedded in those frameworks. Across disciplines, feminists dis-cover the contradictions of "adding woman" to constructions that are literally defined by their "man-ness": the public sphere, rationality, economic power, autonomy, political identity, objectivity. The systematic inclusion of women—our bodies, activities, knowledge— challenges categorical givens, disciplinary divisions, and theoretical frameworks.

> It became increasingly clear that it was not possible simply to include women in those theories where they had previously been excluded, for this exclusion forms a fundamental structuring principle and key presumption of patriarchal discourse.
> It was not simply the range and scope of objects that required transformation: more profoundly, and threateningly, the very questions posed and the methods used to answer them . . . needed to be seriously questioned. The political, ontological and epistemological commitments underlying patriarchal discourses, as well as their theoretical contents required re-evaluation.[46]

The *reconstructive* project marks the shift "from recovering ourselves to critically examining the world from the perspective of this recovery . . . a move from margin to center."[47] Not simply seeking access to and participating within (but from the margins of) androcentric paradigms, feminist reconstruction explores the theoretical implications of revealing systemic masculinist bias and systematically adding women. Not surprisingly, the shift from "women as knowable" to "women as knowers" locates feminism at the heart of contemporary debates over what constitutes science and the power of "claims to know." This is difficult terrain to map, so I start from a vantage point that I hope is reasonably familiar.

Key to the feminist reconstructive project is the relational concept of *gender*: the socially constructed dichotomy of masculine-feminine (man-woman, maleness-femaleness) shaped only in part by biologically construed male-female distinctions.[48] What renders this concept systemic and transformative is the feminist claim that "all of social life is gendered."[49] As Harding notes:

> Once we begin to theorize gender—to define gender as an analytic category within which humans think about and organize their social activity rather than a natural consequence of sex difference, or even merely as a social variable assigned to individual people in different ways from culture to culture—we can begin to appreciate the extent to

which gender meanings have suffused our belief systems, institutions, and even such apparently gender-free phenomena as our architecture and urban planning.[50]

Feminist scholarship, both deconstructive and reconstructive, takes seriously the following two insights: first, that gender is socially constructed, producing subjective identities through which we see and know the world; and, second, that the world is pervasively shaped by gendered meanings. That is, we do not experience or "know" the world as abstract "humans" but as embodied, gendered beings. As long as that is the case, accurate understanding of agents—as knowable and as knowers— requires attention to the effects of our "gendered states." For example, ". . . if gender patterns who we are, it also patterns how we think, and our views of science cannot escape this."[51] Thus, knowledge claims are transformed by recognizing gender as "an independent analytical category"[52] and gender hierarchy as a system that is not reducible to some other form.[53]

Distinguishing sex as biology from gender as social construction expands feminist analyses in a number of significant and interrelated ways. First, gender decenters biologistic explanations that have effectively disabled our understanding of *social* relations. Rather than a choice between nature *or* culture, the concept of gender enables us to examine meanings imposed on the body, to understand how women (and men) "are made not born." In this sense, the concept of gender resonates with other contemporary critiques of ahistorical, essentialist frameworks and emphasizes instead that our construction as feminine and masculine is an ongoing, complex, and often contradictory *process* that must be studied as such.

Second, gender refocuses our understanding of how the terms of man-woman and masculine-feminine are related. Rather than categorically separate, independent categories, the terms are mutually constituted and interdependent: they presuppose each other. The appropriate metaphor is not "A and B" or "A1 and A2" but "A and not A." "Man," "masculinity," and "male worlds" are literally defined by their exclusion of (and disdain for) that which constitutes "woman," "femininity," and "female worlds." This has systemic implications for evaluating androcentric knowledge claims since the "zero sum" construction of A–not A, man-woman, and masculine-feminine suggests that "A" (man) cannot be fully understood without knowledge and understanding of "not A" (woman) *and vice versa*.[54] In contrast to examining women or "the feminine" in isolation, gender focuses our attention on the interdependence of masculine and feminine. Thus, women's studies is not peripheral to but transformative of men's studies; it is not simply "about women" but about how masculine constructions (e.g., science, states, realism) *depend upon* maintaining feminine ones (and vice versa).

Third, attending to context in order to examine systems of interaction displaces essentialist, atemporal renderings in favor of multiple empirical and historical analyses. "Because gender is relational rather than essential, structural rather than individual, analyzing gender requires consideration of changes in systems over time."[55] Moreover, recognizing gender simultaneously as structural and as a component of individual identity prompts attention to the interaction of macro and micro "structures" without privileging one at the expense of the other. Feminist scholarship thus attends to the subjective and everyday while relating these to the historical and structural relations within which specific data or studies are situated.

Fourth, gender as a social construction can be examined from diverse perspectives and with attention to multiple dimensions. Questions addressing interactive processes become central: How are gender identities constituted and re-enforced? What distinguishes cultures that identify more than two genders? Whose interests are served by "naturalizing" (de-politicizing) gendered dichotomies? Are heterosexual relations more accurately understood as erotic, contractual, or exploitative? How do symbols, language, art, and technology interact in constructing "the feminine"? How is the international division of labor and resources also gendered? To what extent does militarism (or instrumentalism, classism, imperialism, monotheism, racism, capitalism, ageism) depend upon masculinism? How are ways of being and ways of knowing related? And how do they affect the politics—the power relations—of claims to "know"?

These questions suggest how far we have come from asking, Where are the famous women? They go, as feminist scholarship has, to the heart of contemporary debates about the status of ontological and epistemological claims and the politics thereof. In many unanticipated ways, "adding women" exposes the constructed nature of "to what?" and disrupts many of the previously unquestioned foundations of Western discourse and its knowledge claims. Even science—most significantly—is not sacrosanct.

Feminist critiques of science and the development of specifically feminist epistemologies now comprise an extensive and sophisticated literature.[56] Of course, feminists are not alone in challenging conventional positivist-empiricist accounts of science and the notions of rationality, objectivity, and value-free method that they privilege. Necessarily embedded in historical context, feminist theorizing both shapes and is shaped by cross-disciplinary debates on the nature of science and claims to know. The contours of these debates are now familiar and will not be reviewed here. What is less familiar, and central to this volume, is how feminist reconstructions are similar to and different from other critiques of science and of its instrumentalist dynamics: that is, what do they add to and how do they transform nonfeminist orientations?

Situating Feminist Critiques and Contributions

To situate feminist critiques and contributions, I identify three ongoing conversations—all concentrating on knowledge and its politics but differentiated by epistemological and critical commitments. These are conversations in which feminist theorists participate along with others, including IR theorists, and to which feminists add a distinctive voice. It is the distinctiveness of the feminist voice—the "difference that gender makes"—that I hope to clarify here.

The focus of the first conversation is the empirical adequacy of knowledge claims. "What counts as knowledge must be grounded on experience. Human experience differs according to the kinds of activities and social relations in which humans engage."[57] Not only feminists, but theorists of other marginalized groups—e.g., colonized populations, racial and ethnic minorities, the underclass—argue that knowledge claims about humans that are based upon only the partial experience of elites are simply inaccurate: they in fact distort our understanding of actual social relations. This conversation resonates primarily with the commitments of feminist "deconstruction" as articulated above: revealing the exclusion and trivialization of women's ways of being and knowing and insisting that women's lives be "taken seriously" in constructing knowledge claims about social reality.

The distinctiveness of the feminist voice in this conversation is fairly straightforward: it is *women's* bodies, activities, and knowing that must be included if we are to accurately understand human life and social relations. For example, including women "corrects"—by rendering them less partial and less distorted—our conventional understandings of political economy and social reproduction. As Aristotle recognized, "women's work" in the domestic sphere is not peripheral to but a necessary condition of "men's work" in the public sphere. The work of contemporary Western women includes not only child care and the physical maintenance of the household but caring for the ill and elderly, sustaining familial communications, transforming resources into services that meet human needs, mediating between public agencies and family demands, and servicing males personally, sexually, and emotionally.[58]

The characterization of women's work as "servicing" applies to paid as well as unpaid labor: "Not only are women the majority of workers in the service sector, they also do 'servicing' [emotional caretaking, appearing submissive, working overtime and without benefits] when they are employed in other sectors."[59] In the global economy, women also do the "servicing" work: as fuel, food, and water suppliers in developing countries, as "docile" and dexterous assemblers in offshore industries, as part-time and nonunionized labor in industrialized countries, as sources of emotional and sexual gratification in tourist enterprises, and as caretakers and crisis mediators worldwide.[60] Women's production, reproduction, and "servicing" are essential components of the world we live in. We do not accurately understand how that world is "made," nor how it "works," when we ignore the work that women do.

The focus of the second conversation shifts toward epistemological issues. Here postpositivist feminists share with other antifoundationalists (ethnomethodologists, phenomenologists, poststructuralists, interpretivists, postmodernists) a critique of the positivist model of science.[61] These theorists specifically reject simplistic notions of objectivity, rationality, and the neutrality of method(s). Rather, they emphasize "the ways in which science is a human activity and, as such, reflect[s] the ways in which particular activities are defined, understood, given meaning, and evaluated by the particular society."[62] Thus, objectivity, understood as a "perspectiveless gaze," is impossible in a socially constructed world; rationality is not transcendental but historically specific, learned activity; and methods are necessarily contextual, and therefore shaped by culture and particular values.

Feminists bring to this conversation the insights of the reconstruction project: the theoretical implications of "taking gender seriously." Here the distinctiveness of the feminist voice consists in extending antifoundational critiques by identifying objectivity, rationalism, and even science itself as specifically male/masculine ways of knowing (derived from male ways of being under patriarchal relations). That is, feminists locate masculinism at the "roots of Western epistemology, even Western culture itself" and argue that "the fundamental dichotomies . . ." between subject-object, rational-irrational, culture-nature, and reason-emotion are all derived from the male/masculine-female/feminine ". . . hierarchy that is central to patriarchal thought and society."[63]

Arguments in support of characterizing "Western philosophy as male" take a variety of (not mutually exclusive) forms. One argument is that Western philosophy as practice has been monopolized by elite males; as subject matter it has construed "men's nature" as human nature and focused on "men's" public-sphere concerns (politics, justice, universal truth); and as an institution it has reproduced the authority and legitimation of patriarchal experience and world view.[64]

Another argument is provided by feminist object relations theory (an adaptation of psychoanalytic theory), which explicates the development and institutionalization of dichotomized masculine (objectifying and autonomous) and feminine (empathizing and relational) identities and cognitive styles.[65] Science is "genderized" through "a network of interactions between gender development, a belief system that equates objectivity with masculinity, and a set of cultural values that simultaneously (and conjointly) elevates what is defined as scientific and what is defined as masculine."[66]

Additionally, some French feminists draw upon Lacanian psychoanalysis to argue that the phallocentrism of the Western symbolic order privileges masculine qualities of "unity, stability, identity, and self-mastery" over and at the expense of feminine forms of "body, spontaneity, multiplicity, loss of self."[67] Finally, feminists draw upon the work of Derrida to argue that the binary logic of Western metaphysics generates asymmetrical oppositions as philosophy's characteristic form.[68] Following Mies,[69] I refer to these as "colonizing dualisms" wherein the first (colonizing) term is assumed to be prior and superior to the second term, the latter perceived as threatening the values that the first asserts.[70] As in the dichotomies noted above, the "positivity" of the first term is identified with masculinity/man/"self" and the "negativity" of the second with femininity/woman/"other."

In general then, what feminists contribute to the second conversation, about epistemological issues, is an insistence that gender hierarchy is not coincidental to but in a significant sense constitutive of Western philosophy's objectivist metaphysics. Modernity's expression of that metaphysics, positivist science, (re)inscribes the identification of masculinity—as objectivity, reason, freedom, transcendence, and control—against femininity—as subjectivity, feeling, necessity, contingency, and disorder. Women are thus excluded from the authority of knowing, and from authority more generally, by the exclusion of "woman" from privileged rationality (objectivity, transcendence, autonomy). Construed as irrational, "woman" is virtually "not fully human. She is, rather, the passive object of man's active, transforming knowledge."[71]

The distinctiveness of the feminist contribution has specific and significant implications for those participating in, or listening to, this second conversation. First, to the extent that masculinity remains privileged and positivism is identified with masculinity, all critics of positivism meet resistance not only to their argumentation per se but to the "demasculinization" of science their argument entails. Second, to the extent that objectivist metaphysics constitutes, and is constituted by, the colonizing dualism of masculine-feminine (as these feminists claim), moving beyond objectivism/positivism requires moving beyond essentialized gender identities as well.[72] In other words, taking postpositivism/postmodernism seriously demands taking seriously as well the feminist analysis of gender "as an outcome of social processes of subordination";[73] failure to do so leaves essentializing objectivism—and its distortions—in place.

In the third conversation, participants address empirical and theoretical concerns in varying proportions; what they share are critiques of modernity's interlocking systems of domination. Here, Frankfurt-vintage "critical theorists," ecologists, neomarxists, world system theorists, peace proponents, and social change activists speak of moving toward a more just, less terrifying world. They explore multiple contradictions and contemporary crises—of technical rationality, accumulation, legitimation, ecological deterioration, the welfare state. Their work specifically criticizes processes of objectification—variously imposed by industrial capitalism, scientization, militarism, and bureaucratization—that render people and nature "objects" whose manipulation and/or exploitation is taken for granted. Thus, the focus is not only domination practices but how they are legitimated, reproduced, and institutionalized by rendering them "natural," and therefore not political.

Sharing the concerns of the conversational group, feminists in this case have distinctively contributed historical, empirical, and analytical evidence that gender hierarchy is fundamental to domination in its many guises.[74] I am arguing, first, that females suffer disproportionately under systems of domination because females constitute at least one-half of most (though not all) subordinated groups and are systematically rendered more vulnerable to sexual violence, other forms of violence, inadequate health care, political subordination, and economic impoverishment.[75] Second, the naturalization of women's oppression—taking male supremacy as "given" rather than as historically, politically constructed—serves as the model for depoliticizing exploitation (of other groups or nature) more generally. As a historical matter, early state formation marked the effective centralization of political authority and accumulation processes, institutionalization of gender and class exploitation, and ideological legitimation of these transformations. At least since Aristotle, the codification of man as "master" and woman as "matter" has powerfully naturalized/de-politicized man's exploitation of women, other men, and nature.[76]

For example, Lerner argues that the appropriation of women's double labor (productive and reproductive) provided the model of subordination and exploitation that subsequently legitimated institutionalized slavery in early states. Similarly, Mies argues that hierarchical divisions of labor "which have developed throughout history . . . [up to today's unequal system of global capitalism] . . . are based on the social paradigm of the predatory hunter/warrior who, without himself producing, is able by means of arms to appropriate and subordinate other producers, their productive forces and their products."[77] Perhaps most familiarly, feminists have exposed the politics of defining "natural resources" as "there for the taking": no permission required, no obligations incurred. Thus defined in the modern era, women's labor and bodies, the earth, and native peoples become "objects" under the control, possession, and sometimes "protection" of scientific, governmental, and military elites.[78]

The mutually interactive projects characteristic of modernity—the making of states, science, militarism, and industrial capitalism—share an instrumentalist dynamic roundly criticized by the participants in this conversation. Feminists argue that all of these projects—and instrumentalism itself—are profoundly gendered and that this gendering has implications for the tasks of effectively criticizing and transforming the social relations constituted by instrumentalism. Nonfeminist analyses of these relations necessarily remain partial and, to that extent, less effective: neorealist theories of the state and neomarxist theories of "civil society" leave the patriarchal foundations of the state in place; critics of structural violence disregard male violence against women and the alternative models of community generated by feminisms; anti-militarists overlook the role of masculine identity in effectuating and legitimating war; and ecologists hesitate to draw parallels between the domination of nature and the domination of women, thereby failing to challenge the exploitative world view at its roots.

Feminists argue that domination—of woman/women, nature, and all who are constructed as "other"—is not a consequence of "essential," atemporal qualities but must be understood in the context of socially constructed, historically contingent practices. Perhaps most significant for critical discourses is the feminist deconstruction, in the Derridean, poststructuralist sense, of domination as natural or as the inescapable consequence of marking "difference." Eliminating the justification of oppression (as "natural") does not eliminate oppression, nor preclude other justifications of it. But, in today's world(s), the hegemonic ideology of "domination as natural" serves powerfully to legitimate and reproduce social hierarchies, through the internalization of oppression, the silencing of protest, and the de-politicization of exploitative rule. Thus, feminist critiques of "naturalized" subjection offer rich resources for (re)visioning, resisting, and transforming social relations.

This is emphatically not to posit a feminist "conflict-free" utopia, nor to argue that feminist critiques necessarily take precedence over other emancipatory discourses, or that gender hierarchy is always the most salient dimension of oppressive dynamics. It is to argue that feminist voices offer alternative visions, and that gender domination is not reducible to some other form of oppression. Liberation movements, therefore, must also be *women's* liberation movements. Moreover, while not always the most salient form of domination, gender is rarely lacking as a dimension of oppressive relations. Thus, "taking it seriously" improves our critical understanding and possibilities for change. In sum, we do not effectively contest objectification if, by ignoring gender, we leave the objectification of "woman, native, other"[79] in place.

From the vantage point of feminist critiques, these conversations might be characterized as follows. The first conversation presupposes (elite) male experience as the "human" norm and thus naturalizes essentialist (and elitist) androcentrism. The second conversation presupposes masculinity as disembodied qualities of rationality, abstraction, and objectivity; here, masculinist transcendence is naturalized. The third conversation problematizes particular forms of domination but not the gendered foundations of instrumentalism and "power over," thus leaving gendered objectification and masculinist control "natural." As indicated above, feminist voices "add to" and transform each conversation by revealing and "correcting" its gendered selectivity and consequences. By reference, then, to these three conversations, feminism is empirically, epistemologically, and politically/normatively relevant.

Opening Feminist-IR Conversational Spaces

Of course, feminist and IR scholars engage independently and variously in these, and many other, conversations. In this volume, contributors seek and explore specifically "feminist-IR" conversational openings. The metaphor of "conversations" and reference to "openings" are very much to the point: I want to emphasize the processual, interactive dynamics and fluid boundaries of conversations, as well as the exploratory nature of shifting perspectives and gaining new vistas. Two objectives of this section are to identify ongoing feminist-IR conversations in relation to essays in this book (following from the three conversations sketched above) and to elaborate additional contributions of feminist scholarship—in particular, how "adding women" transforms fundamental categories and, therefore, theory; and how the epistemological shift to postpositivism need not be atheoretical or apolitical. The latter contributions emerge from recognition of the interdependence of the three conversations; that is, feminism not only contributes a unique voice to each conversation but confirms the connections between them in ways that additionally illuminate the workings of our world(s).

To the extent that IR theorists and other scholars engage primarily in empirical research and analyses, adding women's activities and perspectives generates more comprehensive and accurate knowledge claims. In Halliday's terms, IR theorists might fruitfully explore how gender issues and values affect international relations and how international processes—military, economic, political, and ideological—have gender-specific consequences.[80] In terms of empirical adequacy, the inclusion of women, their activities, and their ways of knowing generates more "scientific" knowledge claims: "surpass[ing] androcentric accounts because in their systematicity more is examined and less is assumed."[81]

The United Nations Decade for Women greatly increased awareness of and systematic research on global gender dynamics. The "women in development" literature is probably the most familiar gender-sensitive research, but a variety of feminist-IR conversations are increasingly visible: for example, women's rights as a dimension of international human rights discourse;[82] the history and contemporary relevance of women's peace and ecological activism;[83] research on "women and politics" in terms of women's political activities within the state, independent of the state, and transnationally;[84] and the role of gender in militaries, nationalism, foreign policy, and international politics broadly construed.[85]

To the extent that feminist scholarship is gender-sensitive, it necessarily participates in and contributes to the rectification of androcentric (male-as-norm) knowledge claims. In this sense, all feminist scholarship—and all contributions to this volume—variously engage in "adding women." At the same time, we can distinguish degrees of emphasis on specifically policy-oriented, historical, empirical, and/or theoretical treatments. In this volume, for instance, Tetreault adds the dimensions of family structure and women's roles to analyses of revolutionary movements and proceeds to outline an analytical framework. Grant describes women's traditional relationship to the symbols and practices of war and security, then explores the implications of women's increased presence in the military establishment of Western nations. Sylvester presents examples of women's concrete struggles in order to demonstrate their disruption of conventional IR givens. And through a historical-empirical lens, Peterson examines gender dynamics in state formation in order to specify women's structural in/security.

Like feminist scholarship in other disciplines, "adding women" to IR reveals how international politics is, in fact, systemically gendered and suggests how approaches that take gender seriously reconfigure fundamental categories and disciplinary "givens." In other words, in a world structured pervasively by gender hierarchy, adding women empirically often entails transforming categories themselves; as fundamental categories are reconfigured, so are the frameworks—the theories—in which categories are embedded. As noted earlier, this demonstration of the interdependence of empirical and theoretical claims, which bridges the first and second conversations, is an additional contribution of feminist scholarship (though not exclusive to it).

For example, as the earlier discussion of feminist deconstruction and reconstruction revealed, what appears at first to be simply "adding women" (an empirical gesture) turns out to be more complicated. To the extent that "adding women" means adding "that which constitutes femininity" to categories constituted by their masculinity (the exclusion of femininity), a contradiction is exposed. Either women as feminine cannot be added (i.e., women must become men) *or the category must be transformed* to accommodate the inclusion of women (as feminine). The (masculine) gender of the original category (for example, the assumption of masculine experience in conventional constructions of the public, political identity, and politics per se) is exposed. Because the categories of masculine and feminine are mutually constituted, a new category accommodating women/feminine necessarily reconfigures the gendered meaning of the original category— including the construction of masculinity it presupposed. Therefore, not only is understanding of the public sphere and politics transformed, but (to the extent that masculinity is constituted by political activity, political identity, etc.) the *meaning of masculinity is also altered.*

Thus, the boundary between empirical-theoretical (practice-theory, fact-framework) is problematized by the shift from adding "sex as a variable" to

understanding gender as an analytic category. Because empirical-theoretical—
like the categories masculine-feminine, mind-body, and subject-object—are
mutually defined (presuppose each other), transforming one necessarily
transforms not only the other but the boundary between them. That is, rather
than essential (therefore categorically "separable") categories, the terms of
dichotomies are relational and their meaning embedded in historically specific
contexts. As the project of "adding women" to politics demonstrates,
reconfiguring "empirical" categories involves theoretical revision: shifting
boundaries between terms, their relationship to explanatory frameworks, and
therefore the frameworks themselves.

Drawing upon the resources of feminist reconstruction more generally,
feminist-IR conversations that reframe conventional categories and "givens"
figure prominently in this collection. For example, "security" is refocused
through Grant's examination of women in the military, through Peterson's
feminist lens on state systems, and through Harrington's critique of power
that is socially unaccountable—i.e., not based in the state. Autonomy, and
its twin, sovereignty, are recast by Sylvester's comparison of feminist and IR
constructions; Elshtain re-views sovereignty as indivisible power and
"masculinized deity"; and Runyan links it to imperatives toward "control
over." The meaning of political community figures prominently here: in
Tetreault's analysis of revolutionary movements; in Walker's interrogation of
the discourse of sovereignty; in Runyan's depiction of unity and harmony as
an Enlightenment objective; and in Elshtain's genealogy of self and nation
identification. Political identity is also reconfigured: Peterson's analysis of
state making reveals political identity as gendered and elitist; Walker relates
political identity to an account of the sovereign subject; Elshtain considers
its essential role in marking "home"; and Grant reframes its relation to
masculinity and citizenship. Many other fundamental constructs—for
example, nationalism, realism, authority, liberalism, citizenship, and
protection—are (re)visioned in this collection and in many of the works cited
here.

Finally, postpositivist feminists not only theorize (as other
postpositivists do) the interdependence of categories and frameworks but
expose the gender *politics* of categorizing practices. For example, feminist
critiques of the public-private dichotomy reveal not only the masculinism
presupposed in these constructs, and women's exclusion from the public
realm (political identity, public sphere activities, and "politics" per se),
but the power/politics of defining—in other words, "bounding"—public
and private. Defining family dynamics, sexuality, domestic work,
childrearing, and social reproduction generally as "private" *de-politicizes*
them, leaving in place the structural inequality and power relations they
currently entail.

My earlier sketch of the third conversation suggested two distinctive
contributions of the feminist voice: revealing the gender-specific dimensions

of domination systems and revealing the legitimation of objectification in general as an extension of masculine domination in particular. Essays in this volume exemplify both dimensions. Harrington specifies the particular vulnerability of women to transnational economic power and bureaucratic decisionmaking. Runyan recalls the interactive objectification of women, "nature," and people of color as the new "order" of Enlightenment was imposed and legitimated. Tetreault analyzes the "forgetting" of women's revolutionary contributions and demands as centralized authority is reconsolidated, and *systemic* transformation postponed. Peterson examines gender-specific consequences of interacting (and sometimes contradictory) systems of domination and their (re)production of gendered identities and ideologies.

Before turning to the chapter summaries, I would like to clarify one of the contributions of the feminist perspective that I identified at the beginning of this section but did not explore in detail: i.e., that the epistemological shift to postpositivism need not be atheoretical or apolitical. There are many complex issues here, not the least being the widely varying use of terms that are themselves difficult to grasp. For instance, I have grouped under postpositivism, no doubt too readily, a variety of distinctive epistemological and ontological orientations (note 60). For me, the crucial point of the "post-move" (whether characterized as postpositivism, postmodernism, poststructuralism, antifoundationalism, genealogy, or the interpretive turn) is its rejection of *transcendental* (decontextualized) criteria for assessing epistemological, ontological, and/or normative claims and therefore the *necessity* of taking responsibility for the world(s) we make—including the criteria we construct for assessing epistemological, ontological, and normative claims.[86]

I am indeed arguing here that the post-move problematizes conventional accounts of objectivity, by denying a single, ahistorical standard, and politicizes "claims to know"—in the specific sense of bringing to conscious awareness their "contingent rather than inevitable" status.[87] Through this lens, knowledge and power cannot be categorically separated, because knowledge claims are necessarily embedded in social relations and their power dynamics. I am also arguing, however, that recognition of this embeddedness does not *entail* either nihilism or "absolute relativism," in the sense of "anything goes" and/or that "criticism itself must be local, *ad hoc*, and nontheoretical."[88] It appears to be the continuing hold of objectivist/positivist dichotomizing that casts the denial of a single, atemporal order as necessitating the denial of all orders/ordering. With others (note 60), I argue that systematic inquiry and comparative evaluation of intellectual and normative claims are not precluded by the post-move—*but they must be contextualized.*

As a move in that direction, I suggest understanding claims to rationality as claims to *consistency*. The latter immediately directs our attention to context: consistent with what? compared to what? Many theorists acknowledge that comparison is implicit in making knowledge claims; the post-move makes this explicit and insists that we contextualize. Moreover, explicitly asking "compared to what?" reminds us that our "choices" (of constructs, questions, theories, objectives, visions) are never independent of but always embedded in historically contingent social relations: they are never "neutral" but always complex "trade-offs," and what we trade off has both intended and unintended consequences. These consequences are political to whatever extent power differentials are affected.[89]

I believe that the misleading identification of postpositivism with the denial of all "ordering" principles contributes significantly to an exaggerated disavowal of postpositivism. Theorists committed to systematic inquiry and/or political change may be rejecting the post-move because of a mistaken understanding of its implications. I make these points in order to suggest the value of specifically postpositivist feminist approaches.[90] Feminists are by definition and determination critical of status quo social relations and committed to political transformation: feminists insist on *situating* knowledge claims in order to "become answerable for what we learn how to see."[91] In contrast to the "apoliticism" and/or "theoretical anarchism" postpositivists are—often falsely—accused of, the critical commitments of feminists compel us to take the relationship between reason and power, knowledge and domination, seriously. Postpositivist feminist scholarship therefore speaks directly to the concerns of those who resist the post-move out of the belief that it denies the pursuit of systematic inquiry and/or the possibility of locating "grounds" for critical action. Like conventional science (and all "movements"), postpositivism contains both progressive and regressive tendencies:

> It is a challenge for feminism and other contemporary countercultures of science to figure out just which are the regressive and which the progressive tendencies brought into play in any particular scientific or feminist project, and how to advance the progressive and inhibit the regressive ones. The countercultures of science must elicit and address these contradictory elements in the sciences and scientific consciousness (and feminists must continue to do so with their various feminisms). The alternative is that regressive forces in the larger society manipulate these contradictory features and mobilize the progressive tendencies for their own ends.[92]

As argued here, feminism is not just "about women," nor the addition of women to male-stream constructions; it is about transforming ways of being and knowing. In sum, I have argued that a feminist orientation is valuable in multiple ways: for increasing empirical accuracy and adequacy, for demonstrating the interdependence of dichotomized constructs (e.g., empirical-theoretical), for revealing masculinist bias in epistemological as well as empirical constructs, for bridging postpositivist and political, critical approaches, and for denaturalizing objectification dynamics, thus enabling alternative visions.

Situating and Summarizing the Chapters

The gendered state presupposed in international relations is the focal point of this volume; gendered security, sovereignty, and political identity are themes connecting all of the essays. Appropriately, contributors share points of departure but are diverse in their consideration and exploration of new conversational spaces. As arranged here, the chapters move from feminist treatments of the state more directly to feminist critiques of IR more generally. The first two chapters concentrate most specifically on feminist analyses of the state as a set of institutions and practices with identifiable, gender-differentiated consequences.

In "Security and Sovereign States: What Is at Stake in Taking Feminism Seriously?" Peterson explores contemporary meanings of in/security, and possibilities for "world security," through a postpositivist feminist lens on states and their interactive structural dynamics. Historical examination of early, Athenian, and modern (European) state formation reveals gendered patterns in the interlocking imperatives of state making: the centralization of political authority, accumulation, militarism, exploitation, and legitimation. In the modern era, objectivist science, masculinism, and liberal capitalism converge in mystifying the structural violence constituted by sovereign state systems; yet their sometimes contradictory trajectories can yield transformational opportunities. New spaces for rethinking world security are explored in a final discussion of protection rackets, structural dependency, and protector-protected identities.

Approaching the state from a different vantage point, Mona Harrington insists that we ask, as the title of her chapter does: "What Exactly Is Wrong with the Liberal State as an Agent of Feminist Change?" Within a global order still premised upon capitalism, Harrington outlines the hazards—especially to those most structurally vulnerable—of prematurely rejecting liberal states as the most effective democratizing power in the face of socially unaccountable international economic forces. It is not "chill-hearted contractarianism" but *social* liberalism and its historical actualization in social democracy and welfare states that Harrington promotes. Because state-based, legislative power is more socially responsible than executive/bureaucratic power based in international organizations or elites, Harrington urges us to resist further shifts from national to international regulation. Holding on to state authority "as the most progressive move possible," Harrington outlines a *re-formed* feminist liberal nation as a means by which the dispossessed can secure structurally necessary protection and gain politically effective voices.

Exploring the gender relations of states through a lens on military and revolutionary activities, the next two chapters offer additional insights on security and possibilities for system transformation. At the beginning of "The Quagmire of Gender and International Security," Rebecca Grant notes that feminist enquiry must take the experience of women as its starting point. She goes on to problematize this observation by reference to recent increases in women's participation in the military. The traditional focus of international relations on war and security has constrained the discipline's interest in and ability to analyze gender issues, since the historical nexus of manhood, citizenship, and military activity renders war and security exclusively masculine domains. Grant explores the implications of increasing participation of women in the military establishment: if women are no longer excluded from the security apparatus of the state, can their experience in the military offer an alternative understanding of international security? She concludes that the gap between women's experience within masculinist/male-dominated institutions (e.g., war activities) and women's conventional experience of "security" (e.g., caretaking activities) problematizes any ready construction of an alternative epistemology based upon "women's" experience. Rather, "there is a need to judge and select," even within a feminist perspective.

In "Women and Revolution: A Framework for Analysis," Mary Ann Tetreault addresses the need for research agendas. As background to her argument, Tetreault reviews the nonfeminist literature on revolutions and Western accounts of the relationship of family and society/state. Drawing upon—and attempting a synthesis of—both structural and cultural approaches, Tetreault considers "gender as class" and "family as structure" in order to develop a framework for analyzing the interaction of women, family forms, and revolutionary movements. The relationship between revolutionary movements and successful system transformation depends not only on shifts in political and economic power but their congruence with cultural and ideological changes. Families, as fundamental sites of socialization and cultural re/production, are key to analyzing sources and outcomes of revolutionary movements. The framework that Tetreault develops for analyzing "women and revolution" does not simply "add women" but (re)visions our normative and analytic understanding of the relationships among gender, families, states, and revolutionary change. This transformational aspect is elaborated in Tetreault's discussion of "what we can learn by studying women and revolution."

The remaining essays explore the masculine gender identity of sovereign man/sovereign state. Variously construed and/or manifested as authority, autonomy, sovereignty, or political identity, state power is revealed as masculinist—with multiple implications for developing feminist analyses and realizable alternatives. Anne Sisson Runyan's chapter, "The 'State' of Nature: A Garden Unfit for Women and Other Living Things," bridges "nature," "states," and "authority." Runyan identifies the metaphysics of the modern Western state as reading "order, unity, and an intolerance of difference into both nature and the body politic." In order to impose its particular order, the state seeks to "master" nature and all recalcitrant subjects by bringing them under the control of white patriarchal culture. The instrumental and exploitative power of the state is legitimated by defining as "natural" that which threatens man/state's control (for example, animals, women, people of color). However, ecocentric and gynocentric conceptions of "nature" as essentially a source of order, unity, and harmony are also problematic. Drawing upon recent ecofeminist analyses, Runyan posits an alternative ethics and politics of "fractious holism" through which to (re)vision relationships among humans and between humans and "nature." This politics of difference resists the images and claims of appropriation and transcendence exemplified by the exploitative man/state.

State power understood as masculinized mastery recurs in Jean Bethke Elshtain's chapter on "Sovereignty, Identity, Sacrifice." Surveying historically the theme of obligatory sacrifice, Elshtain explores the identification of self and nation and its gender-differentiated effects. The "idea and ideal of sacrificial political identity" goes back to the hoplite warfare of classical Greece; on tombstones, men were honored only if they died in war, women only if they died in childbirth. The medieval expression was that of *publica caritas*, semireligious devotion to the *regnum* as *patria*. In the twentieth century, states secure obligatory sacrifice through nationalist appeals to an "imagined community." To understand this sacrificial identification of self and nation, Elshtain explicates our need for community, for civic identification, for being "part of a way of life," for requiring a "home." But the notion of a homeland is "double-edged": a sense of unity and order (associated with a "masculinized deity") within is purchased at the expense of disorder and hostility without. Constrained by the nation-state system, we cannot exit the discourse of war and politics; we can only "try to tame and limit the demands of sovereignty." Elshtain calls for a move from political identity as sacrifice to an ethics of responsibility in a complex moral universe.

The last two chapters more directly challenge the grounds of traditional IR theory. As her title suggests, in "Feminists and Realists View Autonomy and Obligation in International Relations," Christine Sylvester draws on the work of numerous feminist and IR theorists. She argues that "autonomy" in IR theory presupposes liberal contractarian philosophy, and that it therefore stresses freedom from nonvoluntary obligations. Through this lens, international *relationships* are denied or mystified by the "language of liberal exchange-oriented contracts." In contrast, some feminists develop the notion of "autonomy" in relational terms, drawing on modified psychoanalytic accounts of gender identity formation and/or analyses of social relations as structurally gendered and interdependent. Realism establishes self-perpetuating "reactive autonomy" as a norm of states and IR; neoliberal institutionalists offer less static and more relational accounts, yet remain "bound" by realist "vigilances"; and otherwise critical approaches to IR continue masculinist and utilitarian biases. Through multiple examples of women's concrete struggles, Sylvester exposes the selectivity of realism and "its corollary that gender is insignificant in international relations." Feminisms do not simply "replace" realism but disrupt its aura as given, reveal its gender specificity, and open spaces "for women, theory, and alternative practice."

Opening alternative spaces is a theme continued in Rob Walker's chapter, "Gender and Critique in the Theory of International Relations." Focusing on the resolutions of political identity expressed by the principle of state sovereignty, Walker identifies multiple questions that feminists, and other critics of IR, must necessarily engage in pursuing *world* politics. It is not simply a matter of "adding certain excluded voices" but profoundly challenging the grounds of contemporary IR theory and its historically specific (masculinist) account of political identity and community. Problematically, it is state sovereignty, as the constitutive principle of modern political life, that must be seriously interrogated; yet this is only to begin unraveling the dense web of connections that renders IR theory, and modernist accounts, so resistant to feminist and other critiques. Walker sketches five avenues of inquiry for revealing what IR theory renders invisible and for confronting a pervasive and insidious "politics of forgetting" that naturalizes systemic hierarchies. In his conclusion, Walker identifies implications of his argument for further feminist-IR conversations and, especially, for a feminist "world politics."

These contributions to a feminist-IR are simply that. They are not intended to bound, but to open, conversational spaces. While varying in emphasis, analysis, and prescription, they share an understanding of gender as constitutive of, not coincidental to, international relations. Taking gender seriously, then, enhances not only empirical "accuracy," but theoretical adequacy and emancipatory possibilities.

Notes

I am grateful to Albert Bergesen, Judith Grant, Donna Guy, Mona Harrington, Stacey Mayhall, Mark Neufeld, Nicholas Onuf, betts putnam, Anne Runyan, Michelle Saint-Germain, Kathleen Staudt, Christine Sylvester, Ann Tickner, Thomas Volgy, and an anonymous reviewer for comments on earlier versions of this chapter.

1. Whitworth, "Gender and International Relations," 266.
2. Halliday, "Hidden from International Relations," 420.
3. Recent and forthcoming books on gender and international relations include Enloe, *Bananas, Beaches and Bases*; Grant and Newland, *Gender and International Relations*; Runyan and Peterson, *Global Gender Issues*; Sylvester,

Feminist Theory and International Relations; Tickner, *Gender in International Relations.*

4. See my "Security and Sovereign States" (this volume) for an elaboration of feminist scholarship on the state; also Charlton, Everett, and Staudt, *Women, the State and Development*; Parpart and Staudt, *Women and the State in Africa*; MacKinnon, *Toward a Feminist Theory*; Burstyn, "Masculine Dominance"; Afshar, *Women, State, and Ideology*; Connell, "State, Gender and Sexual Politics"; Sassoon, *Women and the State*; Eisenstein, *Radical Future* and *Feminism and Sexual Equality.*

5. Carnoy, *State and Political Theory*, 3, emphasis in original.

6. Easton, "Political System," 303; also Ferguson and Mansbach, *Elusive Quest*; Abrams, "Notes"; Rosenau, "State in an Era of Cascading Politics."

7. Halliday, "State and Society," 217.

8. See discussions in Mann, *States, War and Capitalism*; Carnoy, *State and Political Theory*; Thomas and Meyer, "Expansion of the State"; Caporaso, *Elusive State*; Hall, *States in History*; Krasner, "Approaches to the State"; Skoçpol, "Bringing the State Back In"; Halliday, "State and Society"; Ferguson and Mansbach, *State, Conceptual Chaos.*

9. See, for example, Skoçpol, "Bringing the State Back In"; Caporaso, *Elusive State.*

10. Krasner, "Approaches to the State," 225.

11. Skoçpol, "Bringing the State Back In," 7.

12. Especially, Ferguson and Mansbach, *State, Conceptual Chaos*; Rosenau, "State in an Era of Cascading Politics."

13. Franzway, Court, and Connell, *Staking a Claim*, 33; Mann, "Autonomous Power of the State."

14. Migdal, "State in Society," 1–2.

15. Abrams, "Notes," 79.

16. Halliday, "State and Society"; Keohane, "International Institutions."

17. Skoçpol, "Bringing the State Back In," 8; Caporaso, *Elusive State*; Ikenberry, "State and Strategies."

18. Mann, *Sources of Social Power* and *States, War and Capitalism*; Tilly, *Formation of National States*; Levi, "Predatory Theory of Rule."

19. Migdal, "State in Society," 3.

20. Kirby, "State, Local State, Context and Spatiality"; Kratochwil, "Of Systems, Boundaries, and Territory"; Rosenau, "State in an Era of Cascading Politics"; Foucault, *History of Sexuality.*

21. Keohane, "International Institutions."

22. Tilly, *Formation of National States* and *Coercion, Capital and European States*; Ruggie, "Continuity and Transformation"; Corrigan, *Capitalism, State Formation, and Marxist Theory*; Corrigan and Sayer, *Great Arch*; Hall, *States in History*; Anderson, *Passages from Antiquity* and *Lineages of the Absolutist State*; Poggi, *Development of the Modern State*; Mann, *Sources of Social Power.*

23. Krasner, "Approaches to the State," 225.

24. Keohane, "International Institutions," 386.

25. Mann, *Sources of Social Power*; Yoffee and Cowgill, *Collapse of Ancient States*; Tilly, *Coercion, Capital, and European States*; Chase-Dunn and Hall, *Core/Periphery Relations in Precapitalist Worlds.*

26. Chase-Dunn and Hall, *Core/Periphery Relations in Precapitalist Worlds.*

27. Lawrence, "Strategy, the State and the Weberian Legacy." Nationalist ideologies work to legitimize central authority by "inventing" a community of shared culture and identifying it as congruent with the political, territorial unit. In today's world, decentralization and centralization are two sides of the same (state

system) coin. Thus, processes of decentralization (for example, the breakup of the USSR) are simultaneously processes of centralization (for example, the consolidation of centralized authority in new states/republics). The latter invoke new nationalisms, that is, different inventions of ostensibly shared culture and therefore community.

28. Chase-Dunn and Hall, *Core/Periphery Relations in Precapitalist Worlds*.

29. Cox, "Gramsci, Hegemony and International Relations," "Social Forces, States and World Orders"; Kratochwil and Ruggie, "International Organization."

30. Corrigan and Sayer, *Great Arch*, 7–8, emphasis in original.

31. Foucault, *History of Sexuality*.

32. Giddens, *Nation-State and Violence*.

33. Corrigan and Sayer, *Great Arch*, 3.

34. Connell, "State, Gender and Sexual Politics"; Cohn and Dirks, "Issues and Agendas"; Anderson, *Imagined Communities*.

35. Skoçpol, "Bringing the State Back In"; Mosse, *Nationalism and Sexuality*; Gellner, *Nations and Nationalism*.

36. Skoçpol, "Bringing the State Back In," 21.

37. Spender, "Introduction," 1–2.

38. Tong, *Feminist Thought*; Malson et al., *Feminist Theory in Practice and Process*; Hooks, *From Margin to Center*; Jardine, *Gynesis*.

39. Please note that this use of "deconstruction" is specifically *not* that of Derrida (*Grammatology*) and has no poststructuralist reference when designating this feminist "project."

40. Stimpson, "Women as Knowers"; Harding and Hintikka, *Discovering Reality*; Ackelsberg and Diamond, "Gender and Political Life."

41. Spender, "Introduction," 2.

42. Harding and Hintikka, *Discovering Reality*, x.

43. Ackelsberg and Diamond, "Gender and Political Life," 508.

44. Stimpson, "Women as Knowers"; Bernard, *Female World* and *Female World from a Global Perspective*.

45. Bordo, "Feminist Skepticism."

46. Gross, "Conclusion," 191-92.

47. Brown, *Manhood and Politics*, x.

48. While an important conceptual contribution in the 1970s, use of "gender" is now seen as problematic. To the extent that employing a sex-gender distinction fails to historicize *both* terms, it contributes to—rather than destabilizes—the essentializing of sex as a "given" category. To the extent that "gender" masks the diversity among women, it contributes to a subordination of "others." See, for example, Mohanty, "Under Western Eyes"; Butler, "Gender Trouble"; Haraway, *Simians, Cyborgs, and Women* (chapter 7); Bordo, "Feminism, Postmodernism, and Gender-Scepticism"; Di Stefano, *Configurations of Masculinity*.

49. Nelson, "Women and Knowledge in Political Science," 4; Brown, *Manhood and Politics*, 190.

50. Harding, *Science Question in Feminism*, 17.

51. Farganis, "Feminism and the Reconstruction of Social Science," 207.

52. Scott, "Gender."

53. Jones and Jonasdottir, *Political Interests of Gender*, 7.

54. Generally, I use a slash between forms (for example, domestic/private/household) to suggest some commonality of meaning or reference, while my use of a hyphen (for example, public-private, masculine-feminine) implies contrast.

55. Ferree and Hess, "Introduction," 17.

56. On feminist critiques of positivism and/or science, see Harding and Hintikka, *Discovering Reality*; Keller, *Reflections on Gender and Science*; Harding, *Science Question in Feminism, Feminism and Methodology,* and *Whose Science? Whose Knowledge?*; Bleier, *Science and Gender*; Haraway, "Situated Knowledges, and *Simians, Cyborgs, and Women.* On rationality as gendered, see also Harding, "Is Gender a Variable?"; Fee, "Is Feminism a Threat to Scientific Objectivity?"; Hekman, "Feminization of Epistemology"; Ferguson, "Male-Ordered Politics." For recent surveys of feminist epistemology see the special issue on "Feminism and Epistemology," *Women & Politics* (Fall 1987), especially the comprehensive review and citations in Hawkesworth's "Feminist Epistemology"; and the special issue "Feminism and Deconstruction," *Feminist Studies* (Spring 1988). On my use of postpositivism, see note 60.

57. Harding and Hintikka, *Discovering Reality*, x.

58. Balbo, "Servicing Work of Women" and "Crazy Quilts"; Peterson, "Whose Rights?" 319–321; Gordon, *Women, the State, and Welfare.*

59. Balbo, "Servicing Work of Women," 255.

60. Sen and Grown, *Development, Crises, and Alternative Visions*; Tinker, *Persistent Inequalities*; Nash and Fernandez-Kelly, *Women, Men, and the International Division of Labor*; Mies, Bennholdt-Thomsen, and von Werlhof, *Women*; Seager and Olson, *Women in the World*; Enloe, *Bananas, Beaches, and Bases.*

61. In general, I use the term "postpositivism" to refer to antifoundational critiques understood as the rejection of "essentializing" objectivist metaphysics. (The latter posits an ahistorical "objective reality" independent of "subjective" mediation and available for "grounding" knowledge claims and establishing foundational meanings.) These critiques also reject the categorical separation of subject-object, fact-value, theory-practice, and rational-irrational associated with this metaphysics. Thus, postpositivism recognizes all knowledge claims as socially (intersubjectively) constructed (not "objectively" received through a neutral method); there are no *transcendental* (decontextualized) grounds for establishing truth claims or foundational meanings. As I argue in the text, this does not entail denying "constructed grounds" for evaluating knowledge claims *comparatively*; i.e., I do not understand "absolute relativism" (nihilism) to be entailed by antifoundational critiques. See also Hekman, "Feminization of Epistemology," 65–83; Harding, *Whose Science? Whose Knowledge?*; Rorty, "Solidarity or Objectivity?"; Neufeld, "Reflexive Turn and International Relations Theory" and "Interpretation"; Hawkesworth, "Knowers, Knowing, Known," 533–557; Haraway, "Situated Knowledges"; Gross, "Conclusion"; Fraser and Nicholson, "Social Criticism Without Philosophy."

62. Farganis, "Feminism and the Reconstruction of Social Science," 211.

63. Hekman, "Feminization of Epistemology," 68; also Irigaray, *This Sex Which Is Not One*; O'Brien, *Politics of Reproduction*; Glennon, *Women and Dualism*; Hartsock, *Money, Sex and Power*; Lloyd, *Man of Reason*; Bordo, "Feminist Skepticism"; Berman, "From Aristotle's Dualism"; Lerner, *Creation of Patriarchy*; Peterson, "Archeology of Domination" and "Transgressing Boundaries."

64. Lloyd, *Man of Reason*; Okin, *Women in Western Political Thought*; Harding and Hintikka, *Discovering Reality.*

65. Chodorow, *Reproduction of Mothering*; Gilligan, *Different Voice*; Keller, *Reflections on Gender and Science*; Flax, "Postmodernism and Gender Relations"; Di Stefano, *Configurations of Masculinity.*

66. Keller, *Reflections on Gender and Science,* 89.

67. Bordo, "Feminist Skepticism," 621, citing Kristeva, *About Chinese Women*.

68. Derrida, *Grammatology*.

69. Mies, *Patriarchy and Accumulation*, 210.

70. Peterson, "Transgressing Boundaries"; Ryan, *Marxism and Deconstruction*; Irigaray, *This Sex Which Is Not One*; Cixous, *Laugh of the Medusa*.

71. Hekman, "Feminization of Epistemology," 71, citing Lloyd, *Man of Reason*.

72. Peterson, "Transgressing Boundaries."

73. Brown, "Feminism, International Theory, and International Relations," 471.

74. Peterson, "Archeology of Domination"; Lerner, *Creation of Patriarchy*; Coontz and Henderson, *Women's Work, Men's Property*; Mies, *Patriarchy and Accumulation*.

75. Does the domination dynamic of war contradict this generalization? We are accustomed to war narratives foregrounding the deaths and sacrifices primarily of men. Without trivializing the horrors of war for those most directly and repeatedly engaged, we can note that (1) whatever the earlier distinctions, modern war making engages countless "noncombatants" (men and women) in horrible death and destruction; (2) the wider, less direct, but systemic consequences of war have, arguably, even greater impact on women than men (i.e., dislocation, food and material resource destruction, military allocation of goods and services, displaced aggression, and the effects of disrupting water, food, and health services delivery); and (3) the "invisibility" of war's violent effects on women, at least in U.S. discourse, may be due largely to avoidance of war making within U.S. borders: we have not "lived" the experience of bombing raids, infrastructural deterioration, and systematic destruction of food and fuel resources.

76. Cantarella, *Pandora's Daughters*; Peterson, "Archeology of Domination."

77. Lerner, *Creation of Patriarchy*, 71.

78. Mies, *Patriarchy and Accumulation*.

79. Minh-ha, *Women, Native, Other*.

80. Halliday, "State and Society," 420.

81. Hawkesworth, "Knowers, Knowing, Known," 557.

82. Halliday, "Hidden from International Relations"; Eisler, "Human Rights"; Peterson, "Whose Rights?"; Heise, "Crimes of Gender"; Hevener, *International Law and the Status of Women*.

83. Runyan, "Feminism, Peace and International Politics"; Stiehm, *Women and Men's Wars*; Brocke-Utne, *Educating for Peace*; Ruddick, *Maternal Thinking*; Harris and King, *Rocking the Ship of State*; Reardon, *Sexism and the War System*; Shiva, *Staying Alive*.

84. Randall, *Women and Politics*; Lovenduski and Hills, *Politics of the Second Electorate*; Jayawardena, *Feminism and Nationalism*; Runyan and Peterson, *Global Gender Issues*; Charlton, Everett, and Staudt, *Women, the State and Development*; Parpart and Staudt, *Women and the State in Africa*.

85. Enloe, *Does Khaki Become You?*, "Feminists Thinking About War" and *Bananas, Beaches and Bases*; Elshtain, *Women and War*; Elshtain and Tobias, *Women, Militarism, and War*; Cohn, "Sex and Death"; Harris and King, *Rocking the Ship of State*; Mosse, *Nationalism and Sexuality*; Harrington, "Feminism and Foreign Policy"; and citations in note 3.

86. Harding, *Whose Science? Whose Knowledge?*; Sederberg, *Politics of Meaning*.

87. Boals, "Political Science," 173.

88. Fraser and Nicholson, "Social Criticism without Philosophy," 25. While denying that apoliticism is entailed by post-moves, I am not denying the *danger* of nihilist and/or neoconservative responses to postpositivist understanding.

89. By referring to trade-offs I do not wish to promote utilitarian or zero-sum constructions but to insist on *situating* choices and decisionmaking within social contexts—as having social consequences and political implications. See my discussion in "Security and Sovereign States" in this volume.

90. See also my "Security and Sovereign States" in this volume.

91. Haraway, "Situated Knowledges," 583.

92. Harding, *Whose Science? Whose Knowledge?* 11.

1

Security and Sovereign States: What Is at Stake in Taking Feminism Seriously?

V. Spike Peterson

> The security of states dominates our understanding of what security can be, and who it can be for, not because conflict between states is inevitable, but because other forms of political community have been rendered almost unthinkable. The claims of states to a monopoly of legitimate authority in a particular territory have succeeded in marginalizing and even erasing other expressions of political identity—other answers to questions about who we are.[1]

What does security mean? What can it mean? Who among us feels secure in the face of nuclear proliferation, environmental degradation, economic maldevelopment, and escalating violence? In today's world, more forms of insecurity appear to be systemic. Global economic crises, human rights abuses, and ecological deterioration problematize definitions of security traditionally framed in state-centric, military terms; they call instead for "new thinking" and a broader construction of "common security."[2] Yet even as we increasingly recognize the local consequences of global processes, the transformation required to achieve "world security" is stymied by continued commitments to a system of sovereign states. As Walker notes, while we need "world security," we "have learnt to think and act only in terms of the security of states."[3] How are we to confront this dilemma?

This chapter takes as its starting point that a global crisis of security exists and that our pursuit of world security is impeded by the privileging of state sovereignty and the configuration of authority and political identity it constitutes.[4] Although worldwide insecurities are recognized, *states* continue to monopolize our understanding of how we organize ourselves politically, how political identity is constituted, and where the boundaries of political community are drawn. Unable to imagine authentic politics and/or political community outside of the state, challenges to state sovereignty "seem to imply either an embrace of hierarchical empires or a rejection of politics entirely."[5] Unable to imagine political identity in terms that are not nationalist, appeals to identification with "humanity" seem hopelessly

31

utopian. Thus, *global* citizenship requires rethinking our construction of identities, or seeking, as Walker puts it, "other answers to questions about who we are." In short, moving toward world security requires moving beyond state sovereignty and the limiting construction of political community and identity it has historically imposed: "The demand for world security is, in effect, a demand for a radically new understanding of political identity."[6]

Stated differently, one might argue that "national security" is a contradiction in terms, revealed as such through an international relations (IR) lens on military security (escalation of defense by particular states generates systemwide insecurity), an ecological lens on environmental disasters (state-centric management cannot address global processes), and/or a critical lens on maldevelopment (economic justice within states is precluded by a capitalist world system of structural inequity). This chapter builds upon and moves beyond these starting points, arguing that "national security" is particularly and profoundly contradictory for women. Through a postpositivist feminist lens on the state, the structural violence of gender (and class) hierarchy—i.e., women's systemic *insecurity*—is revealed as an internal as well as external dimension of state systems.[7] Moreover, this lens illuminates the historical gender basis/bias of states, sovereignty, politics, political identity, and "legitimate authority."

That these constructions—and the understanding of security they presuppose—are profoundly gendered has important implications for (re)visioning world security: much more than rethinking security arrangements between and beyond states is required. Structural insecurities internal to states—constituted by gendered (and other) divisions of labor, resources, and identities—as well as androcratic politics generally must be recognized and critically examined. We must understand how extensive and systemic current insecurities are *and* how particular identities produce, and are produced by, this structural violence; we can understand neither without attention to gender. "Radically rethinking security"[8] is one consequence of taking feminism seriously: this entails asking what security can mean in the context of interlocking systems of hierarchy and domination and how gendered identities and ideologies (re)produce these structural insecurities. Moreover, rendering women's insecurities visible does not simply provide historical-empirical confirmation of masculinist domination. Illuminating the gender of core constructs and historical processes both sheds new light on ways of being and knowing and suggests alternative understandings of "who we are" that are then available for (re)visioning.

Only a portion of this larger project is addressed here. Interacting systems of differential power are at work in state making: hierarchical centralization of political authority; military consolidation, internally and externally; exploitative divisions of labor and identities; and legitimation through instrumentalist, elitist, and masculinist ideologies. This chapter offers a historical overview of "gendered states," specifically, the gender dynamics of state formation in early, Athenian, and modern (European) contexts.[9] How the state constitutes and "enacts" gender politics is then fleshed out by reference to "power relations," suggesting more specifically how women are positioned vis-à-vis systemic insecurity. A concluding discussion employs feminist analyses of "protection" and structural dependency both to enhance our understanding of systems of in/security currently in place and as resources for rethinking world security.

Historicizing Gendered States: Early State Formation

Most international relations scholars focus on the modern period of European state formation and the contemporary interstate system. This selectivity impairs our understanding of how states centralize authority, (re)constitute individual and collective identities, consolidate and maintain coercive power, and especially, institutionalize the legitimation of structural violence. Neglect of the Athenian polis is particularly significant: not only because modern states replicate many of its features, but because classical Athenian texts established constructions of authority, identity, politics, public-private, and security that powerfully shaped subsequent theory and practice. While the continuing influence of Thucydides, Plato, and Aristotle is conventionally noted, we too frequently ignore the context of their writing: in the interactive processes of state formation, the emergence of objectivist metaphysics, and reconfigurations of individual and collective identities.[10]

While patriarchal customs precede and enable state formation, it is with early states that systemic masculinist and class domination is *institutionalized*; the exploitation of women as a "sex/gender class" is here backed by the coercive power of the state, and the *reproduction* of gender hierarchy is ensured through a reconfiguration of legitimating ideologies.[11] In early states this stunning transformation in social relations and identities has not yet been "naturalized"; thus the interplay of emergent structures is readily discernible, perhaps especially so in classical Athenian texts. Consequently, critiques of state systems and political identity are enriched by attention to early and Athenian state making, where these systemic transformations historically occurred and are clearly visible.

As noted in the introduction to this volume, contemporary theorists argue that states are not evolutionary givens, unilineal developments, or completed and accomplished facts; they are ongoing projects that must be understood in historical context and in relation to what they are formed "against."[12] Given the resistance to early centralization,[13] how do we account for the actual transition to—the historical "success" of—state orders? As key to the transition, Cohen articulates a positive feedback loop that amplifies centralized political (and military) control:

> There are multiple roads to statehood, . . . produc[ing] similar results.
> . . . The reason for this is clear. Once a society begins to evolve more
> centralized and more permanent authority structures, the political realm
> itself becomes an increasingly powerful determinant of change. . . . The
> hierarchical structure itself becomes a selective determinant that feeds
> back to all the sociocultural features to make them fit more closely in its
> overall pattern.[14]

Understood in historical context and in relation to what they are formed
"against," early states mark a transition from corporate, kin-based
communities to the *institutionalization* of centralized authority, gender and
class stratification, organized warfare, and justificatory ideologies. The
concentration of resources made possible by appropriating the labor of
women (and subsequently of war captives and slaves) was crucial for
accumulation processes. Moreover, the invention of writing—historically
concomitant with state formation and under the control of elite, androcentric
power—was crucial for author-izing and reproducing centralized rule.[15]

The early state's displacement of autonomous kin communities had
specific and largely negative consequences for women. I shall summarize
these consequences by reference to the construction of women's experience
through the interacting relationships of authority, property, "work," and
sexuality. Communal and kin-based societies do not distinguish "domestic"
or "economic" from social practices more generally; state formation marked a
shift to relatively independent "domestic/household" units of production/
reproduction distinguished (retrospectively) from a "public/political" sphere.
That is, the "family" household—and women's subordination within it—does
not precede but is historically constituted by state centralization.[16] As the
basic socioeconomic unit defined by the state, the individual household marks
citizenship claims and facilitates labor mobilization, resource extraction,
conscription for military and public works service, regulation of property
(including women), and legal control more generally.

In kin-based systems authority depends a great deal on relationships, not
simply abstracted attributes; rules are complex and permit claims to authority
by diverse people, depending on the specifics of context.[17] In a newly
constituted "domestic/household" sphere, women's identities are narrowed to
reproductive functions "because they represent control over present and future
workers and the subordination of local kin group reproduction to the
reproduction of the emerging class-based society."[18] In the process, women
lose kin claims to property, become transmitters of property, and are treated
as property themselves. Moreover, the establishment of individual household
units renders women more vulnerable to and dependent upon fathers and
husbands, while weakening their access to countervailing power and support
from larger kin networks; women's status/identity shifts from "sisters" (a
relation of autonomy and potential gender equality) to lifelong dependency as
daughters and wives.[19]

With the emerging significance of inheritable claims to private property and citizenship, sexuality becomes a focus of state regulation. For example, women's adultery becomes a crime against the state and, significantly, is publicly punished.[20] Simultaneously, status differentiations *among* women are instituted through customs and laws distinguishing "respectable" women—protected property transmitters—from those who are outside of the protection of a father or husband.[21] Finally, transformed cosmologies and world views historically accompany and legitimate emergent male domination as the state supports masculinist "religions" (gradually displacing a variety of belief systems that included reverence for and celebration of female deities and woman-identified fertility) and/or masculinist "philosophy" (fostering the privileging of male-identified reason, abstraction, autonomy, and agency as distinct from mere animal, "natural" existence).[22] Control of newly invented writing significantly augmented elite power in instituting ideologies justifying gender and class domination: altered cosmologies were author-ized and fed back into the stratifying dynamic.

This brief summary oversimplifies what are complex and often contradictory processes and, especially, neglects the varying effects of resistance to the centralizing project. It suggests, however, the extensive transformation in gender (and class) relations and identities that is institutionalized and, significantly, "naturalized" long before modern state formation.

Historicizing Gendered States: The Athenian Polis

The Athenian polis exemplifies the gendered pattern of state making: altered property and authority relations (women losing prior claims to property on their own behalf, becoming merely transmitters of property and lifelong dependents); fragmentation of kin-corporate subsistence/domestic re/production units (formation of the *oikos*/household as basic socio-economic unit, distinct from "sphere" of collective decisionmaking; gender and class divisions of labor); institutionalized militarism (celebrating a reconfigured "masculinity"); and transformed ideologies (elaborating and privileging masculinist cosmologies and world views that subordinate that which is marked as feminine). In Athens, the shift from aristocratic kin-based societal organization to centralized political authority occurred in the context of expanding agricultural, commercial, and military activities. The increasing wealth and power of a middle class and impoverishment of nonpropertied citizens and small farmers led to demands for land redistribution and debt cancellation. "In the final stages of progress toward the middle-class city state," tyrants and/or lawgivers frequently appeared as "conciliators of social factions."[23]

In general, tyrants put a temporary end to crippling conflicts, furthered peasant independence, and strengthened the economic position of the middle class. Lawgivers attempted to stabilize socioeconomic relations by codifying citizenship and regulating property relations (slavery, debts, marriage, inheritance); for example, Solon's legislation displaced aristocratic principles, establishing both property-based citizenship and a new notion of "alienable" private property in which individual family holdings were freed from obligations to the clan. The independent household (oikos) became the key social, economic, and political unit of the polis: "the whole of the productive output of this small corporation was appropriated by its male head as the basis for his claim to participate in the state."[24]

In Athens, citizenship claims based on property (and/or military service) effectively excluded women. Relegated to the private sphere, "women spent their lives acting under the authority of a male guardian. . . . [A woman's] status was derived entirely from kinship with males, and her primary function was to produce a male heir. . . . Adultery was for this reason a severe offense. . . ."[25] Thus, women's sexuality was strictly regulated, with laws also codifying a distinction between respectable women (providers of legitimate heirs) and not-respectable women (providers of men's pleasure). Wherever located, women's sexuality was placed at the service of and under control by men, who exercised that control individually and collectively through the patriarchal state. For example, Solon's legislation regularized a double standard, exemplified in his establishment of state-owned brothels staffed by slave women.[26]

For Aristotle, it was the public realm of politics where free men achieved the highest good: political action; that realm was radically distinguished from the private realm of necessity, where women, slaves, and children achieved the production and reproduction that was a precondition of the public. Only equals could seek immortality by pursuing the highest good. The higher order was thus reserved for men, who could there transcend the demands of necessity, the needs common to humans and animals. Because necessary, the private could not be abolished, but "necessity" could not be permitted to contaminate the activities and relationships of the superior association. A "radical bifurcation" of asymmetrical public and private spheres was the result.[27]

Not only spheres of action but other ways of being and knowing were asymmetrically dichotomized. In the Athenian polis, objectivist metaphysics (dualisms of Western philosophy), essentialized sexual identities (mutually exclusive male and female principles), and hierarchical state making (exploitative social relations) were mutually constituted.[28] As one consequence, the public-private dichotomy legitimating the political order maps on to the culture-nature (subject-object) dichotomy of objectivist metaphysics, legitimizing domination practices (such as "objectification" of women, nature, "other") more generally. Implicit in the dichotomy of culture-nature (subject-object) is the intention of domination or control—fending off the unpredictability or instability of nature by imposing predictability and order through the power of classificatory systems and/or actual physical control. The construction of maleness underpins these dichotomies. Through the male-identified capacities for reasoning, abstracting, and formalizing, the man/masculine identity becomes the agent/subjectivity uniquely capable of transcending the realm of necessity—understood as nature, material and sensual embodiment, and concrete reproduction (femaleness/woman/feminine).

For instance, in the *Symposium*, Plato spurns the concrete entanglements of the body and desire, associates them with unruly female passions, and denigrates the merely mortal creations (children) of women's labor. Male (pro)creativity, the ability to give birth to ideas, exceeds that of women by begetting immortal creations. In the *Republic*, Plato's solution to the factionalism and disruption associated with the private was to eliminate the strife by subsuming private interests within the public, collective domain. In contrast, Aristotle deemed the private realm a precondition of the public, so retained it as a necessary but inferior level.[29]

If Aristotle presented a different resolution of public-private tensions, he nonetheless replicated Plato's hierarchical model—indeed, he provided what has proven to be a lasting rationalization of domination utilizing the fundamental, "natural," and Platonic dichotomy of soul over body (reason-affect, culture-nature, transcendence-contingency). It is important to note that the nondemocratic nature of Plato's and Aristotle's moral and political philosophies precludes their grounding in concrete practices and participatory interaction. Both Plato's model of "philosopher-kings" and Aristotle's model of the "public" institute rule by those explicitly separated from and untainted by "necessity." Indeed, their claim to rule is premised upon their unique capacity to remain disassociated from the necessary labor of maintaining the social system, both productively and reproductively, and from all personal "attachments" of an affective nature: the preferred moral and political self is viewed as "*disembedded* and *disembodied*."[30]

I note here two of the many consequences of this hierarchical division of labor and identities. First, negating the centrality of reproduction, men "relegated" this work to women and denied its profoundly political nature.[31] This exclusion from political theory impoverishes our understanding of how sociopolitical relations—especially social identities and legitimating ideologies—are *in fact* reproduced. As a corollary, ignore-ance of social reproduction masks objectivist tendencies to reify, rather than explain, social "reality." Second, men surrendered *systemic* participation in childrearing and dependent caretaking experiences, thereby, presumably, shaping systemically their ways of being and knowing themselves, with important implications for *reproducing* gendered systems.[32]

Historicizing Gendered States: Modern European States

Centralization processes in Europe cover tremendous regional and cultural diversity yet reproduce, in general, the gendered patterns marking early and Athenian state making. My discussion of the modern period generalizes across Europe in regard to the interactive development of science, state making, and capitalism. I then focus on the gender dynamics of militarism and nationalism, as preface to the concluding discussion.[33]

Like Athens, European state making occurred in the context of expanding commercial and military activities; new technologies permitted global exploration and, for Europeans, the accumulation of resources that facilitated the consolidation of centralizing processes. Unlike Athens, the European context included a philosophy of individualism, an increasingly secular world view enhanced by the development of "science," and expanding relations of production associated with the rise of capitalism. The modern era is also characterized by a vast increase in what Mann refers to as the "infrastructural power" of states: "the capacity of the state to actually penetrate civil society, and to implement logistically political decisions throughout the realm."[34] Similarly, Giddens emphasizes the enhanced "information storage" and surveillance capacities of modern states, including expanded means of violence, available for deployment both internally and externally.[35]

The state's enhanced infrastructural power permits the maintenance of centralized rule less through direct violence and more through indirect violence; thus *legitimation* processes become key to maintaining (reproducing) state power—and therefore become pivotal to our understanding of that power and the in/securities it constitutes. Ideologies assume centrality in our analyses not because they are *more* potent (determinative, ultimate, primary, etc.) than physical coercion but because they secure the reproduction of social hierarchy with less resort to (but no less reliance upon) physical coercion. Most of *us*, most of the time, reproduce gender, class, race, and countless other relations of domination *unreflectively*. This "forgetting" of human costs and possible alternatives is ideological, even as the consequences are graphically concrete. "Raw," material power/violence is not here eliminated or disregarded: it is the menacing but mystified presence backing up (en*forcing*) ruling elite claims to authority (e.g., "legitimate control of the means of coercion," law enforcement and economic regulation). Without recourse to means of coercion, legitimating ideologies would "carry no *force*." But by minimizing direct coercion, the location of power and domination is mystified, *systemic* domination and its insecurities are obfuscated, the contradictions of, for example, national security are masked, and possibilities of resistance profoundly altered.

Of course, the state is not unique in combining physical, economic, and ideological means of power: militarism, capitalism, and patriarchy all embody such combinations. However, the state is unique in a *"sociospatial and organizational* sense. Only the state is inherently centralised over a delimited territory over which it has authoritative power."[36] Recall Cohen's positive feedback loop: once centralized authority structures are established, "the political realm itself becomes. . . . a selective determinant that feeds back to all the sociocultural features to make them fit more closely."[37] Technological developments amplify this feedback process and its effectuation of centralized—yet mystified—control.

Moreover, state formations constitute power relations (gender, class, race hierarchies), and the state "has the exclusive right to use force to maintain those relations."[38] Thus, while there are many sources of power shaping our social relations and in/security, the state is strategic in three senses: it acts as the *centralized* "main organizer" of gendered power;[39] it "exercises legitimate violence and defines what is illegitimate";[40] and it institutionalizes and reproduces (through sanctions, cultural forms, education, policy, regulation, law) the *legitimation* of social hierarchy.

In European state making we observe, as in Athens, the *interaction* of exploitative accumulation, military consolidation of state power, and patriarchal control over and regulation of women's productive and reproductive powers. We also note a revival of the power of reason, its identification with male principles, and a denigration of that which does not accord easily with this new ordering. For example, independent—especially deviant/defiant—women, their procreative powers, and their identity as "knowers" were, both in Athens and in modernizing Europe, perceived by many as threatening to the emergent order. Similarly, women and their association with "nonrational" cultural forms were suppressed in favor of masculinist principles of rationalism, emergent "professionalization," and sovereign, hierarchical authority.

With the development of capitalism in tandem with technology, boundaries in the division of labor and identities shifted as the "scientific" world view increasingly penetrated into all social relations. Feminists and nonfeminists alike acknowledge science and rationality as inseparable from and mutually supportive of the social transformations understood as modern state formation and capitalism. By compressing a great deal of literature, we can view these interactive projects through a feminist lens and gain considerable insight into gendered identities and politics.

The Rise of Science

The scientific revolution marked a shift in our understanding of "the world" and the position of "man" within it. A now rich feminist literature argues that the rise of science marked not only a transformation in "ways of knowing" but in gender relations and gender symbolism—a transformation in ways of being as suggested by reconfigured identities and new metaphors.[41]

Merchant argues that insofar as woman was identified with nature, "by reconceptualizing reality as a machine rather than a living organism, [science] sanctioned the domination of both nature and women."[42]

As in Athens, scientific reasoning was explicitly constructed as male and explicitly promoted as superior to and *exclusive of* that which was marked as female/nature/feminine, and significantly, that which implied emotion, passion, and connection. As Keller notes, this is not to suggest the imagery employed was a direct reflection of "actual relations between the sexes," but very much a "[concern] with the definition of gender, especially of what it meant to be a man, and what it meant to 'raise a Masculine philosophy'."[43] The "rational spirit" that was required for science, as well as for capitalism, discriminated against women in a material sense, as evidenced, for example, by the witch persecutions and by the rise of professionalization, which excluded women and eliminated sources of their authority. But the more immeasurable damage had its source in the symbolic dimension of the persecution: the long-term and insidious identification of woman—and nature and nonreason—with that which was categorically distinguished from and of lesser value than man—who was identified with science and reason. Man positioned himself in "the world" as "knower" and agent/subject, categorically separated from woman as "known" and object. This process effectively "naturalized" again the subordination of "woman" as well as of "nature."[44]

Our attention is drawn here to what the state is formed *against*. As centralized power is consolidated, "state activities more or less forcibly 'encourage' some [ways in which social life could be lived] whilst suppressing, marginalizing, eroding, undermining others. . . . This has cumulative, and enormous, cultural consequences; consequences for how people identify (and in many cases, *have* to identify) themselves and their 'place' in the world."[45] After the seventeenth century, "rational" ways of knowing dignified "rational" ways of being such that alternatives were increasingly marginalized, at best, and often "erased."

The Rise of the Modern State

In the modern period, the process by which "authority" was constructed was key to the legitimation of centralized power. The feudal order had been characterized by a decentralized, "latticelike network" based upon "conditional property"—carrying with it specific social obligations—and "private authority," which resided personally in the ruler.[46] Common traditions of religion, law, and custom, based upon inclusive natural rights, legitimated these relations. Ruggie argues that a legitimation crisis of "staggering proportions" was entailed in the transition to absolute private property (the right to exclude others) and to public authority (the "integration into one public realm of parcelized and private authority"). What we regard today "as the modern classics in political theory and international legal thought were produced in direct response to this legitimation crisis."[47]

For present purposes, John Locke is the most significant figure among the many who responded to this crisis.[48] Locke's model of human nature, social contract, and state-society relations continues to shape modern understanding, and his methodological individualism has proven no less significant than his political individualism. Locke specifically wrote in response to the debates of his time: how can one justify absolute individuation (of person, of property, of territorial states) while providing a basis for political community?[49] How can the contradiction between the particularity of individual choice (in the private sphere of religion or market) and the need for collective order and identity be resolved?

Prior to Locke, political authority was often legitimized by reference to the "natural" authority of the father, an argument formalized by Sir Robert Filmer in defense of the absolute authority of kings. While Locke's *Second Treatise* is rightly associated with the "defeat" of Filmer's "classic patriarchy," he by no means rejected patriarchy altogether. As feminist scholars have shown, Locke retains and "naturalizes" patriarchal relations within the (now private) "family"; he places limits on the absolutist rule of fathers and husbands while re-enforcing the rule of male over female as "natural."[50] Thus, rather than standing "irrevocably opposed," liberalism and patriarchal relations are reconciled in Locke's work. Liberalism, as derived from Locke's theory, must be understood as in fact liberal patriarchalism.[51]

Locke articulates a political sphere of "free individualism" in contrast to the private sphere of "natural subordination" in the family. As in Athens, kinship is not eliminated as an ordering principle but redefined and restricted to the sphere of domestic relations—the family of co-resident kin—which is, in turn, contrasted with the public sphere of specifically political relations. As Nicholson argues, modern political theory "is primarily about what has been seen as distinct from the family . . . [with] 'politics' . . . being about forms of interactions or types of institutions whose nature and history exist independently of the family."[52] Thus, for both Locke and Aristotle, politics was based on convention, humanly constructed practices, understood as categorically separate from the activities of domestic/household/familial arrangements.

Locke (re)established the family as "natural" and naturally hierarchical in Western political theory. The significance of this "essentializing" move can hardly be overstated: by discrediting history Locke not only reified the "family," but lent his authority to the *erasure* of *actual* history: resistance, specificity, alternatives. This was a powerful, political move: that which is outside of history is "naturalized," is outside of politics, and cannot be contested. Moreover, by mystifying the masculinism of the state/public and the contingency of the family/private, Locke obscured the gendered politics of both spheres and, importantly, the *politics of defining the boundary between them*. Not only are women and nonpropertied men excluded from "politics," but all of the activities associated with the domestic/familial sphere, which are in fact quite laden with power relations, are excluded as well. (These include, for example, biological and social reproduction, emotional and physical caretaking, maintenance of the household, and affective/sexual relations.)

The politics of separate spheres is further complicated, and significantly so, when we consider the various meanings of public and private and the shifting boundary between them.[53] In Athens, the "private" referred to the household sphere of production as well as reproduction: "economics" was encompassed within this sphere; residents in the household included domestic slaves. Moreover, the "social" was yet to be delineated as separate from the public/political sphere. In modern liberalism, the "private" referred to the "family" understood as co-resident, biologically related kin responsible for reproduction. "Necessary" subsistence production, understood as "women's work," took place in this sphere and was increasingly differentiated, as industrialism developed, from market, exchange relations that were understood as "men's work." Thus, a new dimension characterized as "social/economic" (in contrast to either political or familial/personal) emerged as market relations gained in significance. That is, outside of the family, in the sphere dominated by men, a second public-private distinction was established: differentiating between the public understood as political/state/power/coercion and the private understood as the social/market/economic/voluntary.[54] As Pateman points out, in *this* version of the public-private, the private begins to command more attention than the public.[55]

The Rise of Industrial Capitalism

What we are witnessing, of course, are the effects of capitalist production relations on categorizations of "work" and the separation—and then reification—of family, economy, and state. As industrialism developed and "productive" labor left the household, the third sphere took form. This sphere, the realm of "real" work that included wage labor, commodification, exchange, and market relations, was also marked as masculine. Reifying the economy as separate from the family (as well as from the political) vastly altered the shape of people's lives and cultural forms—all with profound gender consequences. Moreover, the introduction of a third sphere, the social/market/economy, while retaining the dualistic labeling of public and private, has obfuscated the relationships among the spheres and, especially, the politics of defining them.[56]

As one consequence, the family/household—already subordinated to the public/political—drops even further from sight as subsequent references to "state-society," "state-civil," and even "public-private" relations are understood to refer to relations between a nexus of state/political activities on one hand and social/market/economic/voluntary activities on the other; the familial/domestic sphere is effectively "erased" from conscious consideration and analysis in these phrases. Likewise, the politics and economics of gender relations within the family/household are also erased and evaded.

The process of "separating" these particular spheres spanned several centuries, with a pace specific to particular states. In spite of considerable regional variation, however, a sequence of changes was repeated as "successful" states consolidated territorial control, expanded commercial—and plundering—activities, and established industrial capitalist production relations.

In the transition from feudalism to early states, smaller household/domestic production predominated and, until industrialization was generalized, "production and family life" for most people were inseparably entwined. The "household was the center around which resources, labor, and consumption were balanced."[57] In this context of social production within patriarchal households, wives were subordinated but hardly "dependent"; their work was essential to the survival of the unit and to that extent respected.[58] Gradually, the industrialization process removed labor and resources from the household, and the site of "production" shifted to the factory.

The structural and ideological separation of "family," "economy," and "politics" was clearly a gender-differentiated process with far-reaching consequences. First, the family/household sphere was associated with the "natural," necessary activities of daily material maintenance, body and emotional sustenance, sexuality, and the caretaking of dependents. Second, economic activities—"men's work"—gained in esteem: private property, the wage contract, and the "free market" now represented the valued sphere of productive activity. Labor associated with the household—"women's work"—was devalued: it received no, or disproportionately low, wages. Third, as "family" and "work" were separated, gender identities were reshaped to conform to bourgeois ideologies of respectability: woman/femininity as care-taking, affective, responsible homemaker, and man/masculinity as hard-working, responsible employee whose alienation at work was compensated for by "leisure" at home.[59]

The bourgeois family form existed only for the privileged few and had to be "created" for the working class. What we might call "the making of the nuclear family"—attempts to generalize the ideology of this model beyond elite families—characterizes the interaction of patriarchal, state, and capitalist transformations in the nineteenth and early twentieth centuries. The "nuclearization" of the family was orchestrated by the state through law and public policies as well as "by various private, secular, and religious groups acting under the authority of the State."[60] As the coordinating and regulatory powers of the state expanded, public authority encroached upon male dominance within the "private" familial sphere: state intervention eroded the power and authority of family patriarchy as the state's recognition of women's legal and economic rights reconfigured the relationship between male heads of households and female dependents.

This did not, however, have the effect of undermining male dominance more generally. "Instead, the state moved to replace the family as the main force that structured patriarchy in the broader society."[61] As feminists argue, the shift from "private patriarchy" (between individuals, within the family) to "public patriarchy" ("publicly-centered monopolization of jobs, law, property, knowledge, etc., by men") altered the form but not the premise of gender hierarchy.[62] No fundamental transformation occurred, because "woman" continued to be defined through masculinist lenses as wife and mother—as a dependent rather than autonomous person or worker. That is, welfare systems have historically responded to women's *demands* by ameliorating some conditions without challenging the patriarchal ideologies or sex-segregated labor markets and pay inequities that render women structurally dependent.[63]

We should not, however, lose sight of the complexity and contradictions embedded in these systemic transformations: there is no simple or "essential" relationship between the commitments of patriarchy, instrumental reason, liberalism, industrial capitalism, and state centralization. These dynamic systems of power develop differentially (they are not reducible to each other) yet inextricably (they are mutually constituted through historical process). Moreover, these interactive transformations have both liberating and oppressive dimensions: given their distinctive priorities, gains for one "system," or a subgroup of a system, may facilitate *or* obstruct gains elsewhere:

> Protective labor legislation, for example, was both a practical victory for working women in a number of female-dominated trades who obtained relief from harsh working conditions, as well as a practical defeat for women in male-dominated trades who were removed from their jobs. It was an ideological defeat for women since it justified sex-based legal classification, while also an ideological victory for workers generally who would benefit from the demise of the principle of laissez-faire in the law of employment.[64]

This overview suggests that historical processes of state making constitute divisions of labor, institutions, and identities that are profoundly gendered, with systemic implications for the production and reproduction of women's insecurities. In the following section, I augment the meaning of "gendered states" by more specific reference to power relations internally and externally: how contemporary states "in practice" constitute and "enact" gendered power and in/security.[65]

Gendered Power Relations

In multiple ways, the state is "the main organizer of the power relations of gender."[66] The "scale and coherence" of the state are readily apparent in official expressions of authority and violence such as executive power, legislation, policing, and wars. But the scope and coherence of the state are also crucial in defining terms and categories—for example, politics, citizen, prostitution, consent, private, security, national interests—and in shaping cultural institutions and norms, such as the division between public and private, what counts as "work," who gets to count, what bounds "public morality," how "acceptable limits" are set, what language is spoken, and which symbols are privileged. That is, the state exercises power through its claim to legitimate violence but also through "state activities, forms, routines, and rituals" that constitute and regulate "acceptable forms and images of social activity and individual and collective identity."[67]

Of particular significance here is the state's mystification of "its patriarchal base by not only constructing but also manipulating the ideology describing public and private life."[68] The state constitutes itself as the realm of political action and promotes a definition of politics that narrowly construes power relations. In contrast, claiming that "the personal is political," feminists argue that "relationships we once imagined were private or merely social are in fact infused with power, usually unequal power backed up by public authority."[69] Moreover, feminists claim that "the political is personal," that men who dominate public life "have used their public power to construct private relationships in ways that bolstered their masculinized political control."[70]

For example, definitions of citizenship are formal expressions of "who counts" politically, and the history of suffrage struggles documents how actively states have resisted "counting women." But the separation between public and private affects far more than who goes to the ballot box; it constitutes and regulates political identity as masculinity.[71] The condition for women's entry into the public sphere is that we "become like men."[72] Many feminists are critical of political identity premised on transcendence and on the denial of "body, need, and necessity,"[73] insisting instead on redefining "the scope of politics, the practice of citizenship and authority, and the language of political action."[74]

The state is additionally a "bearer of gender" by reference to male domination of the top personnel of states and to the cult of masculinity among these personnel. Similarly, gender differentiation is evident in the disproportionate number of men in the coercive apparatus of the state (military, police, prisons) and in infrastructural services (railways, power, construction), while women overwhelmingly sustain the service sectors (teaching, health and welfare services, clerical support) and are found disproportionately in part-time, nonsalaried positions.[75] Moreover, as the centralized agent of social control, the state "exercises legitimate violence and defines what is illegitimate."[76] It uses force and its threat in the name of maintaining social order, i.e., security. Feminists ask, How does the state employ coercion and its threat to maintain patriarchal power?[77] How are the costs and benefits of the social order distributed? Whose well-being is in fact secured?

Women are the objects of masculinist social control not only through direct violence (murder, rape, battering, incest), but also through ideological constructs, such as "women's work" and the cult of motherhood, that justify structural violence—inadequate health care, sexual harassment, and sex-segregated wages, rights, and resources. The state is implicated in all of these. Its construal of sexual violence and the threat of violence, however, as "private" and not, therefore, a public or political concern, is particularly lethal for women. Documentation of this violence is now extensive and harrowing: in the United States (according to 1980 FBI statistics), one of every two women experiences some form of battering, one of four experiences incest, one of four is raped, 97 percent of all male-female violence is against females, and 26 percent of all homicides are murders of women by their husbands.[78] While its particular manifestations vary cross-culturally ("bride burning" in India, gang rapes in the United States, clitoridectomies in Africa), male violence constitutes a "global war against women."[79] The grueling consistency of this violence contravenes explanations couched in terms of "isolated incidents" or "individual deviance." More coherent is Hanmer's conclusion that "force and its threat is the basis for the extraction of all benefits that men make from women; that is, economic, sexual, and prestige gains."[80]

The state is complicit "directly" through its selective sanctioning of non-state violence, particularly in its policy of "nonintervention" in domestic violence. It is complicit "indirectly" through its promotion of masculinist, heterosexist, and classist ideologies—expressed, for example, in public education models, media images, the militarism of culture, welfare policies, and patriarchal law. When the state *does* intervene, it typically does so from within a patriarchal ideology that at best "protects" women while simultaneously reproducing masculinist givens that ensure women's "need for protection."

This is *not* to suggest simply that women can or should avoid the state and its potential support. It is to insist on asking structural questions about the processes by which male domination and violence are reproduced. For example, if we fail to notice that the state regulates rape but does not prohibit it, we fail to ask *why* women are being raped and how the state is complicit.[81]

> Similarly, applying laws against battery to husbands, although it can mean life itself, has largely failed to address, as part of the strategy for

state intervention, the conditions that produce men who systematically express themselves violently toward women, women whose resistance is disabled, and the role of the state in this dynamic. Criminal enforcement in these areas, while suggesting that rape and battery are deviant, punishes men for expressing the images of masculinity that mean their identity, for which they are otherwise trained, elevated, venerated, and paid.[82]

Finally, the state's authority to exercise and define legitimate violence operates "externally" as well. While liberal pluralist perspectives on the state tend to emphasize its function as securing the collective good, recent historical and sociological literature on state making emphasizes the necessarily militarist dimensions of gaining and consolidating territorial rule.[83] Feminists have examined the gender dynamics of militarism, arguing that (re)visions of security must address the gender of military ideology, practices, and economic priorities. They have also examined the gendered identities embedded in nationalism. The latter is perhaps the most powerful ideology of collective authority and political identity in the modern era; its gendered basis therefore has many implications.[84] Historically, European nationalism (deployed within states as a unifying political/emotional identity and externally as a weapon of imperialism)[85] and Third World nationalism (deployed in independence struggles)[86] have promoted similar constructions of gendered "respectability": the superiority of national culture is demonstrated by "assign[ing] everyone his place in life, man and woman, normal and abnormal, native and foreigner."[87]

Nationalism mapped on to state making is particularly effective in obscuring social hierarchies: the political identity constituted by citizenship collapses diverse, particular identities to a "one-ness" of nation-state membership. To the extent that nationalism is effective, it mystifies the multiple particularities that in fact differentiate those within the state: by gender, ethnicity, class, language, region, etc.

> To speak in the name—and language—of the nation both denies the particularity of what is being said (and who is saying it) and defines alternatives and challenges as sectional, selfish, partial, ultimately treasonable: . . . To define "us" in national terms (as against class, . . . or gender, or religion, . . .) has consequences. Such classifications are means for a project of social integration which is also, inseparably, an active *dis*integration of other focuses of identity and conceptions of subjectivity.[88]

While internal differences are masked, the assumption of external differences is codified: what I call the "sovereignty contract" fixes the trade-off between internal unity/reason/politics and external difference/irrationality/war.[89] Externally, militarism occurs as states consolidate and defend territorial boundaries; constructions of "sovereignty" legitimize the maintenance of the state system in which direct violence is the ultimate arbiter of social conflict(s). Presupposing atomistic, self-interested and acquisitive individuals (and states), the "exclusionary logic of the contract" frames the construction of politics and security.[90] Peace, in these constructions, can only be "negative peace" as violence can only be regulated but not transcended; justice, and associated constructions of peace and security, can only be established by direct violence, as domination, or by indirect violence, through enforcing abstract, universalist contractual claims.

In mainstream literature, women's participation in war and militarism is obscured by the dichotomy associating women with peace/nurturance/ passivity and men with war/violence/agency. Yet feminist interrogations expose how crucial gender is for sustaining military activities. Women may form only a small percentage of combatants and the upper echelons of military, paramilitary, and intelligence decisionmaking,[91] but these are profoundly gendered domains. Discomfort with women combatant roles reflects the continued gender dichotomies of protector-protected, active-passive, and subject-object and suggests how entrenched our "essentializing" of sexual identities remains.[92] The ideological and cultural conflation of manhood, combat, militarism, and national chauvinism not only reproduces violence but glorifies it as a "natural" expression of masculine and nation-state "identities."[93] We might well ask, Is militarism without masculinism possible?

In a discussion of feminism and militarism, Enloe suggests that the two principal nonfeminist theories of militarization—one centering on capitalism, the other on the state—assume that "men are the natural actors under militarism so that women are considered only in terms of how militarism affects them, as if they were an off-stage chorus to a basically male drama."[94] She argues that feminists must recognize the "impact-on approach as a *necessary* but not *sufficient*" analysis and explore instead how "gender, and more specifically, the subjugation of women for the sake of sustaining male privilege—patriarchy—actually *causes* militarization and the wars that flow from it."[95] We must examine how militarism and masculinity—while not identical—have become so entwined.

First, how are constructions of masculinity and femininity related to war making? How do these vary across cultures and contexts? How do the processes of war, state making, and nationalism produce gender, class, and race identities and in/securities? How is the mystique of combat gendered and what is its significance—for "equality of opportunity in violence," for gendered constructions of immortality, and for gendered dynamics of protector-protected relations?

Second, what *are* the gender-differentiated effects of war making and militarism? For example, how are women specifically affected by the economic costs of militarism, the structure of labor markets serving the military-industrial complex, and the embodied consequences of war (as victims of violence, as caretakers of the disabled, as refugees)? In what ways does the presence of military bases affect local women? *How* is the presence of women in the military affecting gender relations?

Third, what would a feminist theory of militarism/militarization look like? How are differences among women (e.g., class, race, occupation, sexual orientation, geographical and geopolitical location) related to militarization and its effects? How might a feminist perspective point beyond dichotomies of us-them, protector-protected, war-peace? How is our understanding of security gendered? Having constructed a vision of feminist security, what strategies can we identify for achieving it?

Discussion: Protection Rules

> Despite all the social changes and legal and political reforms over the past 300 years, the question of women's subordination is still not seen as a matter of major importance, either in the academic study of politics or in political practice.[96]

Quite simply, and with deadly monotony, women's systematic *oppression*—and insecurity—is not taken seriously; to the extent that it is "visible," either gender hierarchy is justified by "nature is destiny" beliefs, mystified by apparent "equal opportunity" options, and/or its transformation is deferred until "after the revolution." The problem, however, is far deeper than our failure to take women's oppression seriously. My focus here on *gendered* states is not intended to mask but to illuminate other forms and expressions of structural violence. The problem—of and for world security— is that structural violence per se is not considered to be a matter of major importance: there is no collective outrage against the terrifying costs of masculinist, classist, and racist inequities. This is not to deny progressive intentions and commitments altogether; it is, of course, a matter of degree. But my point is less to argue the question of degrees than to ask, How has the systematic exploitation and degradation of human lives—and of our ecological support system—become so acceptable, so apolitical, so natural?[97] How have the current "rules of the game" been so effectively "authorized" that we take them as "givens"—inevitable, and therefore acceptable? How has our understanding of security been framed by sovereign state systems that themselves constitute profound and pervasive *in*securities?

I respond to these questions by exploring how situating gender and states in relationship to each other "systematically" reveals their relationship to structural violence and its reproduction. This essay has so far illuminated both the insecurities constituted by historical processes of state making and, more specifically, their implications for women's systemic insecurity. Rethinking world security requires, in part, this more accurate understanding of existing insecurities: it requires *politicizing* structural violence as historically constituted—as contingent rather than natural—and specifying some of its implications and consequences. This understanding confirms that structural violence can be changed and identifies some of the changes necessary to pursue world security. But rethinking world security also requires more accurate understanding of the identities and ideologies that (re)produce and, significantly, depoliticize structural violence and its insecurities. This is to query ways of being and knowing; to privilege questions of "who we are," how we learn to know who we are, and how particular identities—who and what we identify with—shape political possibilities.

We can employ the lens of "protection"—here understood simply as the exchange of obedience/subordination for (promises of) security—to explore how state systems (re)configure the meaning of and possibilities for system-wide security. The focus of our lens is sharpened by examining "protection rackets," structural dependency, and protector-protected identities. More specifically, I submit that rethinking "protection," and its constructions of security and identity, is a crucial component of efforts to address world security.

I begin with various forms of protection that states promise:[98] protecting citizens from each other, protecting rights to privacy, protecting property rights, and protecting citizens from external threats. Because security assumes so many guises, most people—regardless of their hierarchically differentiated positions within systems—experience *some* sense of participating in one or a number of these forms of "having" security: for example, through identification with a "secure" class, gender, role, age group, occupation, ethnic group, nation, etc. All people (at the least, as dependent children) have experienced the need for protection, and seeking some form(s) of security, however defined, appears to be a ubiquitous construction of human needs. As a justification for state power, therefore, "protection"—understood as providing forms of security—seems quite compelling.

Yet this is to gloss over the ambiguities of "protection": "With one tone, 'protection' calls up images of the shelter against danger provided by a powerful friend, a large insurance policy, or a sturdy roof. With the other, it evokes the racket in which a local strong man forces merchants to pay tribute in order to avoid damage—damage the strong man himself threatens to deliver. The difference, to be sure, is a matter of degree . . ."[99]

Worse, it is not simply a matter of degree (suggesting linear, single-variable comparisons) but a matter of trade-offs (suggesting interactive, multiple dimensions, always in process). The *interaction* of systems of in/security (patriarchy, instrumentalism, state making, industrial capitalism) renders complexities and contradictions such that apparent gains can mask actual costs. The degree of gain or loss depends on the specifics of context, on factors such as what time frame we adopt, how we perceive the gain or threat and our position in relation to it, and our access to resources for dealing with or reconfiguring the situation. That is, the evaluation of actual gains and trade-offs cannot be done in the abstract but requires contextualizing attention to interacting practices, institutions, and systems.

What do we know about large-scale protection systems? Defining a racketeer as "someone who creates a threat and then charges for its reduction," Tilly pursues the analogy of state making and war making as "quintessential protection rackets":

> To the extent that the threats against which a given government protects its citizens are imaginary or are consequences of its own activities, the government has organized a protection racket. Since governments themselves commonly simulate, stimulate, or even fabricate threats of external war and since the repressive and extractive activities of governments often constitute the largest current threats to the livelihoods of their own citizens, many governments operate in essentially the same way as racketeers.[100]

As Tilly notes, this is not to argue that "government authority rests 'only' . . . on the threat of violence. Nor does it entail the assumption that a government's only service is protection."[101] Rather, the argument is that effective state making *depends upon* militarism, extraction, capital accumulation, and ideological legitimation. In the absence of "escape routes" or sufficient power to resist centralizing forces, options for seeking security are severely limited; lacking "secure" alternatives, one is "forced" to participate in state forms of protection.

Similarly, feminists have explored the dynamics of marriage as a protection racket: systemic male violence against women and our position in the labor market "force" us into marriage as protection from these systemic threats to our security.[102] The gender politics of marriage and the family cannot be understood without recognizing women's vulnerability: women select marriage as a form of protection in large part because their choices— within systems reproducing structural violence—are severely limited. Like state protection rackets, this is not to argue that negative constructions of "protection" exhaust the meaning of marriage; protection rackets do permit (but do not in fact guarantee) some forms of security (economic support, sex/affective pleasures, privacy), especially those denied to nonparticipants.

The point is, of course, that as protection *rackets*, states and marriage are implicated in the reproduction of hierarchies and in the structural violence against which they claim to offer protection. It is illuminating to review how the systemic costs and insecurities of protection rackets are so effectively mystified. First, individual participants making "rational" choices to "accept" protection, simultaneously act "irrationally" by reproducing systemic dependency. Benefits to individual units appear secured but at the expense of either system-based equity and justice or long-term system sustainability. For example, in the case of states the appearance of protection is paid for in the perpetuation of structural violence and in the security dilemma posed by the state system, global ecology, and capitalist economics. Second, the decentralization of units and their linkage through the protector/"center" (rather than "locally") obscures the "collective interest" that the protected may have in a transformation of the system itself. Preoccupation with maintaining whatever security one can, or jockeying for marginal improvements, may resituate certain protectees but reproduces the asymmetrical system dynamics and "competition" for "scarce" security. Similarly, to the extent that protection is "working," the protected lack incentives to risk destabilization and/or potential loss of what security they have.

Third, protection systems reproduce nonparticipatory dynamics while obscuring accountability of protectees for maintaining boundaries, hierarchies, and identities that are the medium and outcome of protection systems. Distance from protector roles leaves decisionmaking and threat assessment to those with particular interests that are only ambiguously related to "collective interests." Identification of the protected with their protectors (as opposed to other protectees), as well as identification of protectors with each other, further complicates alliance formation directed at transforming the system itself. Protection systems also distort the meaning of "consent" by both mystifying the violence that backs up the systemic inequality and perpetuating the illusion of equality among parties to "contractual obligations."[103]

Finally, while we can acknowledge the structural asymmetry of protection rackets, we cannot ignore the reality of threats; once institutionalized, protection systems render disengagement risky at best, and possibly devastating. This, of course, is especially true for those most vulnerable and poses enormous difficulties in assessing strategies for change. There are no simple win or lose options, but double binds (in fact, multiple binds):

> One of the most characteristic and ubiquitous features of the world as experienced by oppressed people is the double bind—situations in which options are reduced to a very few and all of them expose one to penalty, censure or deprivation. For example, it is often a requirement upon oppressed people that we smile and be cheerful. If we comply, we signal our docility and our acquiescence in our situation. We need not, then, be taken note of. We acquiesce in being made invisible . . . We participate in our own erasure. On the other hand, anything but the sunniest countenance exposes us to being perceived as mean, bitter, angry or dangerous. This means, at the least, that we may be found "difficult" or unpleasant to work with, which is enough to cost one one's livelihood; at worst, being seen as mean, bitter, angry, or dangerous has been known to result in rape, arrest, beating and murder. One can only choose to risk one's preferred form and rate of annihilation.[104]

Again, choices are always *trade-offs* shaped by context. This understanding is crucial for comprehending the complex relationship between our resistance to and complicity in oppressive systems. It informs Enloe's call for refining "the concept of cooptation"[105] and Eisenstein's declaration that "'freedom of choice' is always an inadequate model for those who do not have power."[106] In the contemporary world, we are all situated in multiple, overlapping, and sometimes contradictory "systems" of in/security (the effects of patriarchy, instrumentalism, classism, imperialism), though some of us are situated much more favorably than others. Protection racket analogies can illuminate the "structure" shaping our locations and choices within this complex configuration, revealing especially how the dynamics of force, and its threat, generate our participation in—and apparently willing reproduction of—structural dependency.

However illuminating, this exploration of protection privileges masculinist constructions that I now want to problematize. The interaction of "systems" and the complexity of our "locations" suggests that, in evaluating choices or strategies for change, we must ask not simply, Is it the right or wrong choice? but, Compared to *what*? What are the trade-offs, the alternatives? The latter question forces our attention to situational and system context and to the lenses—for example, social identities—through which we make choices. *"Through" what identity do we seek "security"*? How are particular ways of being and knowing the medium and outcome of "protection" systems?

Stiehm's analysis of protector and protected is helpful in this regard. Situated in the context of women's exclusion from state-sanctioned roles of protector or defender,[107] Stiehm's discussion resonates with many of the points made in this chapter regarding protection dynamics: the protected are dependent (cannot choose to defend themselves); the degree of threat one is being protected from is in part defined by the protector ("whose interest may be to exaggerate the threat"); the distance of the protected from actual defensive activities surrenders assessment of risks and threats to protectors; frequently, protection is simply not in fact possible; protectors sometimes identify more with other protectors than with the protected; the status of "protector" depends on structural demands for protection and their embodiment in the "protected."

Of particular interest is Stiehm's analysis of the protector's dilemma: he has dependents representing "both a burden and an expanded vulnerability"; if protection fails, he has failed; dependents can also be "unruly and draining" and require provisioning; the protector is in fact dependent upon the relationship to establish his status, and gains of autonomy or power by the protected can threaten that status; once a threat to other protectors, the protector may also become a threat to the protected. Stiehm also employs the protection racket analogy:

> How does it happen that so many situations which are said to enhance
> safety end in decreased safety? Is it possible that the greatest threat to
> one's existence comes not from a vicious enemy but from one's own
> protector(s) who may (1) deliberately exploit one, (2) manipulate and
> harm one in the interests of better control or of guaranteed safety, (3)
> attract violence by organizing one's protection, and/or (4) turn on one?
> Many governments, after all, simply *are* the military, and even in many
> civilian governments the military represents the largest budget item.[108]

How do these dynamics shape social identities? Stiehm quotes a phrase
from the wall of a POW camp cell: "Freedom—a feeling the protected will
never know." The phrase is now also inscribed on a wall of the U.S. Air
Force Academy.[109] Clearly, the role of protector is embedded in heroic
narratives, suggesting how "feelings of unity, sacrifice, and even ecstasy"
frame combat expectations.[110] The experience of protecting can also be
simply hellish; it all depends. How the protected construct their experience
no doubt varies as well, but is unlikely to be couched in heroic terms; as the
above saying suggests, dependency is not to be preferred to "freedom."

These accounts of protection rackets and the protector-protected
dichotomy are powerfully gendered. Protector-protected roles are embedded in
constructions of masculine autonomy (freedom, control, heroics) and
feminine dependency (passivity, vulnerability, woman as adored but also
despised). Cast in this fashion, dependency is demeaning, a status indicative
of subordination and one shunned by the free man—by the political man in
Aristotle's terms. Transcendence is preferable: seeking freedom from the
entanglements of (mere) material necessity. Masculinism may celebrate
protector roles to the extent that they permit heroism (transcendence again),
but *being* protected is an identity to be avoided as much as possible. This
version of protection constructs dependency in narrow, dichotomous terms
that obscure (inter)dependent relations as a pervasive feature of social reality.

As long as we remain locked in dichotomies, we cannot accurately
understand and are less likely to transform social relations: not only do
oppositional constructions distort the contextual complexity of social reality,
they set limits on the questions we ask and the alternatives we consider. True
to their "origin" (Athenian objectivist metaphysics), the dichotomies most
naturalized in Western world views (abstract-concrete, reason-emotion, mind-
body, culture-nature, public-private) are both medium and outcome of
objectification practices. Retaining them keeps us locked in to their
objectifying—reifying—lens on our world(s) and who we are.

As clarification of these points and to suggest (re)visioning strategies, I
turn briefly to rethinking three dichotomies. First, the separation of public-
private and production-reproduction has surfaced repeatedly as an organizing
principle of modern state making. Historically, this separation has not only
framed "spheres" of activity oppositionally, but insisted on the elevation of
one at the expense of the other. Thus, the various forms of "women's work"

are denigrated and literally de-valued. Clearly, failing to take seriously reproductive activities—both biological *and* social—has had systematic consequences for women's lives and choices. But it has also been costly to our ways of knowing (and being): our understanding of social reality is distorted and weakened by marginalizing what are in fact key practices and processes. Specifically, ignore-ance of women's work impoverishes our understanding of *social reproduction*: everyday maintenance securing the reproduction of social identities, group cohesion, legitimation ideologies, and indeed, social formations. Moreover, static, economistic ways of knowing not only preclude taking seriously women's work, lives, and identities but also preclude expanded *vision*. Stuck in ahistorical categorizations, dynamic possibilities are rendered in-visible. One conclusion, a staple of much feminist writing, is that the division of labor needs to be transformed in the direction not simply of adding women to what men do, but of greater engagement by men in reproductive and caring work. Furthermore, in relation to protection dynamics, the acknowledgement that we are *all* situated in various dependencies (re)visions social relations, with specific implications for transformation strategies.

The separation of public-private also expresses the second dichotomy, whose poles can be recognized as reason-affect, mind-body, freedom-necessity, abstract-concrete, culture-nature. As Brown notes: "When the reproduction and maintenance of life are organized oppressively and regarded as demeaning, transcendence of life appears as the only road to recognition, continuity, and creativity."[111] In denying the body/materiality/necessity and seeking transcendence, masculinist philosophy constructs politics as disembedded and disembodied. Another staple of feminist work is the critique of these decontextualized, abstract accounts of how to be in the world. Rather, feminists insist on (re)visioning politics and "bringing the body back in." We seek a politics *not disembedded* but situated in historical and cultural contingency, recognizing dimensions of power (politics) in asymmetrical social relations and various cultural forms, and acknowledging the complex and sometimes contradictory interaction of systems of power. We seek a politics *not disembodied* but situated in material processes, a politics that recognizes dimensions of desire, affect, and emotion in all social relations and cultural forms, including rationality, and that acknowledges the interaction of desire, knowledge, and power. Again, what is required is *not* simply the addition of women to masculine abstractions but a transformation in our understanding of politics, power, and political identities.

Third, the hierarchical separation of protector-protected (re)produces masculinist constructions of dependency as necessarily undesirable; it is a very short step, as we have seen, from despising dependency to despising dependents. In fact, practices construable as "protection" are extremely diverse: from maternal caretaking to faculty mentoring to organized crime to state executioners. The dichotomy of protector-protected misrepresents the complexity of our "security" arrangements and, especially, the meaning of security in the context of human interdependence. An alternative lens reminds us of the many ways we seek security: through emotional support, caretaking, meaningful production, and everyday reproduction of human community.[112] Through this lens, (inter)dependency is resituated from degraded status to centrality: life quite literally does not go on, much less feel good, in isolation from caretaking, "servicing," and processes of reproduction. That these activities have been positioned as marginal to the "real work of producing the world" reveals masculine power to re-present the world through the particularist lenses of elite men. Finally, the dichotomies of protector-protected, direct-indirect violence, and war-peace are interwoven; denying them as oppositional *dichotomies* means recognizing the complexity of (inter)dependence, the interrelationship of oppressions,[113] and the uncertainty of security.[114]

I have argued that historically interacting systems of domination (patriarchy, state making, instrumentalism, capitalism) engender structural violence; their mutuality suggests that transforming the domination relations of any one—or combination—of these systems requires transforming the objectifying practices of all. Through currently dominant lenses (positivist, "realist"), this may seem an impossible task. But as the historical review of state making suggests, systemwide, revolutionary transformations have occurred before: our social relations are "made not given."

As socially constructed and frequently contradictory systems, even "protection rackets" are vulnerable to transformation. In the current context, interacting local, national, and global crises confirm the fragility, and therefore transformational possibilities, of large-scale systems—even those of long duration. We are experiencing multiple crises of legitimation as various authorities are increasingly unable to deliver on providing protection, securing order, and/or maintaining safety. How the failure to deliver expected benefits affects people cannot be determined abstractly; at a minimum, such failures raise legitimation questions that are potentially transformational.

The priorities of various systems can come into conflict, exposing the dynamics of particular exploitative practices. As contradictions are revealed and confronted, identities are reshaped, with potential for new answers to who we are, to who and what we identify with. Women in paid jobs for most of their lives challenge the myth of the dependent wife and expose the contradiction of idealized nuclear family models. Workers in advanced industrial economies lose jobs as multinationals seek lower wage costs in less developed countries. The welfare state cannot meet the minimum needs of increasing numbers of dependents. Environmental crises respect no borders. Multiple "indirect threats"

> are the result of the kind of society that the current global political economy produces. Industrial activity, agricultural monocultures and

rampant individual consumption of "disposable" items (all of which are attempts to enhance some forms of human welfare through domination and control of facets of nature) produce other forms of insecurity which undermine the security provision that is the ostensible reason for many of these activities in the first place.[115]

The emergence of critical social movements suggests awareness of systemic crises and possible new identities. Moreover, crises are strategically important in that legitimations of exploitation previously deemed "natural" are exposed as constructions. To the extent that the current "rules" and the structural violence they constitute remain in place—and remain depoliticized—because they appear natural, as givens, this disruption is a necessary, but not sufficient, condition of system transformation. The proliferation of crises only establishes that changes are happening; it does not ensure movement in any pregiven direction.

The identification of appropriate strategies becomes crucial: How can we most effectively move toward world security? In addressing the extent and complexity of global insecurities, I argue for a postpositivist feminist lens as the most promising orientation for the (re)visioning required.[116]

Through a *postpositivist* lens, the rules of objectivist metaphysics are revealed; reductionist dichotomies are sighted and their domination dynamics exposed. Postpositivist (re)visioning deconstructs the oppositional dynamics of myriad dichotomies: mind-body, culture-nature, protector-protected, public-private, production-reproduction, reform-revolution. This (re)visioning does not deny the distinctions these dichotomies posit, but resituates them contextually: in relation to divisions of labor and identities, institutions, structures, and possibilities for systemic transformation. A postpositivist lens rejects "naturalized" constructions, whether as essentialized identities (of woman, man, nation) or depoliticized categories (the family, natural resources, contract, truth, security). Rather, postpositivism compels our attention to context and historical process, to contingency and uncertainty, to how we construct, rather than dis-cover, our world(s). It thus denies the illusion of the "perspective-less gaze,"[117] and the arrogance and power of claims to objectivity understood as independent of bodies and contexts.

Through a *postpositivist feminist* lens, the rule of dichotomizing and the dichotomies it generates are gendered, the consequence of masculinist experience and standpoint. Feminist (re)visioning exposes essentialized sexual identities and their hierarchical construction at the core of interacting objectification processes. Through this lens divisions of labor are inseparable from divisions of social identity; as historically constructed, these have relied upon an essentializing of masculine-feminine and on the deployment of that "naturalized" hierarchy as justification for interrelated, though differently embodied, domination relations. As postpositivists expose dichotomies generally, feminists extend that critique to the cultural forms dichotomies have historically taken, exposing their gendered dynamics, their politics.

Feminism and postpositivism are similar in their critiques of dominating ideologies, objectivist metaphysics, and the constitution of body/power/ knowledge.[118] But our critical and transformational commitments also move us to *situate* knowledge claims in order to "become answerable for what we learn how to see."[119]

Finally, as we reach toward world security, we can ignore neither the limited security afforded by gendered (welfare) states nor the objective of moving beyond states of gender (territorial states and states of mind). These are not oppositional but, like reform and revolution, interactive components of long-term, systemwide transformations. There are no easy "answers" in the face of "multiple binds." While we seek revolutionary transformations required for world security, we must also care for and about those who are structurally vulnerable—and realize that means all of us.

Notes

Portions of this essay were included in "Beyond Gendered States," paper presented at the 15th World Congress of the International Political Science Association in Buenos Aires, July 1991. I am grateful for feedback and support from Carol Bacchi, Mona Harrington, Stacey Mayhall, Nick Onuf, Ralph Pettman, betts putnam, Anne Runyan, Ann Tickner, and an anonymous reviewer.

1. Walker, "Sovereignty, Security and the Challenge," 6.
2. Tickner, "Redefining Security."
3. Walker, "Sovereignty, Security and the Challenge," 1.
4. On rethinking global security see, for example, Tickner, "Redefining Security"; Dalby, "Rethinking Security"; Barry Buzan, *People, States and Fear: The National Security Problem in International Relations* (Brighton: Wheatsheaf Books, 1983); Chase-Dunn, "World-State Formation"; Johan Galtung, *True Worlds* (New York: Free Press, 1980); Mel Gurtov, *Global Politics in the Human Interest* (Boulder, CO: Lynne Rienner, 1988). On state sovereignty in relation to political identity see Grant, "Feminist Criteria"; Walker, "State Sovereignty, Global Civilization," "Sovereignty, Security and the Challenge," and "Sovereignty, Identity, Community"; Ashley, "Untying the Sovereign State" and "Living on Borderlines."
5. Walker, "Sovereignty, Security and the Challenge," 12.
6. Walker, "Sovereignty, Security and the Challenge," 13.
7. On postpositivist feminism see my "Introduction" in this volume. Because this essay focuses on *insecurities*, it is extremely critical of state systems. This is not to argue that states offer *no* benefits, are responsible for all insecurities, or represent the worst conceivable organization of social life. It is to argue that we must examine the gender dynamics of sovereign states if we are to accurately understand and effectively reconfigure "security." The state is not the only or arguably even the main "problem," but its historical and ongoing role in the construction and reproduction of the *legitimation* of violence and domination—specifically, its "depoliticization"—warrants our closest attention. Feminist critiques of "naturalized" subjection offer rich resources for (re)visioning social relations and particularly (I believe) for moving beyond gendered states and their security dynamics. For important feminist treatments of women and welfare states see Harrington (this volume); Gordon, *Women, the*

State, and Welfare; Sassoon, *Women and the State*; Wilson, *Women and the Welfare State*. My focus here is on the historical conditions that make state welfare/"protection" necessary."

8. Dalby, "Rethinking Security."

9. For elaboration and further references see Peterson, "Archeology of Domination," "Transgressing Boundaries," and "Gendered States" (the latter includes twentieth-century state making); Runyan and Peterson, "Radical Future of Realism." My approach to states is informed by transdisciplinary, postpositivist, critical, and feminist commitments; I understand the state not as a thing but as historically varying and very complex processes (see especially Abrams, "Notes"). Following Connell ("State, Gender, and Sexual Politics," 510), references to the state "as an object or as an actor" mean "the set of institutions . . . subject to coordination . . . by a state directorate." Specifically in regard to women's insecurities, there are important differences between states and between classes, races, etc., within them. However, my focus in this paper is on the *patterns* of *gendered* states and I accept, therefore, the overgeneralizing risks of macrolabels, e.g., "the state," "women," "feminist." I undertake the hazards of such macro-sociopolitical study from, first, the observation that "macro" treatments of *gender* hierarchy are still "underdeveloped" (especially in IR) and, second, a conviction that understanding how domination is gendered is necessary but not sufficient for transforming domination practices more generally.

10. Peterson, "Archeology of Domination," and "Transgressing Boundaries."

11. In this essay patriarchy, masculinism, and gender hierarchy are used interchangeably to refer to male domination—individually and as a "class"—through the appropriation/control/regulation of women (our bodies, labor, knowing); it includes meaning systems (e.g., privileging that which is associated with "maleness") accompanying and legitimating patriarchal relations. Particular forms of male domination must be understood in historical context; here I focus on patterns of gender hierarchy as revealed in state formation processes. For nonfeminist treatments of early state formation see Cohen and Service, *Origins of the State*; Claessen and Skalnick, *Early State*; Haas, *Evolution of the Prehistoric State*; Carneiro, "Theory of the Origin of the State"; Mann, *Sources of Social Power*. For feminist anthropological reviews of early state formation see Lamphere, "Anthropology"; Rapp, "Anthropology"; Atkinson, "Anthropology"; Gailey, "State of the State," *Kinship to Kingship*; Silverblatt, "Women in States." For additional feminist scholarship on the historical development of gender hierarchy, see Lerner, *Creation of Patriarchy*; Burstyn, "Economy, Sexuality, Politics"; Janssen-Jurreit, *Sexism*; Coontz and Henderson, *Women's Work, Men's Property*; Mies, *Patriarchy and Accumulation*; Peterson, "Archeology of Domination." Theories assuming social domination is "natural" are not addressed here; see Gailey's treatment of these ("Women and Warfare," *Kinship to Kingship*); also Sacks, *Sisters and Wives*; Leacock, *Myths of Male Dominance*; Bleier, *Science and Gender*; Fausto-Sterling, *Myths of Gender*.

12. Corrigan and Sayer, *Great Arch.*

13. Mann, *Sources of Social Power.*

14. Cohen, "Introduction," 8.

15. Lerner, *Creation of Patriarchy*; Peterson, "Archeology of Domination."

16. Arthur, "Liberated Women"; Nicholson, *Gender and History.*

17. Gailey, "Evolutionary Perspectives."

18. Gailey, "Evolutionary Perspectives," 20.

19. Sacks, *Sisters and Wives*; Silverblatt, "Women in States."

20. Lerner, *Creation of Patriarchy.*

21. Chevillard and Leconte, "Slavery"; Lerner, *Creation of Patriarchy*.

22. Gimbutas, *Goddesses and Gods of Old Europe*; Stone, *When God was a Woman*; Robbins, "Tiamat and Her Children."

23. Arthur, "Early Greece," 27.

24. Arthur, "Liberated Women," 67. Women's roles in the accumulation process are rarely acknowledged in state formation literature. Three brief points in regard to the Athenian case: (1) women's domestic labor—free and nonfree—would appear to be significant, especially in nonindustrial, primarily rural-agricultural economies as exemplified by Athens; (2) as Aristotle noted, this labor (in addition to men's slave labor) was a precondition of the participation of male heads of households as citizens; (3) the appropriation of women's labor—free and nonfree—meant reproductive as well as productive resources.

25. Foley, "Conception of Women in Athenian Drama," 130.

26. Pomeroy, *Goddesses, Whores, Wives and Slaves*; Arthur, "Early Greece"; Keuls, *Reign of the Phallus*.

27. Elshtain, *Public Man, Private Woman*, 455.

28. A series of binary oppositions, premised upon the categorical separation of subject-object, culture-nature, reason-affect, etc., characterizes objectivist metaphysics (Derrida's [*Grammatology*] metaphysics of presence) and the positivist science it underpins. (See also Rorty, *Philosophy and the Mirror of Nature*; Ryan, *Marxism and Deconstruction*; Hodge, Struckmann, and Trost, *Cultural Bases*.) A reorientation of meaning systems accompanies—in order to legitimate—state making. I have argued elsewhere (through historicizing the polis and interpreting classical Athenian texts) that objectivist metaphysics—and specifically the public-private dichotomy at the heart of Western political constructions—serves to justify Athenian, and by extension, other (civil) state exploitation ("Archeology of Domination," "Trangressing Boundaries"). Moreover, the mutual constitution of instrumental (objectifying) metaphysics, essentialized and hierarchical sexual identities, and oppositional self-other, us-them social relations has implications for transformational strategies. As further developed in this chapter, the domination dynamic in any one or combination of these orientations (i.e., instrumentalism, sexism, and classism/racism/imperialism) cannot be transformed without taking their mutual constitution seriously.

29. Other Athenian texts—drama and poetry—"reflected" the shift to new masculinist principles of order and control. My remarks here oversimplify a complex literature; clear differences exist in the *portrayal* of gender relations (for example, in prose vs. poetic texts) (Foley, "Conception of Women in Athenian Drama") as well as among retrospective *interpretations* of women's situation.

30. Benhabib, "Generalized and the Concrete Other," 81, emphasis in original.

31. Clark, "Rights of Women"; Vickers, "At His Mother's Knee."

32. See Chodorow, *Reproduction of Mothering*; Gilligan, *Different Voice*; Di Stefano, *Configurations of Masculinity*.

33. My discussion does not distinguish between liberal capitalist and socialist states. This is due in part to space limitations but also to the lack of distinction between the two in terms of gender relations: specifically, the double workday for women; asymmetrical sex-segregated employment patterns; male monopoly of political, military, and top decision-making positions; and masculinist ideological discrimination (Burstyn, "Masculine Dominance"; Cameron, "Sexual Division of Labour"; MacKinnon, "Feminism, Marxism, Method"; Mies, *Patriarchy and Accumulation*). For elaboration of the argumentation in this section and a discussion of twentieth-century Third

World states (which replicate the pattern cited above) see Peterson, "Gendered States."

34. Mann, "Autonomous Power of the State," 189.

35. Giddens, *Nation-State and Violence*. See also Foucault's articulation of "disciplinary power" (*Power/Knowledge*), Bourdieu's "theory of practice" (*Outline of a Theory of Practice*), Gramsci's theorization of "hegemony" (*Selections from the Prison Notebooks*); Carnoy, *State and Political Theory*; and T. J. Jackson Lears, "The Concept of Cultural Hegemony," *American Historical Review* 90 (1985): 567–93. The extensive literatures building upon these insights are all relevant.

36. Mann, "Autonomous Power of the State," 198.

37. Cohen, "Introduction," 8.

38. Grossholtz, "Battered Women's Shelters," 60.

39. Connell, "State, Gender and Sexual Politics," 519.

40. Franzway, Court, and Connell, *Staking a Claim*, 105.

41. Runyan in this volume; Merchant, *Death of Nature*; Keller, *Reflections on Gender and Science*; Harding, *Science Question in Feminism*; Bennett, *Unthinking Faith and Enlightenment*; Schiebinger, *The Mind Has No Sex*; Lloyd, *Man of Reason*.

42. Merchant, *Death of Nature*, xvii.

43. Keller, *Reflections on Gender and Science*, 53.

44. These processes in Europe have imperialist corollaries: like "mother earth" and women, the colonies were deemed "natural resources." With the rise of capitalism, "nature" was economically defined as "everything that was to be free of costs, that is, free for unrestricted appropriation. . . . This concept then included women, the earth, water, other 'natural resources' and also the native peoples, the land, and the peoples in the colonies" (Mies, "Introduction," 8; von Werlhof, "On the Concept of Nature").

45. Corrigan and Sayer, *Great Arch*, 4.

46. Ruggie, "Continuity and Transformation," note 30, 274.

47. Ruggie, "Continuity and Transformation," 275–276.

48. Locke is highlighted here because of his centrality to Western constructions of liberalism, individualism, social contract, and the dichotomy of state-family (public-private). All of these have particular relevance to gender relations/identities and the continued legitimation of state authority.

49. Ruggie, "Continuity and Transformation," 276.

50. Elshtain, "Political Theory Rediscovers the Family"; Pateman, *Problem of Political Obligation* and *Sexual Contract*; Eisenstein, *Radical Future*; Nicholson, *Gender and History*.

51. Pateman, *Problem of Political Obligation* and *Sexual Contract*; also Richard Krouse, "Patriarchal Liberalism and Beyond," in *The Family in Political Thought*, ed. Jean Elshtain (Amherst: University of Massachusetts Press, 1982). According to Pateman, the liberal ideology of the social contract and related concepts of rights, interests, individualism, and representation mystify the masculinism and structural subordination underpinning these constructions. In *The Sexual Contract* she argues that in the name of new freedoms, social contract theorists mystified the establishment of new slaveries: contracts about "property in the person" are always about obedience (exchanged for protection) and subordination. The tradition of contract is masculinist because the social contract presupposes a sexual contract, and the latter presupposes patriarchal relations, with men and women embodying essentialized (and mutually exclusive) male and female sexual identities and heterosexual roles.

52. Nicholson, *Gender and History*, 1.

62 V. Spike Peterson

53. Benn and Gaus, *Public and Private in Social Life.*
54. Pateman, "Feminist Critiques of the Public/Private Dichotomy";
Norton, "Contemporary Critical Theory and the Family"; Dahlerup, "Confusing
Concepts"; Cohn and Dirks, "Issues and Agendas."
55. Pateman, "Feminist Critiques of the Public/Private Dichotomy."
56. Kerber, "Separate Spheres, Female Worlds"; Nicholson, *Gender and
History.*
57. Tilly and Scott, *Women, Work, and Family,* 12.
58. Zaretsky, *Capitalism, the Family, and Personal Life,* 29.
59. Cameron, "Sexual Division of Labour."
60. Laurin-Frenette, "Women's Movement and the State," 28.
61. Boris and Bardaglio, "Transformation of Patriarchy," 72.
62. Brown, "Mothers, Fathers, and Children," 240; Eisenstein, "State, the
Patriarchal Family, and Working Mothers," 84.
63. See Gordon, *Women, the State, and Welfare.*
64. Baron, "Feminist Legal Strategies," 496.
65. Sex/affective relations (family/intimacy/sexuality/household) and
economic relations (labor market/"work"/wages/welfare) are not separate from but
interact with "power relations" in constituting women's (and men's) systemic
insecurities. Through legislation, public policies, and less formal but no less
effective "official discourses," states regulate sexual practices and reproduction
options, reinforce particular constructions of femininity and masculinity, and
promote the model of heterosexual, nuclear households. Similarly, states regulate
labor practices and workplace options, reinforce particular constructions of
"women's work" and "men's work," and promote the model of a dependent-wife
wage system. The gender dynamics of these relations contribute decisively to
structural violence. For elaboration and references see Peterson, "Gendered
States."
66. Connell, "State, Gender and Sexual Politics," 520.
67. Corrigan and Sayer, *Great Arch,* 2–3.
68. Eisenstein, *Radical Future,* 26.
69. Enloe, *Bananas, Beaches and Bases,* 195.
70. Enloe, *Bananas, Beaches and Bases,* 195.
71. Hartsock, *Money, Sex, and Power*; Brown, *Manhood and Politics*;
Jaggar, *Feminist Politics and Human Nature*; Okin, *Women in Western Political
Thought.*
72. Jones, "Citizenship in a Woman-Friendly Polity," 792.
73. Brown, *Manhood and Politics,* 196; Pateman, "Introduction"; Peterson,
"Whose Rights?"
74. Jones and Jonasdottir, *Political Interests of Gender,* 9.
75. Connell, "State, Gender and Sexual Politics"; United Nations, *World's
Women.*
76. Franzway, Court, and Connell, *Staking a Claim,* 105.
77. Hanmer, "Violence and the Social Control of Women"; Dobash and
Dobash, *Violence Against Wives.*
78. Vera Taylor, "The Future of Feminism in the 1980s," in *Feminist
Frontiers,* ed. Laurel Richardson and Vera Taylor (New York: Random House,
1983), 442, citing Susan Henry, "Commonwoman," *What She Wants* (April
1981); Grossholtz, "Battered Women's Shelters"; see also United Nations,
World's Women.
79. Heise, "Crimes of Gender." Equally telling is our failure to acknowledge
that sexual violence is the most *pervasive* human rights issue. Key to this

"denial" is our treatment of sexual violence as "private" and not political, as a domestic not international issue. On the androcentrism of human rights see Peterson, "Whose Rights?"

80. Hanmer, "Violence and the Social Control of Women," 219.

81. MacKinnon, "Feminism, Marxism, Method."

82. MacKinnon, "Feminism, Marxism, Method," 643.

83. Giddens, *Nation State and Violence*; Tilly, "War Making and State Making," *Coercion, Capital, and European States*; Mann, *Sources of Social Power* and *States, War and Capitalism*.

84. Mosse, *Nationalism and Sexuality*.

85. Gellner, *Nations and Nationalism*; Mosse, *Nationalism and Sexuality*; Anderson, *Imagined Communities*.

86. Enloe, *Bananas, Beaches and Bases*; Jayawardena, *Feminism and Nationalism*; Janice Newberry, "Women and the Moral Boundaries of the Nation," unpublished ms. (1991); Chatterjee, "Colonialism, Nationalism and Colonised Women."

87. Mosse, *Nationalism and Sexuality*, 16.

Nationalist ideologies attempt to legitimate particular forms of rule in the name of (invented) collective identities. Their moral/normative power lies in claims to cultural superiority. In modern state making, particular nationalisms have constructed their claims to superiority in gendered terms. For example, Europeans invoked bourgeois respectability—specifically, claims to sexual control/regulation and an "economy of reason" (both senses)—to legitimate imperial rule. The model of bourgeois respectability was the Victorian family with its specific gender divisions of labor and identities; these symbolized the norms of civility and civilization being imposed on colonized peoples. In throwing off imposed rule, independence movements drew similarly on gendered constructions of nationalist identity. For example, the model of respectability among Islamic peoples was the gender division of labor and identities symbolized by the moral purity of the veiled Muslim woman—she represented the superiority of the "traditional" culture.

88. Corrigan and Sayer, *Great Arch*, 195.

89. Also Walker, "State Sovereignty, Global Civilization," "Sovereignty, Security and the Challenge," and in this volume.

90. Leonardo Paggi and Piero Pinzauti, "Peace and Security," *Telos* 63 (1985): 3–40.

91. Burstyn, "Masculine Dominance," 6.

92. Segal, *Is the Future Female?*; Runyan, "Gender Relations"; Mies, *Patriarchy and Accumulation*; Enloe, *Does Khaki Become You?*

93. See, for example, Hartsock, *Money, Sex, and Power*; Enloe, *Bananas, Beaches and Bases*.

94. Enloe, "Feminists Thinking About War," 529.

95. Enloe, "Feminists Thinking About War," 529–30, emphasis in original.

96. Pateman, *Sexual Contract*, 219.

97. To argue for "improvements," even revolutionary, system transforming improvements, is not to suggest human suffering or social conflict will or can be eliminated. To maintain that the current degree of structural violence is the best we can hope for ensures that it is.

98. This discussion focuses on—and does not distinguish between— contemporary states. I take the risk of generalizing across states because it enables a view of macropatterns—e.g., systemic interactions of structural

violence—that is necessary for understanding systemwide dynamics. Again, my critique of states is not to argue there are easy alternatives or that states are responsible for *all* insecurities.

99. Tilly, "War Making and State Making," 170.

100. Tilly, "War Making and State Making," 171.

101. Tilly, "War Making and State Making," 172.

102. Runyan, "Gender Relations"; Susan Brownmiller, *Against Our Will* (Toronto: Bantam Books, 1975); MacDonald, "Drawing the Lines."

103. See Pateman, *Sexual Contract*.

104. Marilyn Frye, "Oppression," in *Racism and Sexism*, ed. Paula Rothenberg (New York: St. Martin's Press, 1988), 38.

105. Enloe, "Feminists Thinking About War," 535.

106. Enloe, *Does Khaki Become You?* 44.

107. Stiehm, "Protected, the Protector, the Defender"; see also Runyan, "Gender Relations."

108. Stiehm, "Protected, the Protector, the Defender," 373. Consider Mann's research: "It was not until 1881—probably for the first time in world history—that a Great Power (Britain) actually spent more money on domestic civil functions than on its military defence and aggression, and this was not stably the case until after the First and Second World Wars" (Mann, *States, War, and Capitalism*, xi).

109. Stiehm, "Protected, the Protector, the Defender," 370.

110. Stiehm, "Protected, the Protector, the Defender," 371, citing J. Glenn Gray, *The Warriors* (New York: Colophon, 1959).

111. Brown, *Manhood and Politics*, 204.

112. See, for example, the feminist work on caring (Tronto, "Beyond Gender Difference"; Waerness, "On the Rationality of Caring"), women's servicing (Balbo, "Servicing Work," "Crazy Quilts), and maternal practices (Ruddick, *Maternal Thinking*; Trebilcot, *Mothering*).

113. Tickner, "Redefining Security."

114. Sylvester, "Feminist Postmodernism, Nuclear Strategy"; Klein, "After Strategy"; Ferguson, "Toward a New Anarchism."

115. Dalby, "Security, Modernity, Ecology," 113.

116. See also my "Introduction" in this volume.

117. Haraway, "Situated Knowledges."

118. Fraser and Nicholson, "Social Criticism without Philosophy."

119. Haraway, "Situated Knowledges," 583.

2

What Exactly Is Wrong with the Liberal State as an Agent of Change?

Mona Harrington

The title of this chapter is a question that needs much more careful exploration by feminists than we have given it so far. In fact, I raise the question in a somewhat belligerent tone because I am inclined to think that the liberal state is a suitable, even elegant, agent to advance a feminist agenda in both domestic and international relations. Yet most of my feminist colleagues who are probing the gendered nature of the state vastly mistrust the liberal tradition and seek to formulate a politics that will displace it. My aim here is to join some of their arguments before a consensus forms that liberalism is beyond the pale of seriously critical feminist analysis. But let me hasten to say, before irreversible misunderstanding sets in, that what I am contesting is the meaning, the content that antiliberals generally assign to liberalism. The object of most of their criticism is actually one variant of the liberal tradition, and I think it is crucially important that we recognize another, more morally spacious, set of liberal ideas and that we help to develop its deeper promise.

I will review the antiliberal arguments in some detail and answer them presently. First, I want to suggest why the whole argument is important.

The crux of feminist challenge to the liberal state is essentially an antistate analysis with demonstrations that liberalism, while promising to divest the state of its destructive features, does not do so. In this analysis, states are inherently oppressive and exploitative organizations of power. They are run by hierarchies in control of deadly force deployed to protect the privileges of elites, which are, for the most part, capital-controlling, white, and male. In short, feminist antiliberal, antistate analysis is similar to already established Marxist criticism of the state but with added attention to gender. States are not only instruments of class interest but also of patriarchy. They perpetuate not only class conflict and violence but also gender conflict and violence. And liberal systems that supposedly democratize power and wealth simply mask the underlying fact of elite rule. Where can this analysis lead but to a call for deconstructing the present sovereign state system?

At this juncture in history—I am writing in the winter of 1990–91 with the Soviet Union and Eastern Europe decommunized, the Cold War over—other calls for deconstructing nation-states are also in the air. Internationalists see the first opportunity since the mid-1940s to put a functioning system of international organization in place, starting with a revived United Nations and extending, in some versions, to complex networks of denationalized, depoliticized regimes rationally and efficiently organizing the world's business.

In other words, the state as a dealer in power, a wielder of weapons, an inherently violent institution, is the object of suspicion and resistance by both antiliberal feminists and liberal internationalists. And, especially now, when the international system is undergoing immense change, pressures for denationalizing change—certainly discourse arguing for it—will be persistent.

In the face of such pressures, I believe that feminist critics of the present state system should beware. The very fact that the state creates, condenses, and focuses political power may make it the best friend, not the enemy, of feminists—because the availability of real *political* power is essential to real democratic control. Not sufficient, I know, but essential.

My basic premise is that political power *can* significantly disrupt patriarchal and class (which is to say, economic) power. It holds the potential, at least, for disrupting the patriarchal/ economic oppression of those in the lower reaches of class, sex, and race hierarchies. It is indisputable that, in the nineteenth and twentieth centuries, it has been the political power of states that has confronted the massive economic power privately constructed out of industrial processes and has imposed obligations on employers for the welfare of workers as well as providing additional social supports for the population at large. And the political tempering of economic power has been the most responsive to broad public needs in liberal democracies, where governments must respond roughly to the interests of voters.

Of course, this is not the whole story. The nation-states of this period have also perpetrated horrors of torture and war, have aided the development of elite-controlled industrial wealth, and have not sufficiently responded to the human needs of their less powerful constituents. But I believe it is better to try to restrain the horrors and abuses than to give up on the limits that state organized political power can bring to bear on the forms of class-based, race-based, sex-based power that constitute the greatest sources of oppression we are likely to face.

Here I think feminists should be particularly alarmed about the new structures of international economic power proliferating and forming linkages to the political internationalism just noted. The giantism of the corporations—private, semiprivate, multinational—now organizing the international economy staggers the imagination. And it is a commonplace that complex organization and negotiation allow multinational corporations to keep their social obligations limited. To a great extent, they can operate around national tax laws, minimum wages, worker protections, food and drug regulations, waste controls, and environmental safeguards.

This is where the appeal of international organization is strong: form transnational institutions that can match the size of world-ranging corporations and thus bring them to social accountability *and*, at the same time, dissolve the dangerous power of warmongering nation-states. But it is an appeal that feminists should strenuously resist as, I believe, they should resist denationalizing appeals in general. To move from national to international regulatory arenas is to shift policymaking further than it has already gone from legislative to executive bases—that is, from potentially democratic and constituent-based to definitively bureaucratic and elite-based authority.

Robert Keohane, arguing *for* a move toward reduced state sovereignty, identifies precisely this problem. As economic interdependence shifts power to international institutions, he says, some means for decentralizing authority must develop. "Otherwise, the decline in states' operational sovereignty will be accompanied by a further attenuation of democracy, and the growth of international institutions could come to mean the rule of impersonal public and private bureaucracies responsible to no one except each other."[1] Exactly. But I doubt the efficacy of decentralizing mechanisms within a political structure that is highly internationalized.

We have seen an excellent and worrying instance of executive aggrandizement through internationalization in the Gulf crisis of 1990–91, with the Bush administration's turn to the United Nations rather than the Congress to authorize the use of force to compel the withdrawal of Iraq from Kuwait. The president, adopting the stance of his recent predecessors, adamantly refused for months to acknowledge that his massive deployment of US troops abroad required a Congressional declaration of war. And this presidential move was applauded by proponents of international organization. Thomas Franck, director of the Center for International Studies at New York University Law School, for example, argued that Congress had no proper authority over war in the Gulf once the United Nations had acted. The United Nations Charter, he maintained, displaces national authority over war and peace, and fortunately so, because the United Nations system, long stalled by the Cold War, "may finally replace vigilante violence with global police-enforced security."[2] Franck's views reflect the age-old hope for an end to international anarchy, the containment of the dangerous violence of nations by international rule of some kind. But what kind? And whose rule? Who would be making decisions about "global police-enforced security"? Who instructs the delegations to the United Nations? National executives do. National legislatures do not. International rulemaking enthrones the outlook and interests of professional foreign policy elites. In the United States, this means the virtually all white male priesthood whose mentality Carol Cohn so precisely documents: insulated from electorates, wrapped in secrecy, as distant as officials in a democracy can get from the outlook of constituencies different from themselves.[3]

As a feminist, I would hold on to state sovereignty as the most progressive move possible in a world of intertwined transnational functions—the one most likely to allow women, racial minorities, and the poor to disrupt the reigning hierarchies of privilege. In fact, I find myself in a kind of reverse Schumpeter position. I see the state, as Schumpeter did, championed by economically atavistic groups clinging to national identity for survival while the logic and power of new economic systems sweep across national borders as if they were not there. But while Schumpeter applauded the erasure of old dividing lines and the fading of their irrationally generated hostilities, I want to keep the lines somehow in place.

Specifically, I am proposing that a re-formed liberal state could well serve feminist purposes and values and, more specifically, that a reconceived liberal pluralism could serve to bring presently dispossessed voices into political discourse and dispossessed people into political decisionmaking. Again, please note the words "re-formed" and "reconceived." The liberalism I am talking about is *not* the version generally identified and rejected in feminist discussion. What follows is an argument about some of the feminist antiliberal charges and the sketching out of a different feminist liberalism as it might operate domestically and internationally.

The fundamental liberal flaw for feminist critics of the tradition is the conception of the individual as an autonomous being, atomistic, related to others only on terms each person chooses. An ideal liberal state based on this premise allows each individual the widest possible freedom of choice. Connections among members of a society are created by contract; society, in fact, consists of myriad contracts, networks of them, and government, of course, operates under a megacontract, the social contract by which governing authority depends on the consent of the governed. The problem feminists see with liberalism thus defined is that the theory supplies no concern for the fate of individuals beyond their freedom, and that it does not take sufficient account of the unequal power among contracting parties to exercise freedom. Specifically, it takes no notice of socially imposed, group-defined identities that individuals do not choose, and that systemically disempower whole categories of people. Women, people of color, the poor, have less bargaining power than men, whites, the rich. A system of supposedly free contract is actually a system of systemic privilege. Also, it is a system with no moral ground except freedom. Right and wrong depend on individual choice. It is a system that denies inherent social relation or social obligation. It is concerned with process, not outcomes—although historically, its proponents have operated on the assumption, uninformed by recognition of unchosen social debilities, that its outcomes would be just.

Some critics of contract liberalism see its tenets operating internationally as well as nationally by their incorporation into principles of realism. In this view, each sovereign state, like an unfettered individual, is a law unto itself. If it has the power to resist domination by another, it is subject to no obligation except those it chooses.

One line of feminist thought links the liberal valuing of individual autonomy to a psychic drive to autonomy implanted in the male psyche by early socialization. Nancy Chodorow, most notably, theorizes that the tradition of female child-raising makes separation from the mother or mother-surrogate harder for boys than for girls as boys must establish themselves as definitively different from the women who raise them. In the process they become deeply concerned with separateness, otherness, clear bounds between one person and another—autonomy, in short.[4] Transposed to international relations, masculine concepts of autonomy produce a view of separate sovereign states as embodying a unitary interest in confrontation with other states and as properly engaging in competition and self-interested change.

In other words, liberalism, by making individual autonomy its highest value, by relying on contract as its primary process, and by not recognizing unchosen, group-based systemic inequalities among members of a society, sets in motion, perpetuates, and legitimizes a social Darwinist order within states and among states. And it is possible that the impetus (or an important part of it) behind this order is a child-rearing dynamic that cultivates personal autonomy as a dominating element of masculinity, lending a crucial emotional push to a politics of separation. Thus, for its feminist critics, the liberal state is virtually fixed in a posture of competition and incipient violence. With autonomy at its heart, its behavior must be marked by boundedness, suspicion, hostility, and efforts to control whatever forces might threaten the sovereign self.

But I do not see the liberal state as so firmly fixated by the goal of autonomy as this description implies, and I especially want to contest and complicate the idea that national boundaries in some important way serve male psychic needs for extreme separation. I do not think we can leap from a finding of boundedness/competition/control/violence in the male psyche to an ascription of these traits, taken together, to states—and thus to a conclusion that the state is necessarily a pathological political form, a bounded unit, xenophobic, nationalist, hostile, easily violent.

Typically, the most passionate advocates of a securely bounded nation are groups that are seriously insecure, economically and politically. I would not, however, include those who are the most insecure, because deeply impoverished groups with virtually no political influence and little hope of gaining it do not tend to identify strongly with the nation or with politics generally. In fact, as Christine Sylvester has noted, some groups (she refers to specific groups of women in African societies) are so completely disconnected from state functions that they effectively "exit the state"—live as if they were not citizens of the state at all.[5] But groups who have, or have had, some influence but not enough to shape events, and not enough to control their own destinies, do tend to be vocal politically and do tend to seek an identity—that of the nation—to enlarge and bolster their own. Conversely, the most powerful groups, at least in modern societies, are the least nationalist in outlook and identity, tending, in fact, to be antinationalist in their politics.

In US politics, this distinction is apparent in debates between isolationists and internationalists before and immediately after the Second World War and subsequently in debates over forms and degrees of anticommunism. Actually, the two debates pitted the same groups against each other, the most virulent anticommunists advocating a new isolationism—the military obliteration of communist enemies and then a return home to comfortable disengagement from corruptions abroad. Internationalists joined the anticommunist crusade but urged security alliances and military deterrent strategies rather than warfare and were mainly concerned to build a variety of connective networks—economic, technological, scientific, cultural—around the world.

The strongest isolationists, old and new, have been those groups whose economic ground is relatively local—agriculture, small city business and professions, small business generally—literally the ground of the south, southwest, and mountain states primarily. Think of the political rhetoric of Barry Goldwater, Jesse Helms, Phil Gramm, not to mention Ronald Reagan—and their predecessors, Bryan, Borah, Bilbo, Nye, McCarran. The strongest internationalists are groups attached to and benefiting from the international economy—big business, and, much of the time, the big business labor force as well. That is, groups based on family farms and in small town commerce, places once central to both the economy and the social virtues of the United States but now marginal and chronically insecure, profess an almost desperate attachment to the nation. But the new power holders, the multinational corporate managers and professionals—fly across national borders without noticing them and move billions of dollars around the world in minutes, on electronic beams no border guard could stop.[6]

In pointing out that the most powerful elites in the present day have little attachment to political bounds, I am not arguing that a masculinist connection to bounds and borders does not exist. On the contrary, the political rhetoric of groups for whom the nation is significant is quite literal in its sexual imagery—an imagery of walls and holes. In the isolationist tradition, foreign policies were to seal off the United States from outside entanglement and chicanery. The dominating image was the fortress— Fortress America. Earlier in the century, it was enough to rely on the ocean barrier. After the Second World War, though, when new technologies began to shrink the oceans, the isolationist call was for thick armor—shields of radar, tanks, and planes, ships in both oceans, missiles and missile launchers—tough, hard phalluses bristling in every direction. The Reagan Administration added Star Wars, seeking to raise the fortress barriers into outer space to repel foreign missiles before they penetrated our borders, thus closing one remaining "window of vulnerability."

The window is one of many images of holes in this tradition. We often hear about US strength draining away out of various holes. Foreign aid, for example, is money poured down a rathole. And the politics of isolation has focused obsessively on danger entering the nation through various holes— dangerous ideas entering with foreign intellectuals, dangerous spies penetrating secret spaces, Central American communist armies marching through Mexico into Brownsville, Texas, illegal aliens filing through unguarded borders, foreign disease (AIDS from Africa) infecting America, and so on. The connection between these fears for the autonomous body politic and the penetrable female body seems clear enough, as does the connection between strong, tough borders and masculinity.

The point is that a political fixation on boundedness does seem related to anxiety about masculinity, but, at least in US history and politics, it relates also to a material condition of insecurity. In this age, the strongly bounded nation-state is the political form preferred by the relatively powerless, not the powerful. And since it is the powerful who shape the behavior and uses of the state, we cannot conclude that the state must necessarily reflect the masculinist political pathologies feminists have identified—exaggerated suspicion, distance, hostility, relentless competition, propensity to violence.

This is not to say that these pathologies are not politically significant. The politics of insecurity, while not dominant at least in highly industrialized states, are still important. Constituencies threatened by massive industrial and technological institutions are large and their discontents and anxieties remain politically influential. In the United States, the present Republican dominance of the executive branch depends on the support of these constituencies; and, to some extent, Republican rhetoric, as well as policy, must take this dependence into account. Nevertheless, these are still not the constituencies dominating the United States or other major powers, and their anxieties do not impose unrelenting hostility to others on the behavior of the developed nations.

On the other hand, we do see passionately xenophobic behavior on the part of states—now most notably in the Middle East—whose traditionally agrarian economic and social structures are severely threatened by pressure from industrial/technological economies. That is, countries like Iran and Iraq are, as a whole, in a position of insecurity similar to that of Americans in the old agrarian regions of the United States, and furious proclamations of otherness, especially on the part of religious/political leaders in the Middle East, are similar in spirit to those of US fundamentalist isolationists.

It may seem that I have arrived at a point compelling celebration of the dominant economic elites in developed states because they appear somehow to have escaped the curse of masculinism and overcome the tendency predicted by feminists to act politically from a posture of extreme differentiation. But, never fear, I have not. Rather it seems to me that the ethic of competition and control takes one form in insecure groups and another among the economically powerful. In the latter case, the form is, naturally enough, economic. It involves the use of power to control and to exploit labor and natural resources—and to maintain an exploitative broad-scale division of labor by gender.

The structure of the liberal states, then, does not necessarily reflect the masculine ethic of boundedness and exaggerated differentiation from others. At present, in the developed regions, this structure has become the instrument of elites who seek to use it in support of internationalized economic functions. And this use must be of concern to feminists, because it is not notably responsive to the needs of the nonprivileged. But this is not due to an unstable psychic underpinning inherent to liberal states.

However, this is not the end of the argument about the supposed veneration by liberals of the atomistic individual. If excessive autonomy in individuals and states is not compelled by male psychic conditioning, it still might be driven by philosophic values that make free individual will the highest social principle. In fact, the logic leading from radical individualism to a politics of competitive self-assertion is completely sound. But is it liberalism? What I do not understand in feminist discussions of atomistic liberalism is the lack of equal attention to nonatomistic forms of liberal theory and, even more important, to the actual forms that liberal states have developed historically. I am referring to various forms of social democracy and various forms of the welfare state.

Surely the developers of social liberalism, which Richard Ashcraft now traces back before T. H. Green to John Stuart Mill, have complicated the classical liberal concept of the isolated individual. Robin West, for example, has demonstrated eloquently that John Dewey's theory of social knowledge—and affirmation of relatedness as an element of liberal value—brought social liberalism squarely into US political thought and debate in the New Deal years.[7] In the present, the liberalism of John Rawls vastly complicates the issue of atomism in the tradition. And, in practical terms, the welfare state has organized, within a liberal democratic rubric, complex systems of social security paid for by taxes collected societywide.

I do not want to argue that these systems have, in fact, relieved all serious oppression where they operate. Nor would anyone argue that social liberalism prevails uncontested by atomistic forms in either the world of theory or of politics. Robert Nozick, Richard Posner, George Gilder, and Milton Friedman, not to mention, again, the political heirs of Ronald Reagan, uphold in their various ways the atomistic or contractarian tradition. And so do a number of feminists believe that strict protection of individual rights will provide women and other subordinated groups the maximum chance at effecting their own choices. The current debate over surrogate mothering yields highly developed explications of the feminist contractarian position by theorists justifying the right of women to make contracts to bear children for money.[8]

But the point is, the contractarian argument is part of a debate. The position is contested and, it appears to me, losing. In fact, in the real world, it has already lost. The welfare state is in place and may be shaved around the edges from time to time, but it is not going away—unless the contractarians should succeed in convincing the eastern Europeans that the alternative to the communist systems they have now rejected is a totally unfettered market. But that seems unlikely.

So why are feminists talking about atomism as liberalism's fatal flaw? What atomism? Where? Why *not* talk about the social liberal tradition? To make the leap from individuals to states, the same questions apply. The complex relations of states with each other in alliances and organizations, as well as the thick web of transnational connections among corporations and other private entities, defy any possible description of present-day states as atomistic—or aspiring to be. If there is something fatally wrong with contemporary liberal political forms from a feminist point of view, it is hard for me to see that it is atomism.

A more serious objection, identified by Spike Peterson, is the still unresolved problem built into the liberal tradition of the differentiation between public and private life, the exclusion of private life from the concerns of liberal politics, and the consequent effective exclusion from political attention of many issues affecting the equality of women.[9] In Carole Pateman's terms, liberal theory and practice still suffer from the fact that the sexual contract preceded the liberal social contract and placed restrictions on women's lives—generally responsibility for family life—such that they could not enter public life on equal terms with men even when that sphere was legally opened up to them.[10]

The public-private divide in liberalism is a serious problem for feminists because some large element of private individual choice, free from public rulemaking, is essential to liberalism, but honoring "the private" still holds dangers for women. The pressure of tradition makes it difficult not to think of private realms as including family life—thus threatening to leave women's traditional roles and duties essentially untouched and perpetuating sexual inequality.

No one has analyzed this knot of problems more clearly and completely than Susan Okin, nor, I believe, provided a better set of answers to this dilemma. She argues that, difficult as this problem is, it does not require the abandonment of liberalism by feminists. Rather, feminists can demonstrate the necessity—under liberal principles of justice—for the reformulation of both public and private spheres, and specifically for public involvement in those parts of the traditionally private sphere that actually operate systemically to undermine the freedom and equality of women. The public could assume responsibility, for example, for day care, parental leave, and even reformulated roles within marriages and families.[11]

Again, as Okin's impressive analysis demonstrates (if not in the abbreviated form here, certainly in the book cited and in her other work), feminists need not read into liberal principles the worst-case scenario under the various difficulties the principles pose.

One could go on with feminist objections to liberalism and answers to the objections, but I think this is enough to demonstrate the necessity to recognize within the liberal tradition a multiplicity of views—some antithetical to feminist aims, some consonant with them. In other words, it is possible within the diverse and open range of liberal theory and practice for feminists to enter and help shape the debate over the direction of both. The question, then, is why should we? Why take on the weight of tradition and expend energy on the contests that go with it rather than reject the whole and start anew? How can the liberal system serve feminist principles domestically and internationally?

I see liberalism as a tradition rich with potential for feminist development, in spite of the patriarchal bent to the liberal past. Most important for feminism is what is most important in liberalism and that is its reverence for the individual. Against all social construction of identity, role, and obligation, all pressures for conformity, and all tyrannies—official and unofficial— liberalism insists on the rightness of individual self-possession, individual judgment, individual choice. What is internal to the person—mind, body, emotions, instincts, values, priorities, the entire personal mix—commands ultimate respect in a liberal world. And this is surely the most basic feminist premise as well—that the individual must have social support for self-definition, a resistance against socially imposed identities, stereotypes, limitations to the range of mind, imagination, movement, work, or role.

And none of this means, as feminists have become too accustomed to saying, that a self-possessed, self-defining individual is morally detached from others. Social liberals insist, on the contrary, that one element of human personality is a capacity and need for relation to others, that relatedness is part of individuality, not its opposite. This is the basis for liberal welfare-state politics as opposed to the contractarian mode of laissez faire. And except for those feminisms resting on an outright communal identity, the individual-in-relation provides a strong basis for a feminist politics as well, both domestically and internationally.

As I see the feminist liberal nation, it acts domestically as an agency through which groups with seriously clashing interests confront each other and establish priorities for addressing difference. To be feminist, such a politics must operate on the premise that unchosen group identities establish patterns of dominance and subordination. To be liberal, the nation must recognize unchosen and oppressive relations as wrong and must seek to reduce and redress the consequent harms. This would be the major purpose of national life—to recognize difference, to take clear measure of its conflicts and harms and then seek a fairer distribution of social resources. Further, liberalism offers what I see as an extraordinarily promising technique for feminist political action—the much-maligned tradition of pluralism.

The problem with pluralism, for anyone seeking redistributional change, is that, like radical individualism, it tends to carry social Darwinist overtones. That is, pluralism has come to mean the interest group politics by which Madisonian factions make their demands, lobby, demonstrate, or more recently, form political action committees that channel money to legislators in a process of contestation that invariably favors the biggest and loudest contestants. It is a process that contains no moral monitor by which to judge outcomes. At best, it's a value-neutral series of bargains, at worst, a game of chance with a stacked deck.

But it doesn't have to be. Pluralism could be a morally focused process if we constructed it that way. I see it as an exquisitely apt means for expressing the *voices* of difference and giving them weight in a feminist politics aimed at dismantling privilege. In such a politics, groups subordinated by difference from a privileged norm—in class, race, sex, sexual orientation, or some combination of these—would give direct testimony of their own condition, needs, and agendas. Their own descriptions of themselves and their goals would necessarily be the premises for debate and action. That is, a crucial part of the process of change from the dominance of privileged norms would have to be the displacement of privileged groups as definers of the terms of debate. The privileged could not be the ones who interpret the needs of the subordinated. The point of view from which questions arose and information was generated would have to be that of the subordinated groups themselves.

Such groups would be stating their own interests in their own terms, as interest groups in pluralist politics always have. In a feminist politics, though, the implications would be different. In traditional pluralism, groups like the National Rifle Association, or even the National Education Association, make their demands and claims, and legislators weigh the merits of the claims—along with the electoral or financial strength of the advocates—against the claims and strengths of others to arrive at some kind of conclusion. The contesting groups themselves need not be concerned about the claims of others or the effects of their own claims on others. And legislators can legitimately bring to bear a wide array of values and responses of their own. But in a feminist liberal political system, which recognized subordination by unchosen group identity, the voices of subordinated groups would have to carry particular weight. Their testimony could not be taken as simply another claim. It would require special attention as evidence of an issue the entire society was obligated to address.

Why? This is where the power of the liberal tradition is crucial. Liberal goals, the movement of all members of society toward freedom and equality, still touch US citizens politically and shape their basic judgments. If these goals seem to have receded in the Reagan-Bush era of power and plunder, it is because the society has lost track of what has been blocking the goals. More specifically, reliance on the market and the military as linchpins of domestic and foreign policy consolidates the power of privileged groups and blocks access to power—movement toward freedom and equality—by subordinated groups. Thus these policies are not just unwise but illegitimate in relation to liberal goals. But the issue of legitimacy does not surface because the full significance of group subordination is not yet clear. Feminist analysis makes it clear, and if a feminist liberal polity were in place, members of subordinated groups could draw on the deep-seated force of liberal beliefs to bolster their positions. That is, if US citizens generally accepted subordination by unchosen group identity as a currently operating social fact, their liberalism would, I believe, lead them to give moral weight to the voices of subordinated groups.

In such a liberal order, the national legislative process would not be a morally neutral free-for-all. Pluralism would not consist of a morally meaningless scramble among conflicting interests but rather an accepted decentering of moral authority. It would mean hearing plural voices in order to reach shared conclusions about how to act, whose needs to place first, by how much, and for how long.[12]

Internationally, the feminist liberal nation would take as its primary task the protection of priorities its people arrived at domestically, which would mean protecting from harm the positions of its own most vulnerable people. And this task is the more pressing in our time given the massed forces of international economic power surging through the world. If presently subordinated groups are not to be fixed at the bottom of crushing hierarchies for ages to come, political power close to home must create spaces of freedom for them. States, as political instruments responsive to their people, must be explicitly protectionist in this sense. Just because we have the technical capacity to override geographic space with worldwide economic systems is no reason to do it, or to accept it. We should accept such systems only if they disrupt hierarchies and work against long-established group oppressions, but at present, this is usually not the case. Therefore, it is international economic systems that must be disrupted by political bounds.

But, as Governor Madeleine Kunin of Vermont has said on numerous occasions, we need not assume that in every instance political restriction on private economic choice works in opposition to economic development. The claims of supposedly productive business are finally a matter of accounting, and often the real social costs of an enterprise do not get assigned to the developer or entrepreneur or multinational corporation. They get assigned to the public in some form—too often in the form of environmental degradation for which someone at some time must pay. Requiring realistic accounting for social costs may curb some kinds of enterprise in the short run but encourage more solid, less costly longer-run development.

What, then, would an international system of inward-turned feminist liberal states look like? It would be not at all the liberal international order Woodrow Wilson imagined. It would be contentious, not harmonious. No invisible hand would assure smooth, mutually beneficial transactions flowing around the globe. But perhaps the worst forms of contention, military aggrandizement and war, would not be prevalent either. The central feminist tenet that each society suffers serious splits, serious fractures among its people, means in effect that there can be no such thing as a legitimate *national* interest as the term has, to now, been understood. And the dissolution of the very concept of national interest could undercut the tendency for nations to respond to tense situations with aggressive or imperial action.

The political fact of fractured interest emerged dramatically in the actual world politics of 1990–1991 with the loss of national cohesion in the Soviet Union, Yugoslavia, and other eastern European states. It took less dramatic but still unmistakable form in the deep splits in the US electorate over the Bush administration's preparations for war against Iraq. A *New York Times*/CBS News poll in early December, 1990 revealed a large gender gap on the question whether the United States should start military action if Iraq were to fail to withdraw from Kuwait by the deadline set in a Security Council resolution. The overall percentage of Americans favoring war if the deadline was ignored was 45 percent, but this included 53 percent of the men polled and only 37 percent of the women. Even more remarkable was the breakdown by race, with 48 percent of the whites for war and only 23 percent of the blacks. The poll provided no clear reading by class except to the extent that class is measurable by political party: 57 percent of Republicans favored war as against 35 percent of the Democrats, indicating less enthusiasm among lower than upper classes.[13]

In a polity *recognizing* disparate and conflicting interests based on sex, race, and class, lack of national unity would not be startling. It would be assumed. The concept of national interest would have no legitimacy. No pretense that the joint fortunes of a nation's people could be advanced by war would be politically possible. National unity, after all, in the Soviet Union, in the United States, in most modern states, has to a large extent taken the material form of military hardware—in the richest states, extravagant contraptions exploding underground, blasting through space, dug into silos, creeping along the ocean floors. But the varied classes and races and the two sexes paying for these tokens of national purpose have not benefited equally from their making, nor would they from their use. No nation starting with the question, How can the diverse interests of our people be best served? could conceivably arrive at massive investment in the military as an answer. In other words, the real promise for peace in liberalism may lie in the logic of its pluralism, its fragmentation, not in its generalizing of social interest.

Wilsonians assumed that only the abuse of power by self-aggrandizing elites stood in the way of universal harmony. Remove these elites from the picture through political democracy, and the common interest of the common people everywhere would prevail. As for occasional instances when tyranny and aggression erupted, democratic states practicing collective security in a league of nations could act out of their common interest to confront and defeat the breaker of natural order. In fact, Wilson assumed that the very existence of a collective security organization would deter aggression, and it is this conviction, this hope, that Thomas Franck and other internationalists are reviving as the Cold War ends and the communist states struggle to recast themselves in democratic form. To the internationalists it appears that the Wilsonian prescription may finally be able to work. A world of democracies may now allow the common interests of the common people in peace to prevail.

But the common people everywhere do not hold common interests. No universal principles can comprehend the diversity and conflict of interests within nations and among them. This became evident in the split in the United States over war with Iraq. The Iraqi aggression against Kuwait was the textbook case for a Wilsonian response from the United Nations. As Stanley Hoffmann said, Iraq's leader, Saddam Hussein, "has violated one of the few fundamental principles endorsed by all states: the right of each country to its political independence and territorial integrity; indeed, he has annexed a member of the United Nations." Hoffmann then went on to urge economic sanctions against Iraq and broad negotiations—not war—but he did assume the necessity of war if "all attempts at a peaceful restoration of the status quo fail." In other words, he assumed that international order requires respect for national borders above all. The nation as the only source of international order must be protected. But if a nation's people have deeply divided views on the stakes and costs of a war, must they place the international status quo above all? Must they fight for the sanctity of national borders as such?

As I have argued for resistance to internationalization, for retention of national authority, for feminist faith in states as potential servants of the vulnerable, it may seem illogical for me to question the need for all states to join in mutual efforts to protect national borders. How can states serve as protectors of subordinated groups if they themselves are chronically vulnerable to border encroachments?

A full answer to that question would require knowing why so many women, blacks, and Democrats in the United States opposed war in Iraq in 1991. The polls that registered their dissent did not yield their reasons. It is not clear whether the opposition was to war in general or to that war in particular. Certainly a gender gap on issues of war and peace in general began to appear in the early 1980s, apparently based on opposition to prioritizing military spending over funding for the kinds of programs particularly beneficial to women. In the case of Iraq, US women understood massive spending for the protection of an oil sheikdom and for Western access to oil supplies at advantageous price levels as displacing priorities such as day care for children, medical care for the elderly, drug rehabilitation programs, subsidies for heating fuel, and affordable housing. The National Organization for Women, in a November 1990 resolution opposing US military involvement in the Gulf, stated that "the billions spent for this military mobilization mean further cutbacks in social services . . . which fall heaviest and disproportionately on the backs of women, the poor, and people of color," and further, "the deadly nature of today's weapons, both conventional and biological, will have a catastrophic effect not only on the people, but also on the environment of the Middle East and worldwide."[14]

Blacks opposing the war at that time saw a disproportionate number of black youth in the armed forces and on the front lines where, in a war, they would die fighting other people of color who were themselves subject to the economic and cultural power of the West. Moreover, Kuwait was not a democracy. It was scarcely a functioning society, having to import much of its labor force from the poor of the Middle East, India, and the Philippines, and many of its professionals from the United States and Europe. Why should America's poor protect Kuwait's rich? Why should people of color die for the economies of white privilege fueled by oil?

The point is, what a nation is and does matters. In a feminist liberal international order, the abstract principle of protection for sovereignty, for the integrity of borders, would not be all-compelling. Nations would rightly call for sacrifice by their people to aid other people whose truly liberal, democratic regimes were threatened, where orders protective of vulnerable groups were threatened. The major business of the nation, however, would be internal; its legitimacy would depend on the efforts it made to take account of difference.

What, then, of international law in general? How are we to think of that tradition in feminist terms, or, more difficult still, in feminist terms grounded in social liberal principles that utilize the state as protector of the weak? International law derives from thinking that identifies the state as a generic misfortune, a force intervening between individual will and welfare on the one hand and the potential for international order on the other—an order based on universal norms for peaceful exchange and the peaceful resolution of disputes. From this perspective, the state is a thug, chronically disrupting the law and order that would be possible in a political environment organized by universal standards and rules. In the twentieth century, this was the lesson of two world wars and the horrors of fascist and communist totalitarianism: to the extent that national power is displaced or diminished, the individual gains.

I know this mentality well, as it was my own first political and professional enthusiasm. Entering law school in 1957, I took every course in international law available, proceeded from law school to work for the advancement of international law in the State Department's Legal Adviser's Office, and after that studied the field further by acquiring a Ph.D. in political science in the field of international law and organization. I wrote a thesis on United Nations peace forces in civil wars. I knew the theoretical arguments challenging and defending the existence and efficacy of international law. I knew the ancient and modern case law. I applauded each advance I witnessed, each treaty signed, each small extension of UN authority, each legislative defeat in Congress of what I then saw as Neanderthal forces safeguarding US sovereignty. When I left the State Department for my excursion into academe, one colleague—a career international lawyer long involved in the crusade against economic protectionism, a lifelong worker against the angry suspicions of US isolationists, a true liberal internationalist—clasped my shoulder and said, "Spread the word!" And I thought I would, but I soon fell into confusion about what the word was or should be.

What are the international norms that would displace the retrograde power of the state? Where do they come from? Who defines them? The answer is spelled out in Article 38 of the Statute of the International Court of Justice. The sources of international law are: (1) treaties and agreements, (2) custom, (3) the general principles of law endorsed by civilized nations, and (4) case opinions and the commentaries of legal scholars. Who, though, makes treaties, customs, civilized principles, and legal opinions? A very small class, the elite of elites. The foreign policy and legal establishments of powerful states. White professionals. Men. Decent, high-minded, public-spirited men seeking a better world, yet by no means representative of or responsive to the perspectives of very differently situated groups. In fact, these are people whose strongest convictions shield them from asking in what ways the experience and interests of law definers might shape the content of the law. Spike Peterson shows this mentality operating in the clear androcentrism built into the field of human rights, of all things, in "Whose Rights? A Critique of the 'Givens' in Human Rights Discourse."[15]

When I think of the internationalist establishment, what comes to mind is a skirmish I had with it in graduate school. It occurred in a meeting to which I was summoned by my thesis adviser and second reader. The second reader, a world-renowned European legal scholar, was appalled by my thesis. I was trying to trace an emerging variation of the law of nonintervention in civil wars by examining the actual practice of United Nations peace forces engaged in pacifying such disputes. He thought that the proper place to look for the law of nonintervention was the writing of jurists back at least as far as Grotius. I knew this scholarship but thought it supremely irrelevant to my inquiry into intervention by international organization. I saw new law emerging out of practice on the ground, in Third World countries. I was following the flow of power and ideas and principles as they coalesced into rules that participants in these conflicts observed.

I arrived at the meeting. I was six or seven months pregnant and apprehensive about the trouble brewing, because I wanted the thesis out of the way before the baby was born. Nonetheless, I entered with a cheerful and confident air, in my best, dark wool maternity dress, aiming for an atmosphere of companionable professionalism. But I met a stony face. My antagonist did not greet me, or even look at me, or speak directly to me throughout the entire meeting. He addressed himself solely to my adviser. I did not exist. Pregnant women looking for law in odd places were beyond the pale—and so was any law they might find or propose.

Where do we go with this? Do we give up any concept of international law? Should nations be the final arbiters of moral right? I don't think so. Yet somehow guiding norms must come from the ground up. Their purpose must be to identify and alleviate sources of oppression. They must charge the state with relieving oppression, tracing the effects of international activities on subordinated groups within it, tracing the connections between subordination at home and abroad, working cooperatively with other nations to make effective rules protecting the vulnerable. This would be the nature of international law in a feminist liberal order—an ongoing formulation of rules responding to the particular shape of problems as they arise, rather than a set of generalized prescriptions supposedly responding to the interests of all. Nations would be agents, not sovereigns. International organizations would be agents of agents, not higher authorities. Rules at all levels of political organization would be products of democratic discourse and decisionmaking, through processes giving full voice and weight to groups both defined by their differences and united by their respect for individuals, for their maximum freedom and equality.

Notes

1. "Sovereignty, Interdependence, and International Institutions," in *Ideas and Ideals: Essays on Politics in Honor of Stanley Hoffman*, ed. Linda B. Miller and Michael Joseph Smith (Boulder, CO: Westview, 1992).

2. *New York Times*, op-ed page, 11 December 1990.

3. See Carol Cohn, "Sex and Death," and her "Emasculating America's Linguistic Deterrent," in *Rocking the Ship of State*, ed. Harris and King, 153–170.

4. Nancy Chodorow, *The Reproduction of Mothering*. Berkeley: University of California Press, 1978.

5. Conference on Gender and International Relations, Wellesley College, October, 1990.

6. For a detailed discussion of American localist politics, domestic and international, see my *The Dream of Deliverance in American Politics* (New York: Knopf, 1986). See also Richard Hofstadter, *The Paranoid Style in American Politics and Other Essays* (New York: Vintage Books, 1967).

7. Richard Ashcraft, "Class Conflict and Constitutionalism in J. S. Mill's Thought," in *Liberalism and the Moral Life*, ed. Nancy Rosenblum (Cambridge, MA: Harvard University Press, 1989); Robin L. West, "Liberalism Rediscovered: A Pragmatic Definition of the Liberal Vision," *University of Pittsburgh Law Review* 46 (1985): 673–738.

8. For a detailed exposition of both sides of the argument, see Mary Lyndon Shanley, "Women's Freedom and 'Surrogate Mothering': A Critique of Contractarianism in Feminist Theory." Paper presented at the annual meeting of the American Political Science Association, San Francisco, September 1990.

9. "Gendered States: Disciplinary, Theoretical, Civil-Political," paper presented at Wellesley Conference on Gender and International Relations, October 1990.

10. Pateman, *The Sexual Contract*.

11. Okin, *Justice, Gender, and the Family* (New York: Basic Books, 1989).

12. Iris Young, in *Justice and the Politics of Difference* (Princeton, NJ: Princeton University Press, 1990) brilliantly explicates a politics of difference based on recognition of group subordination and on the effective participation of subordinated groups in the policy-making process. I have drawn on, or find myself in agreement with, much of her argument. She does not, however, seek connections to the liberal tradition, seeing it as focused too strongly on the individual. And she does not project her democratic polity as a nation-state but rather—here her argument is general—as a literally decentralized, regional, public policy-making process, coordinated with systems of democracy in the workplace and in other social institutions. I have not taken up, as she does in provocative detail, the elements of difference that distinguish groups in a positive sense and the ongoing operation of such differences politically.

13. *New York Times*, 14 December 1990, p. A 14.

14. "Resolutions on the Persian Gulf Passed by the National Organization for Women," November 18, 1990. *National NOW Times*, Nov./Dec., 1990, p. 18.

15. Peterson, *Alternatives* 15 (1990): 303–344.

3

The Quagmire of Gender and International Security

Rebecca Grant

Wars have been fought by men, resolved by men, and chronicled by men. By the end of the twentieth century, however, female soldiers will reach higher rank and play an increasingly important role in the military in several nations. Journalists, scholars, and eventually, the historians who write on contemporary warfare will include women in their ranks. In practice, warfare and the process behind the decision to go to war are no longer the exclusive domains of men.

Surely, this is a quiet triumph for feminism. Organized demands for equality and years of action on the part of individuals have given women access to one of the last bastions of male dominance. The participation of women in the state's mechanisms for war also marks a change in the relationship between women and the state. For those who study gender and international relations, there is the potential for a new source of material.

As these developments unfold around us, however, we are left to wonder whether and how they will make a difference to theories of what constitutes security, and how security is attained and lost. Will the participation of women give us insights, or reveal a different set of values, which we can use to make better sense of the difficult choices between the norms of domestic civility and international anarchy? Is the feminist standpoint lost when feminist scholars are no longer confined to "a vantage point at the periphery," a "standpoint of people who have been systematically excluded from power?"[1] Can the experiences of women be used directly to reconstruct some of our views of the historical and current relationship between the state and the military?

All these questions touch on a specific set of assumptions about feminist theory, and the role of a potential feminist epistemology within the security studies subfield of international relations. Women's participation in the military establishment is a narrow topic, but it raises an especially important and controversial set of issues that have relevance for other areas of research on gender. The idea of women as soldiers touches on the question of just how we are expecting to create and use a feminist perspective in international relations theory.

Feminist enquiry can have many forms and different ideological overtones. However, by one definition it must take *women*'s lives as the epistemological starting point. With this in mind, we can return to the issue of how archetypes of the male experience as warrior have contributed to construction of theories of the state. This is not the only source of theory on states and international security. But many explanations—from Thucydides to modern versions of the stag hunt—rest on received foundations of archetypal male experience. With more women in the armed services, previous barriers are disappearing. We could in theory launch a new search for a particular feminist "epistemology," capable either of challenging male archetypes in security policy or of creating other ways to assess the unique aspects of women's experiences.

The difficulty is that we may encounter a diversity of experiences and unexpected currents—such as a lack of distinction between the experience and viewpoints of the male and the female. This brings into question the assumption of difference between the experience of women and men in similar situations, and the criteria for a feminist view of security. Is difference essential, or can it fade as societal boundaries such as the taboo against a public role for women in the state begin to change?

This chapter explores the premise that in the case of security, the experience of women alone is not a clear guide for defining a feminist epistemology. The experience of women in war zones, the end of their exclusion from the security apparatus of the state, etc., all encounter a competing assumption that a feminist perspective should be kept aloof from the grit of war and security policy. The counterintuitive slant of the premise discussed in this chapter is at odds with examples of highly successful feminist scholarship in several other academic fields. In the next section I will argue that a special set of questions is raised by the special place that security, with its set of archetypes of male experience, occupies in the foundation of the discipline of international relations.

Part One: Constraints in the Traditions of International Relations

War and security were the most conspicuous issues in the early development of international relations as a separate discipline. Without the need to draw and defend boundaries we would not have "international" relations as such. This heritage has created constraints on the ability to establish a feminist perspective. Many of the constraints have been reinforced rather than overturned by recent research.

The origin of the problem goes back to the fact that the early development of the discipline was influenced primarily by the Great War of 1914–1919. Another wave of development followed after 1945, in the wake of the Second World War. The background for this second generation of scholars was the effort to establish the principles of the new and unprecedented global security role the United States had undertaken. At the same time, the special problem of nuclear weapons constituted a significant portion of the research agenda, drawing students and younger scholars to the field. Exemplified by E. H. Carr and others who wrote on the interwar period, the postwar scholars were driven in part by the need to develop a better understanding of international conflict in order to prevent it.

Their focus on the problem of war—and of why peace movements failed—became a defining assumption. For the most part, however, international relations was uncritical of the social relations that supported the international role of the state. Specifically, one of the features that escaped attention was the traditional practice of using gender roles as a basis for distinguishing between the morality for the private citizen and the citizen ready to sanction violence as a member of the public. Early international relations theory was ready to be analytical and prescriptive about politics among nations, but was not ready to explore the common basis for sanctioning war. Martin Wight believed, as Michael Howard put it, that international politics dealt with "the very fundamentals of life and death: with the beliefs, the habit structures which shape moral communities and for which it is considered appropriate to die—and worse, to kill."[2] The implications of social roles based on gender are certainly part of that set of fundamental ideas.

The emphasis on war and problems of security perhaps did more than anything else to distinguish international relations as a separate subject. International relations scholars might well agree that basically, this was the right thing to do, since it reinforced the initial premise that one could and should study the international system and its influence, instead of looking at diplomatic interaction purely as a legal or historical process. Although the emphasis on war was necessary to distinguish the new subject, it also created conditions that blocked off feminist enquiry in this discipline from the start. Only male citizens participated in wars. To the early international relations scholars, understanding why *men* acted the way they did was one of the basic questions. When this was universalized into the issue of understanding why "man in the state of nature" or "man in society" acted in certain patterns, it was easy to retain the male gender archetype proffered by political theory.

Without question, the tools available to pioneers of international relations theory were already laden with gender bias. History, philosophy, law, and political theory rarely explored the implications of gender roles for each branch of thought. As the research of many feminist scholars has demonstrated, the public realm of political action was effectively closed to women beginning with the Greeks. Plato, Aristotle, Machiavelli, Rousseau,

Hegel, and others consciously assigned the citizen's role to the male.[3] The
role of the female in society was seen as having little connection to the
practice of politics. The most difficult conception to challenge, however, was
the notion that women had no role in maintaining the security of the state.

What started as a practice of placing a lower value on the female role in
politics became a means of excluding—intentionally or by tradition—many
of the alternative perspectives of human values and behavior. The female
gender role, so conspicuously outside the realm of war, was not considered as
a basis for analyzing international relations. All the assumptions about state
behavior in the international system were predicated on theories of interaction
between male citizens, or men in the state of nature, or other androcentric
archetypes. Assessments of the nature of competition depended almost
entirely on the image of the male, the citizen who abides by one set of laws
in domestic society and who is authorized and encouraged to follow another
set as a soldier.

Given their intellectual tradition, then, and their frequent preoccupation
with war, the early twentieth-century theorists of international relations were
little inclined to deal with the issue of gender in state-society relations. This
intellectual history alone, however, produces too clean a picture. International
relations theorists did more than swallow and perpetuate a tradition of gender
bias that they had learned from political theory and history. The
developments in feminist movements in the early twentieth century were
frankly ignored. They were not seen as part of a wider social and cultural
fabric that might be influencing the international system.

Perhaps some would argue that "feminist enquiry" is even more of a
newcomer in academia than the study of international relations, and that the
early twentieth-century theorists had no feminist scholarship to discover. Yet
this is not entirely the case. Feminism and the study of international
relations are contemporaries. They grew up together and were stimulated by
some of the same events. Both can look back to tracts by Machiavelli or
Christine de Pisan, which set out some of the issues well before either field
had a clear identity.

By World War I, women were beginning to change their relationship to
the state. Shortly before the war, for example, the activities of the suffragists
in Britain reached their peak. The Asquith government was far from
indifferent to the often spectacular activities of these women. During World
War I, women served at the front lines in more prominent roles than ever
before. For many women in the United States and Europe, the cause of peace
was one of the great organizing forces of feminism after the battle for
women's suffrage had been won. While theorists were beginning to piece
together the structure for studying international relations, women were
asserting their political views on an unprecedented scale. Yet this dawn of a
new source of commentary and experience went unnoticed. Some, like Harold
Nicolson, who learned about feminism from his wife, Vita Sackville-West,

and from her lover, believed that the feminine qualities of "zeal, sympathy, and intuition" were "dangerous qualities in international affairs."[4]

Actually the men and the women were proceeding in parallel. The year 1919 provides an example. While the victorious, "satisfied" powers (to quote E. H. Carr) met at Versailles, the International Congress of Women convened in Zurich. The women delegates were deeply concerned over the harsh provisions of the treaty under discussion at Versailles, and many were skeptical that the proposed League of Nations would offset the treaty's retribution. Future Nobel Peace Prize laureate Jane Addams, presiding officer of the congress, and her colleagues were becoming aware of the problems of peace at the same time that John Maynard Keynes and Harold Nicolson were preparing to publish their condemnations of the settlement. The International Congress of Women concluded that "a hundred million people of this generation in the heart of Europe are condemned to poverty, disease, and despair, which must result in the spread of hatred and anarchy within each nation."[5] The analysis was correct. Through the 1920s and 1930s, international organizations of women flourished. Although this was one of the most striking developments of the era, it had little discernible impact on the men who pondered over the nature of relations between states.

It would be too simplistic to argue that while feminists concentrated on peace, male international relations theorists were preoccupied with war, and hence the gender line was reinforced. Jane Addams did assert in testimony before the US Congress that war hysteria came primarily from men, because men were more prone to emotionalism.[6] But Addams's line of thinking did not make the male agenda. The experience of women in the peace movement was ignored by those concerned with relations between states, despite the prominence of individuals like Addams. Men's conceptual schema of interstate relations were not equipped to take note of how gender roles affected activists. The understandable obsession with determining the causes of war was so great that it left little margin for assessing the significance of the feminist peace movements. The new discipline duplicated the sources of gender bias.

The cost has been a discipline unequipped to comprehend the full range of causes that lie behind international events. World War II had at least one cause linked specifically to issues of gender. As Claudia Koonz has written, Hitler's primary war aim was not military triumph but the establishment of a new order in Germany based on race and sex.[7]

Today, the gap between gender issues and the study of security is still wide. Although individual women have reached positions of authority in the foreign policy decision-making structure, the legacy of gender bias has gone largely undisturbed within international relations theory, and most of us are still startled by an assertion like Claudia Koonz's. Even in the trend toward "reflective" work on international relations theory, gender has not been accorded a place as part of the investigation into why states go to war. Most of the theorists writing during periods of reform in international relations theory have not opted to take into account the shifting relationship of women to the state and to international politics.

For example, recent re-evaluations of concepts like security have sought to trace the concept in question back to ancient Greece, in order to clarify the origins of the contemporary dilemma. The aim of a body of research by Jervis, Gilpin, and others has been to look for traces of the neglected roots of cooperation theory in the earliest discussions of the security dilemma, such as are found in the writings of Thucydides. However, returning to ancient Greece does not go far enough to compensate for gender bias. The system of distinction between male and female gender roles was firmly in place during the Pelopponesian Wars. Jean Bethke Elshtain has commented that "for the Greeks, war was a natural state and the basis of society."[8] In Athenian society, the role of women was to produce the next generation of males to defend the city-state. It is tempting to suggest that the prevalence of war weighed heavily on the lack of political rights accorded to women. At the same time, the thinkers of ancient Greece had a final reason to exclude women from roles as citizens in the state: the interest of these thinkers in public society was founded in part on the assumption that war was a natural phenomenon and that only men were important in this realm. This legacy is particularly intriguing because there is evidence in the literature of the period that gender relations were an issue in Athenian society. Nonetheless, the male ruling class resolved the problem at the expense of according citizenship rights to females. All these tendencies implied that it was both desirable and necessary to maintain the distinctions between gender roles.

There is, however, an exception. Thucydides and other writers did acknowledge an archetype of the woman as warrior: the Amazon. Fragments of myth about the Amazons indicate that they were regarded as a coherent, functioning society. In some versions, the men of the society were all dead; in others, the Amazons simply dominated their menfolk the way the Athenians did their women. There was a sense that the Amazons were a powerful "nation," but not a model for rational statehood in the eyes of the Athenians. The fighting prowess of the Amazons was acknowledged, but as a group they were emphatically a society apart from the Athenians; and Athens strove to separate itself from this and other foreign societies. Jason, leader of the Argonauts, dealt with the Amazons he encountered in one time-honored fashion: he married one of them.[9]

In the case of the Amazons, their success as soldiers was not sufficient to entitle them to the attributes of rational political actors. Still, as part of the project of re-examining the Hellenic origins of the state, it would not be inappropriate to reflect on why the Amazons were feared, admired, scorned, and above all, rejected as part of the norm.

The antipathy of the Athenians toward the Amazons indicates how the role of women as warriors was alien to the idea of citizenship and state structure. It is not the actual experience of women but the symbolic power of the female gender role that emerges from the shadows as an important element in the male polity. The female holds in trust both civic and martial virtues. Statues in nearly every capital of the world display figures of women symbolizing victory, glory, freedom, and other virtues. But action in the state belongs to the male.

The woman who pilots an Air Force C-141 transport plane or an army helicopter assigned to the 82nd Airborne Division is still an atypical figure. Even more striking is any imagery personifying the state as female. The very idea of women's values of care, affectivity, and connection smudges the clean division between the role of the female as symbol of ethereal civic values and martial glory, and the role of the male as political agent responsible for decent government. If this division comes into question, it rocks the image of how certain human social roles are categorized by gender in order to make it possible for society to embrace contradictions in what is expected of its members as a whole.

Where international security is concerned, the discipline of international relations resists gender issues particularly well. The answer would seem to be to construct a feminist epistemology—an ordering of criteria based on defiance of the male archetypes and on construction of alternatives drawn from awareness of the female as different. Such an epistemology could cope with gender issues in the state as a factor in war, deliver a feminist view of cooperation, and pursue other avenues of enquiry as well. But the troubling hypothesis explored in the next section is that taking women as a starting point for gender theory may not fulfill the requirements of a feminist epistemology. Erasing the male archetypes by examining an assumed female alternative can point in a third direction that confirms neither.

Part Two: Women in Combat

Nothing illustrates the dilemmas of both feminism and international relations better than the issue of women in combat. This issue catches the discipline of international relations ill-prepared, but it also challenges some feminist approaches. In conventional accounts, women, in their femininity, are not supposed to have a stake in the fortunes of soldiers or to place a value on anything connected to the destructive enterprise of war. Some feminist perspectives have relied on a stereotype of women turning away from war and the numerous messy problems of international security as seen from the perspective of the state.

A crucial distinction must be observed here. The experiences of women in combat are part, but not the sum, of feminist thinking on war and peace. A feminist perspective does not have to follow directly in the wake of the women who push the frontiers of equality in the professional military careers. Feminist enquiry by definition must take women's experience as its starting point. But it cannot, and perhaps must not, seek to value all of these experiences equally, without reference to a set of criteria. Not all experiences of women (or men) in combat are uniform, but it is the potential for similarity across gender lines that could be disturbing in the search for a feminist epistemology. To some extent, the difference constituted by our conception of the female gender role must be preserved if it is to be used as a basis for critique.[10] Taking account of women's views on peace and of the effect of combat experience on women should not be expected to yield a uniform perspective. After all, the example of the mysterious Amazons has done little more than hint that women may be just as good at the arts of war.

At the least, however, the whole issue of women's service in the military and in government posts may offer a partial way to correct the exclusion of women's experiences from theory and to begin to formulate alternative views of security. The presence of women in these jobs is, in the eyes of some, a testament to the effectiveness of feminist movements.

In the United States, women constitute about 11 percent of the armed services. The US military operations in Panama and in the Gulf under the Bush administration have pointed out starkly that the military depends on its female members and that women are now an indispensable part of the instrument of US military power. The Greek model applies no more. An act of Congress still prohibits women in two of the three services from serving in particular areas of armed combat, but it is being challenged, and women will most likely gain the right to qualify for most combat specialties, particularly those reserved for pilots. Few, however, question that women who serve near the front lines as pilots, logisticians, mechanics, medical personnel, etc., are likely to be drawn into combat in the event of war. Twenty years after the start of the second wave of women's liberation, women in the United States have won the right to die for their country.

Death, so rarely mentioned in connection with security, snaps us out of the theoretical reverie on women's experience. How much of a victory is women's participation if it ultimately funnels into the same tragic waste? Here we are face to face with the dilemma of being pleased with equality and dismayed at the lack of transformation. Raising the issue of the actual experience of women neatly provides empirical data but does little to establish criteria for theory or critique. The current structures, both in international relations and in much feminist thought, contain potential pitfalls. It would still be easy for many to ignore the fact that some individuals involved in the fighting will be female. Certainly, the old stumbling block of seeing women as virtuous "beautiful souls"[11] who might inspire civic pride, but who ought to be kept apart from war and combat, can be identified and avoided. Nevertheless, there are more troubles to come. Although women are now closely involved in both politics and the military, the implications of their participation remain ambiguous. Society may come to regard women as equivalents to their male counterparts. By this line of thinking, both gender groups are "individuals" and the distinction of sex becomes irrelevant. On the other hand, a society can take the attitude that while women should be "equals" in most ways, the job of "fighting" should stay with the men. The justifications for this second point of view are extremely diverse. Male chauvinists object that women are not capable of performing an equal role in combat. Ardent feminists suggest that enlightened women should not want or seek to engage in fighting. Either way, the debate cuts to the roots of the concept of citizenship and to the question of whether it is legitimate for the state to send people to war.

Focusing on the actual experience of women in war is another perilous approach. Certainly, it breaks down the cherished stereotype of the "beautiful soul." It also undercuts, however, the idea that for women, the experience of war is essentially and irrevocably different from that of men. This poses a challenge to the relationship between an analytical feminist perspective (one part of which is that women experience the state and its violence differently) and the raw data of women's experience.

The core of the question is whether the experiences of women in the armed forces meet the criteria for use in a feminist enquiry. If they do not, we must rethink the embracing definition of women's experience as a starting point. Women soldiers then become a category difficult to interpret in feminist scholarship. Their tales are undeniably fascinating. They are also compelling as glimpses of the forbidden role of the soldier, a role so familiar to the male gender role. There is a taste of power and perhaps a thread of enlightenment in the idea of women acting outside their socialized feminine identity. The feminist premise, however, that values like care and affectivity have a distinctive place in women's experience, does not come through unscathed.

In actuality, exceptional women have already established a record as leaders and warriors. Feminist historians have done an excellent job of pointing out that women have often been involved in military engagements. Joan Scott Kelly documented the activities of noblewomen who led soldiers in defense of their lands during the early Renaissance period in Italy.[12] Margaret of Anjou, formidable wife of the English King Henry VI, led her armies to the decisive battle of the War of the Roses at Tewkesbury in 1471. A century later, Queen Elizabeth I rallied England to face the threat of invasion from the Spanish Armada. Small numbers of women fought and were killed in the American Revolution and the American Civil War. In the twentieth century, the examples are even more diverse. They range from the women who ferried combat aircraft in Britain and the United States during World War II, to the nearly 800,000 Soviet women who served in the armed forces, many in combat roles. The Soviet women volunteers constituted almost 8 percent of the total armed forces by the end of 1943. They served as combat pilots, tank crew members, and artillery specialists, a record not matched among the Western allies.[13]

The accounts of women who participated in combat roles present another challenge to the assumption of difference. Women's direct experience of war seems to bring out many of the qualities and emotions that are familiar from the stories told by men. Sophia Kuntsevich was a medic in the Ukraine. She recalled that in her first battle: "The bombs started to fall and I started to dig immediately. I only dug a few shovelsful and flung myself down and lay there with my arms covering my head." When the bombing stopped, she heard the cries of the wounded, and ran to one fallen man. "Then I just began, automatically, to bandage him, then another. A new wave of bombing started, but by now I was occupied, so it was not as frightening."[14] In December 1941, Sophia Kuntsevich was wounded; when she recovered, she insisted on returning to the front. Her descriptions echo many themes of the male soldier: fear, uncertainty, the conviction that she was not brave, but just another soldier trying to do her job. Her request to return to frontline duty was a typical sign of the bonding of individuals who shared the dangers of combat.

When the shooting stopped, however, it became clear that gender roles had not been substantially transformed. Society looked askance at the British women who served in mixed antiaircraft crews, especially those few who were stationed abroad after the Normandy invasion in 1944. The veterans pointed out that the exhaustion and filth of war were hardly conducive to romantic affairs. However, women of this era have also noted that the youth of the men and women, and society's taboos on premarital sex, were strong influences even in the pressure of war. Although women were serving in nontraditional functions, the gender roles were hardly eradicated by the experience. A Soviet woman remembered that despite initial discrimination from the men, the male soldiers were helpful, albeit within established roles: "They would help us carry things, when they could, and in return sometimes would ask us to help them wash their clothes or sew on buttons."[15]

Much of the real debate over women in the military is distinct from the question of women's specific roles in war. It is the problem of maintaining adequate peacetime forces that makes recruitment of women indispensable. Furthermore, for the women who join the military, the decision is a pragmatic one. Women recruits cite education, opportunity, advancement in a professional environment, and very occasionally, patriotism, as their reasons for enlisting (a list that does not vary significantly for the male recruits.) The achievements of US women in the military since the mid-1970s have come in peacetime. It is true that in the national crisis faced by the USSR in the Great Patriotic War against the Nazis, restrictive gender roles were dramatically lifted and women funneled into frontline roles; the current debate in the United States over women in combat may focus as well on issues specifically linked to war. This debate, however, is a reflection of old prejudices and traditions in domestic society. In fact, the pressure to ensure equal opportunity for advancement to women pursuing careers in the military is a direct companion to similar demands of women pursing careers in civilian life. The advancement of women in the military is one of the main achievements of the women's movement for equal opportunity. As the French revolutionary Pauline Leon asserted in 1791, women want the honor "of making tyrants see that women also have blood to shed for the service of the fatherland in danger."[16] Two hundred years later, women soldiers are proud of their roles and loyal to their units. They have chosen military careers for the opportunities offered to them, but they are also proud of serving their nation.

Finally, the issue of women in combat leaves observers with a series of uncomfortable conclusions. Does it make war unacceptable when women soldiers are killed in the deserts of Arabia? Apparently not. Do the women serving in combat support branches alter the military psychology of their units in any way? Probably not. The media images of female reservists in Operation Desert Shield and Operation Desert Storm unexpectedly leaving behind their young children were poignant, but the press did an equitable job of pointing out that male single parents in the services faced similar problems. These points challenge the whole idea of gender difference as a basis for constructing an alternative view.

With this challenge comes a broadside against the idea of a complete, alternative "other" (to use Simone de Beauvoir's term) that stands apart and draws sustenance from a source of perception merely waiting to be uncovered. Indeed we must still take women as the starting point, but perhaps we cannot expect a clear road.

Combat makes the experience of women soldiers an ambiguous model for reform. As Ruth Roach Pierson concluded, there is no consistent women's response to the trials of war and revolution.[17] Perhaps, after all, there is more to be learned from the women who did not fight. Yet if that is the case, has the success of the feminist movement in obtaining more equal opportunity been for naught in theoretical terms? Returning to the central question, must we modify the dictum that a feminist epistemology must take the experience of women as its starting point? If we start with a record of experience that demonstrates more similarities to male experience than differences from it, is it possible to construct a distinctive feminist epistemology? To discount women's actual experience seems to weaken the project. More disturbing still is the hypothesis that specific incarnations of the feminine gender role—the beautiful soul set above war and politics—may have to remain in partial use. This is exactly what a feminist epistemology, based on women's experience, is designed to avoid, by giving a genuine reading, not an ideal as seen from the eyes of men. Yet it appears that women's actual experience may not always serve the needs of a critical, transformative project. To be female is not necessarily to be feminist.

Likewise, to experience is not necessarily to know. The brief survey of images of women in combat is enough to indicate that reclaiming experience and histories alone cannot build a feminist epistemology.

Conclusion

The quagmire of gender and international security is thickened by the ambiguity surrounding the experience of women. The findings of this section appear to challenge the adequacy of assuming that the experience of women is enough to construct a feminist epistemology. Writers and scholars who differ on the tenets of feminism have been preoccupied for some time with defining what does and does not constitute feminist insights. However, it is unsettling to see the difficulties reappear so clearly in the discussion of war and security, where one might have expected the lines to be more distinct.

Given this dilemma, it is not unreasonable to ask if taking the experience of women as the starting point must remain at the heart of feminist scholarship. For international security, it might be necessary to identify a framework where states and systems and women are combined as starting points for a feminist epistemology. Under that rubric, the aim of research would not be to fill in a new role for women but to examine how changes in the roles of and attitudes about women shift the three-sided configuration of the state, the international environment, and women. But the effort to work within a feminist epistemology can never stray completely from the prime task of working from women's experience.

Taking women as the starting point is inherently difficult because finding a pure source of "the experience of women" is elusive, even in feminist theory. Feminist postmodernism, as the name implies, develops an epistemology in which postmodern criteria are present. By no means is this a matter of women simply being "added on" to a fully developed epistemology that then marginalizes gender issues. The very complexity, though, of feminist postmodernism, or liberal feminism, or other variations, already means that women are not the *only* starting point. Women's experience is set in a context derived from a discipline or methodology that attaches other values: the deconstruction of texts, the content of language, etc. For example, the idea that language itself represents an accumulated experience of linguistic acts adds in another set of experiences to be considered along with those that are explicitly about women. For the female soldier, her experience is still set in the context of a male-dominated institution and changes in meaning when set outside that context. The feminist perspective cannot stand entirely outside the context it addresses. This obligation also leads to a number of different commitments within feminism, and this in turn fragments the grounds for feminist epistemology.

To those who are familiar with the tides of liberal, radical, and Marxist feminism (and other schools as well), the problem of a fragmented feminist perspective is not surprising. Each of these three broad schools has taken elements of other theories and applied them to feminism. Feminists of these different stripes have differed with each other partly because of their convictions about the agenda of feminism and partly because of the way they have chosen to coexist with other, nonfeminist schools of thought that are important to them. Even radical feminists have made that decision by refusing these other, patriarchal schools of thought. The combination of context and agenda invariably influences what is selected as the basis of knowledge for a feminist epistemology in any subject area. Feminist epistemology in the realm of international security must either decide to curtail the admission of all "women's experience" or accept, as other fields have done, that there is a need to judge and select, even within the feminist perspective. If the theorist chooses to work around the dismaying sameness of women's experience in combat settings, that is her choice, and her potential gain or loss.

The ambiguity of the feminist perspective on women in combat is tenable because it is a gateway to a feminist epistemology, not an epistemology in itself. In the end, a feminist epistemology is not a clear map but a license to draw one. Joan Kelly illustrated this with her work in history, which, as Joan Scott describes it, makes "speculative, generalized, abstract explanations about women in history."[18] Kelly's work has met a reasonable set of epistemological criteria: it started with women as subjects, stayed within the discipline of history, and produced theory. What she concluded about women and their lack of a renaissance was therefore only one of the contributions of her work.

No question, the results can vary widely. The experience of women in combat seems to echo male experience because it emanates from the male-dominated institution of the military. One could argue that the dilemma is simply part of the original problem of exclusion. Or, one could conclude that it is a mark of the universal nature of the human reaction to war. In the latter case, feminist theory becomes redundant. Or, one could say that it signals a way toward a more fully human understanding of the problem of war. This short exercise raises just some of the possibilities and they are not all equally attractive from most feminist perspectives.

We may not readily be able to meet the challenge of incorporating both the experience of women and a discernible set of feminist values into an epistemology that we can call "feminist." What a *feminist perspective* can and should do is to identify gender bias, and provide criteria for a research agenda that leads toward a better understanding of aspects of human behavior that have been marginalized in theories of security. There may still be real value in using selected elements of the generalized feminine gender role as a source of ideas on the better aspects of human behavior. This is not a recommendation to return to the terrible trade-offs of the "beautiful soul" image. If feminine values are to be used as ontological and epistemological starting points, a careful set of criteria must be established by individual researchers. Inevitably the "experience of women" will have to be filtered to formulate a feminist perspective.

What a *feminist epistemology* must do in time is to include tools for confronting the gender bias structured into the theories of security in international relations. It must also resolve the conflict of values between women's experiences in combat, and feminist assumptions about security that feed a feminist epistemology. Finally, a feminist epistemology must define how it functions given the presence of other epistemologies that cover the same agenda of war and security.

Most likely, several versions of a feminist epistemology will emerge, and within them several theories about gender and international security may flourish. Virginia Woolf decried the basis of nationalism that would inspire women to fight when she wrote: "As a woman, I have no country. As a woman, I want no country. As a woman, my country is the world."[19] Not all women may agree with this statement. Pauline Leon evidently did not, judging from the quotation cited earlier. Nor, at present, would the women who have experienced combat. As scholars we may well be more attracted to Woolf's point of view. That is a sign, in part, that developing a feminist perspective is also a normative task, and a heuristic one.

Much will depend on the ability of the international relations discipline, and its personnel, to undergo adjustment and to tolerate a degree of ambiguity in both the feminist perspective and feminist epistemology. Tension remains between the experience of women, and the requirements of feminist scholarship. Still, there is every reason to press forward.

Notes

1. Robert Keohane, "International Relations Theory: Contributions of a Feminist Standpoint," in *Gender and International Relations*, ed. Grant and Newland, 41.

2. Quoted in Michael Howard, *The Causes of Wars* (Cambridge, MA: Harvard University Press, 1983).

3. See especially Elshtain, *Public Man, Private Woman*.

4. Quoted in Carol Miller, "Women in International Relations? The Debate in Inter-war Britain," in *Gender and International Relations*, ed. Grant and Newland, 75.

5. Charles de Benedetti, *Peace Heroes in Twentieth Century America* (Bloomington: Indiana University Press, 1986), 49–51.

6. De Benedetti, *Peace Heroes*, 44.

7. Claudia Koonz, *Mothers in the Fatherland: Women, the Family and Nazi Politics* (London: Methuen, 1988), 392.

8. Jean Bethke Elshtain, "The Problem of Peace," *Millennium* 17 (Winter 1988):441.

9. Ilse Kirk, "Images of Amazons: Marriage and Matriarchy," in *Images of*

Women in Peace and War, ed. Sharon Macdonald, Pat Holden, and Shirley Ardener (Basingstoke: Macmillan, 1987), 27–39.

10. "Gender is not a point to start from in the sense of being a given thing but is, instead, a posit or construct, formalizable in a nonarbitrary way through a matrix of habits, practices, and discourses. Further, it is an interpretation of our history within a particular discursive constellation, a history in which we are both subjects of and subjected to social construction." Linda Alcoff, "Cultural Feminism Versus Post-Structuralism: The Identity Crisis in Feminist Theory," *Signs* 13 (Spring 1988):431.

11. This is Elshtain's term in her *Women and War*.

12. See Joan Kelly, *Women, History, and Theory* (Chicago: University of Chicago Press, 1984).

13. Shelley Saywell, *Women in War* (New York: Viking, 1985), 131.

14. Saywell, *Women in War*, 140–41.

15. Saywell, *Women in War*, 146.

16. Ruth Roach Pierson, "Women in War, Peace, and Revolution," in *Images of War*, ed. Macdonald, Holden, and Archer, 208.

17. Pierson, "Women in War, Peace, and Revolution," 225.

18. "Joan W. Scott "Response to Gordon," *Signs* (Summer 1990):859.

19. Quoted in Ruth Pierson, "Women in War," 221.

4

Women and Revolution: A Framework for Analysis

Mary Ann Tetreault

In *Political Order in Changing Societies*, Samuel Huntington defines revolution as "a rapid, fundamental, and violent domestic change in the dominant values and myths of a society, in its political institutions, social structure, leadership, and government activity and policies."[1] A great deal of attention in the literature is devoted to the consequences of revolutions for state structure, political institutions, class relations, the competitiveness of postrevolutionary states in the international system, and other macrolevel phenomena.[2] Each of these aspects helps to explain the origins as well as outcomes of successful revolutions. Here, however, I would like to broaden the focus beyond these aspects of revolution to concentrate on more "fundamental" issues, those bound up with "values" and "myths" in a very "domestic" context, that of the family. It is my intention to develop a framework that can be used to analyze the interaction between revolution and the role of women in society. If revolutions are indeed fundamental changes in the domestic order, it is reasonable to examine the most elemental structure in that order to see how it fits into the pattern of transformation.

Defining Revolution

The analysis of revolutions from this unconventional perspective is complicated by the fact that revolution as an analytical category of events is problematic in itself. In the earliest political writings of Western philosophers, revolutions are treated as events resulting in the transformation of domestic political structures, including power relations among domestic social groups.[3] Even Aristotle, though, whose analysis of the transformation of domestic political systems is solidly based on empirical information, does not discuss as one of the outcomes of revolution the dawning of a "new age" characterized by the appearance of "new men" and new relationships among individuals. New-age references make their first appearances in Western political thought with the spread of Christianity throughout the Mediterranean world. Significantly, Christian new age thinkers wrote and spoke extensively on reordering gender relations as part of the revolutionary transformation of the world initiated by Christ. Scholars such as Elaine Pagels and Peter Brown see the battles for control of the church, and the alliance of the victorious ecclesiastical hierarchy with the hierarchy of the state, as fought on formal lines drawn by considerations of gender and sexuality in the new age.[4]

In the modern literature on revolution, which, in the West, is shaped by rationalist ideology, many of the treatments of revolutionary transformation explain it as an outcome of structural change fueled by modernization.[5] This kind of explanation goes back to "The Communist Manifesto" of Marx and Engels, which produced a scientific theory of revolution based on dialectical materialism, and to Lenin's writings on imperialism, which explicitly incorporated an external (international) as well as an internal (domestic) arena as appropriate foci of study. Yet even modern revolutions, from the English and the American to the French and the Russian, projected the vision of a new age, a recreation of the individual and the fine structure of society, as important outcomes of revolution. In the French case, for example, revolutionaries made as strenuous an attempt as any early Christian sect to create new social and ideological structures they hoped would survive political reaction and "moral" backsliding as well as signify that the new age had indeed begun.[6] To develop the framework I have chosen to analyze women and revolution, I will draw upon both of these strands—the structural approach that leans heavily on the literature on modernization and state building, and the more recent literature that concentrates on culture—and try to effect a synthesis, or at least a combination, of the processes they delineate.

The three structuralists whose work has influenced this discussion all adopt a modernization perspective, even though each views the connection between modernization and revolution differently and assigns different weights to external causes of revolution. Although none of them considers women as a separate category of participants in revolutionary transformation, their analyses contribute to the development of structural explanations for the pattern of women's revolutionary activities.

Huntington sees revolution as proceeding through one of two mechanisms, both domestic in origin. In the first, those new groups or classes appearing as the result of modernization become mobilized in response to their exclusion from power because of the persistence of the old dominant groups in positions of authority. These new men form new institutions in the domestic periphery that challenge the legitimacy and power of an already partially modernized central government whose relative superiority requires that it be overthrown through violent means. This process may take a very long time to accomplish because of the differences in power and organization of the two opposing forces. Huntington calls this the Eastern pattern. In the second mechanism, revolution occurs as the result of the failure of traditional regimes to respond politically to the demands of a modernizing economy and its associated new classes. Economic crisis or a failure of will (or both) leads to a collapse of the center and its replacement by a highly modernized, i.e., adaptable, successor. Huntington calls this the Western pattern.[7]

Barrington Moore also takes a principally domestic view of revolutions and groups them into three categories: bourgeois or liberal revolutions, such as occurred in England, France, and the United States; revolutions from above, such as occurred in Germany and Meiji Japan; and communist revolutions, such as those in Russia and China. His assignment of a revolution to one of these categories is a function both of its class base and of its outcome. In his model, a bourgeois revolution is shaped primarily by new capitalist, i.e., commercial, classes and results in a liberal democracy. A revolution from above is made by an alliance between capitalist classes and state elites composed of feudal remnants. It results in a fascist state. A communist revolution is made by peasants, intellectuals, and perhaps a nascent proletariat, and results in a communist state. In Moore's view, the presence or absence of a large and mobilized peasant class is the primary differentiator between gradualist, relatively less violent revolutions and the intense and violent upheavals that lead to rapid social change.[8]

Theda Skoçpol regards both the international and the domestic arenas as critical to the formation of the set of conditions under which revolutions are likely to occur. Her main concern is with social revolutions, revolutions that correspond most closely to the ones that Huntington classifies as Eastern and Barrington Moore as communist. Skoçpol distinguishes between social and what she calls political revolutions according to whether they do or do not proceed from class-based revolts from below and whether or not they result in a basic transformation of society's state and class structures. The international dimension takes account of external pressures on the state that might force it to extract more from its population in order to be competitive, and that may also prevent it from dealing with rebellions in the usual way— through effective repression—due to limited resources. The results include the eventual accommodation to a new class within the elite (a political revolution) or growing vulnerability to peasant revolts that are of sufficient magnitude to bring down an old regime and simultaneously destroy its social bases (a social revolution).[9]

All three of these analysts take a structural approach to the study of revolution. That is, they explain the origins and the outcomes of revolts by repressed and excluded classes or groups by focusing on class relations, the nature and adaptability of state institutions, and/or the position of the state in the international system. In seeking primary causes of successful revolutions, this perspective discounts motivation, spirituality, ideology, and other individually-based phenomena that might signify failures of or losses of "legitimacy" in the Weberian sense.[10] If a structural focus is adopted, thus neglecting this dimension of revolution, we lose an important explanation not simply of the process by which revolutionary groups might be mobilized, but also of the particular structure, especially the fine structure, of post-revolutionary society, the new age, that results. Although theorists such as Tocqueville justifiably believed that the old-regime structures of state and society have a remarkable ability to persist into the new age,[11] revolutions both require and make possible fundamental change in at least some of these structures. This, after all, is how we define revolution. The content of revolutionary ideologies, from the rationalism of the French to the Islamic fundamentalism of the Iranians, shapes not only the social and political structures of the new age but, more importantly, the grounds upon which its political battles are fought, the "terms of discourse" that define structural and political power in postrevolutionary society.[12]

This political discourse is embedded in normative and positive theories about political and social systems. The new-age order is least susceptible to challenge when these theories are congruent, that is, when the mechanisms or patterns of order they postulate as natural or preferred are similar to each other.[13] When this occurs, the propositions of these theoretical systems resonate in a hegemonic ideology, the dominant interpretation of empirical observations of real systems.[14] This threefold symmetry is an integral part of the new age order. It becomes the problematique of the theories.[15] As a result, the survival of revolutionary ideology is contingent on social change in the new age. Where postrevolutionary regimes cannot, or will not, effect or mediate changes in social structures congruent with revolutionary ideology and practice, system transformation unravels.

From this perspective, revolutions are attempts to guide the process of political change along a preferred path of system transformation. As such, they are as much struggles over symbols—theoretical concepts—as struggles over political and economic power. The resulting disruption of congruence allows alternative models, i.e., different arrangements of symbols, to be developed, and also provides a political space in which they can be manipulated and made concrete through organization and mobilization. The completion of this process results in a new set of theories, a new problematique, and a new symmetry. The demands of congruence limit transformation to elements reflected in all three patterns. They also explain the high degree of continuity between pre- and postrevolutionary social orders.

Gender as Class; Family as Structure

Two issues must be examined before a discussion of women and revolution can proceed. The first is the question of gender as class: do women and men have different interests based solely on gender? On the one hand, women are perceived to be biologically bound to human reproduction in ways that men are not.[16] The physical facts of pregnancy and lactation are often translated theoretically as embedding women, through their biological role, in the private, subsistence, economy of the household.[17] Women have rarely been viewed as agents in the public, exchange economy of the polis. Indeed, Levi-Strauss argues that women themselves are commodities in premodern exchange orders.[18] The conceptualization of women as human individuals or as members of the social groups into which we categorize men is thereby blurred or even negated. If they have no interests, there is no reason to expect women as women to have a political existence at all.

On the other hand, it might be argued that women and men have substantially similar interests, based on their social class and on other factors such as regional ties, ethnicity, or religion. Indeed, some of the rhetoric of the black power movement in the United States called upon black women to repudiate any feminist alliance with white, generally middle-class women, and to devote their activities to the pursuit of their true interests as oppressed black women in alliance with oppressed black men.[19] Yet history is replete with evidence of gender as class underlying the social order. Scholars from a variety of disciplinary and ideological perspectives have found evidence of gender class consciousness in patriarchal societies.[20] Nevertheless, while men often see themselves as a gender class, women seldom do. The reasons for this are chiefly structural, located in marriage and the family as social institutions.

Marriage in most cultures is arranged so that female partners are inherently less powerful than male partners, even where formal oppressive institutions such as polygyny are absent. For example, social mores in nearly every culture prescribe an age difference in spouses that favors men. Property laws in most cultures also favor men; in most societies about which we have any information, women did not or do not have property rights at all; educational opportunities, the structure of social activities and linkages, and the distribution of political rights generally favor men. On the average, men are larger than women as well. Thus, the modal marriage pairing occurs between a larger, older, better-educated, richer, and legally favored man, and a smaller, younger, less-well-educated, propertyless, and socially and legally less-well-protected woman. The structural disadvantages of such a partnership make it difficult for the weaker partner to assert herself, much less to protect herself from exploitation and violence. The persistence of structural inequality in marriage is visible even in cultures where women's political rights are somewhat better protected than in older societies. One example is the ubiquity of physical violence against women and children in US families today.

Women are also not a new class in the sense that Huntington and others use the term to identify groups of men whose roles and interests did not exist in earlier orders or in the theories and problematiques to which these orders gave rise. New men are important agents of system transformation—their new access to resources enables them to reorder systems in which they exist but have no place, or at least, no place commensurate with their resources. Women also have no place in the public arena, and they have fewer resources than new men have that are suitable for creating such places. When new men make revolutions, they sometimes mobilize women as auxiliaries, but these women do not have a distinct political identity in their own right and thus no claim on the new order for status, power, or justice.[21]

Family structure is a critical factor in the development of a gender class consciousness among women. It also mediates the connection between the family and the larger society that makes the family effective or ineffective as a locus of revolutionary activity. In the next section of this essay, I will describe two basic family structures, the privatized family and the organic family, and examine their potential as agents of the revolutionary transformation of society. Here I would like to indicate in particular the mechanism by which family structure also impinges on gender class consciousness among women. Structures that isolate adult women from one another, especially from their generational peers, reduce the potential for gender class consciousness among women. The classical example of such a family is the nuclear family with a mother who does not work outside the home.[22] The utility of such a family structure for the support of patriarchy is part of the reason why it is so idealized in philosophical and political polemics (see, for example, the discussion of Rousseau below).

A family structure that is alienating as well as isolating can be seen in the traditional Japanese family as described by Ruth Benedict in *The Chrysanthemum and the Sword*.[23] Here, the son brings his wife to the patriarchal home, where she is isolated both from society and from him by her mother-in-law. The isolation of the Japanese wife continues even in modern nuclear families today through social proscriptions against "well-side chat"—female generational peers gathering together for anything other than prescribed and supervised occasions.[24] These examples of family structures that block the development of gender class consciousness among women are also examples of family structures that are poor agents of revolutionary transformation.

Society, Family, and Revolution

Although many scholars believe that one can talk about changes in the status of groups of men without considering the structure of the family and its place in society, few would argue that issues dealing with the status of women can be separated from a consideration of the family. This distinction is due in part to male gender class consciousness and its resulting relegation of women and families to the role of environmental factors affecting—or not affecting—conflicts among classes of men. It is also part of the rhetorical struggle to embed the family within a social and cultural system that reflects the values of individuals and groups contending for political, economic, and private power.

Theories about the origin of the family from the Genesis myth to the more formal arguments of scholars reflect deeply held beliefs about the nature of woman as separate from the nature of man and about the place of the family in the moral order.[25] They also reflect assumptions about the role of the family as an element of society. Roughly speaking, analysts fall into two groups with respect to the latter issue, those who think that the structure of the family is not connected to the structure of the social order and those who believe that it is.

Rousseau, for example, who believed that modern society corrupted human nature, looked back to a "state of nature" predating civilization to determine the basic nature of man, woman, and human society. He postulated the existence of three stages of social development: an original, sexually egalitarian state of nature, where both men and women lived identical lives as self-sufficient, unattached individuals who reproduced the species as the result of random sexual encounters; the society resulting from what he calls the "first revolution," one based on the social equality of patriarchal nuclear families living in relative isolation from one another, within which there was a complete division of labor between the sexes resulting in the economic dependence of women on men; and the third stage, which followed the "great revolution," brought about by the invention of agriculture and metallurgy. Because these inventions led to a division of labor among men, the "great revolution" was also the origin of social inequality in Rousseau's sense—social inequality among men.[26] It is the second stage, where women are totally dependent on and subservient to men while each man is equal to and independent of all other men, that Rousseau regarded as the ideal state of nature in which men's characters could be developed to their highest potentials.[27] After the first revolution, Rousseau believed that the role of women was fixed. He thus separated the family from "particular social and economic arrangements and power relationships,"[28] making women irrelevant to considerations of political and social change.

Friedrich Engels was also concerned about social inequality, but not from a liberal perspective. His discussion of the origin of the family was intended to show how capitalism degraded human relationships and put women in bondage. Unlike Rousseau's, Engels's state of nature was based on the notion of an original organic unity of family and society, the gens.[29] In these early human groups, men and women did not pair off into nuclear families but lived communally. Lineage was traced through the mother, the only parent whose biological connection to the child was unambiguous. This primitive society was imagined to have been classless and egalitarian with respect to gender. Engels believed that women instituted "the pairing family," which, together with the development of a more complex economy, ended the egalitarian Eden.[30] Humanity's "lowest interests—base greed, brutal appetites, sordid avarice, selfish robbery of the common wealth"— precipitated "a fall from the simple moral greatness of the old gentile society."[31] These lowest interests led to the development of private property, which isolated individual pairing families—and what the men in them could seize and hold for themselves—from the rest of the community. Men overthrew traditional kinship forms in order to keep their property to themselves and transmit it to their sons. As a result, women were subjugated, slavery was invented, and economic classes developed. Moreover, in order to perpetuate "this growing cleavage of society into classes [and] also the right of the possessing class to exploit the non-possessing. . . . [t]he state was invented."[32]

More recently, social scientists have shown us that both of these models of the "natural" family are idealizations and overgeneralizations. Family and kinship patterns differ across cultures as well as within cultures over time. Spike Peterson's work on families in ancient Greece and Mesopotamia demonstrates that their evolving structure is tied to the historical event of state formation. She argues that Athenian family structure has been reified as the state of nature in the work of most Western political philosophers, such as Rousseau, even though the developed patriarchy of Athenian high culture came from antecedents that challenge its position as the paradigm of the family in the state of nature.[33]

In his study of the evolution of the family in England from the sixteenth through the eighteenth centuries, Lawrence Stone, like Peterson, also finds explicit connections between the state and family structure. He argues that the patriarchal family in England was fostered by the mutual interests of an absolutist state and postreformation sects in encouraging the development of psychological and physical boundaries between the nuclear family on one hand—where the father was "a legalized petty tyrant"—and, on the other, kin, neighbors, and other elements in civil society likely to challenge the authoritarian state or the authoritarian sect.[34] Stone sees family life prior to the early modern period as much more permeable to the demands of kin and civil society than it later became. Unlike Christine Gailey, however, who studied the transition of Tongan Islands society from a kinship to a kingship system, Stone does not regard the previous kin-based society as especially supportive of women or even of family life as we generally understand it: "The closest analogy to a sixteenth-century home is a bird's nest."[35]

Most analysts who see family structure and political forms in society as contingent do not believe that such contingency is constant. Some family forms are closely integrated with larger social, political, and economic patterns, while others are much less dependent on or linked to macrolevel structures, or what Marxists call the social forces of production. Stone finds multiple family forms coexisting within the same political economy, as a function mostly of social class but also of individual situations and temperaments.[36] The analyses of Rousseau and Engels indicate that the degree of contingency between the family and the political community may well be a function of the extent to which the family as an institution is "privatized" in any given society.

The ideal family of the liberal Rousseau reflects its problematique as a vision of extreme privatization, while that of the socialist Engels embodies a vision of a communitarian past. Rousseau's ideal family exists outside of society and thus is both irrelevant and impermeable to revolutionary transformation. To Engels, both the original communal family and the more recent patriarchal family are linked to the overall organization of the economy and society, a general proposition that Peterson and Stone would probably agree with. As Eli Zaretsky argues, however, the connection between society and the bourgeois family—which is intensely private and socially isolated— more closely resembles the family-society relationship postulated by Rousseau than the one envisioned by Engels.[37] The traditional family may be a point at which revolutionary transformation can be initiated, but Zaretsky's analysis indicates that this is not true for the modern family.

The bourgeois family form is itself an outgrowth of capitalism and thus a product of modernization. This family and its intimacy represent the ultimate in privatization, a totally private personal life severed from the public sphere.[38] Zaretsky traces its beginnings to sixteenth-century England where the family, including nonrelated workers in the family business, replaced the manor as the basic economic unit of production. Although some new-style families were made up of members of the nobility and merchant capitalists, the "most revolutionary sectors" among these families "came from the class of small producers working their own property." The bourgeois family gave rise to a new ideology of the family "linked with the newly emerging ideas of private property and individualism."[39]

Although its economic relations differentiated the bourgeois family from family forms under feudalism, it is its insulation from the rest of society that is its dominant and most remarkable characteristic. The middle-class family and its home began to be separated from work, the workplace, and nonfamily members employed in the family business in England and the Netherlands toward the end of the sixteenth century.[40] This sequestering produced a pattern of gender relations analogous to that of the *oikos* of ancient Greece, within which elite men conducted their private lives and elite women their entire lives.[41] As a result, home and family in the modern period increasingly formed the bases of personal life, a private life oriented around personal relationships outside the public sphere.

This development had a number of unfortunate social consequences. It kept women in their homes, away from the contaminating influences of the public life of economic struggle and political competition.[42] It reinforced the dominance of autonomy as a social and political virtue at the expense of community at the same time that the nation-state as a political form began to take shape in Europe.[43] Family privatization can thus be seen as the new problematique associated with theories of sovereignty and possessive individualism.[44] It reinforced and corresponded to the spread of the normative belief that conflict based on competition is the primary mode in which human beings interact in public realms, such as the domestic economy or interstate relations.[45]

The bourgeois family also contributed to personal autonomy for men. Whereas the relationship between husband and wife had formerly been based on contractual formalities involved in conveying property and ensuring the paternity of offspring, it was now understood to be rooted in romantic love and personal regard.[46] Like the move to patriarchalism in the sixteenth century, this change added to male autonomy by loosening the ties of kinship and contract that bound men to their extended families. At the same time, this development reduced the autonomy of women by removing kinship as a legitimate source of economic and emotional support. The isolation of women in privatized families increased their husbands' control of their lives.

By the end of the nineteenth century, the bourgeois family had enshrined voluntary marriage based on mutual affection as a social ideal.[47] But the substitution of private desires for social constraints did not stop there. By the end of the twentieth century, it was also evident in declining marriage rates, high divorce rates, and widespread sexual abuse of children, although some, like Carroll Smith-Rosenberg, would attribute these to the decline of the bourgeois family rather than to its developmental continuation.[48] Even so, the pattern of increased male autonomy and independence from family obligations continues, and is an important element in critiques of "liberalism" by conservatives in the United States.[49]

As Zaretsky points out, the privatized family resists revolutionary transformation by attenuating the connection between the individual and society. Disappointment and failure are personal, internalized, and attributed to flaws in the individual rather than to the effects of unjust or oppressive social structures. The burdens of failure are carried primarily by the family, and often disproportionately by the mother.[50] Neither state nor society bears responsibility for the results of family ineffectiveness and pathology, which are falsely, but firmly, regarded as independent of the social order. This belief undercuts the legitimacy of attempts to connect family pathology to political and economic forces, and discourages dissatisfied persons and families from organizing to change anything but their own individual situations.[51]

The potential impact of the privatized family on politics can be viewed in a number of ways. This family's insulation from state and society attenuates its ability to reproduce a given set of social and political relations, both by reducing the access of outside forces to the socialization of children and by permitting "deviant"—for example, egalitarian—family relationships to flourish relatively unmolested. Thus, the privatized family is potentially a vehicle for change at other levels because it can disrupt the threefold symmetry underlying stable social systems. Yet, on the other hand, the privatized family can be seen as a dead end, a black hole that absorbs energy that could otherwise be used to transform society. Its deviance can be authoritarian rather than democratic. Its isolation can be viewed as atomization, making it a poor arena for political mobilization. State support of privatized family forms can thus be seen as in the state's interests.[52] Atomized families, like atomized workers, are at a structural disadvantage when making demands on the state.[53] Thus, in a society where the privatized family is the dominant form, one strategy for revolutionary movements is to create new civil structures to compensate for kinship and community networks that were inadvertently lost in the process of modernization or purposely destroyed by an authoritarian state. The Christian base community is an example of such a strategy.

Revolutions that neglect the kin and community aspects of social organization are unlikely to affect family life or women's roles. They are more likely to result in broadened elite competition—a political revolution in Skoçpol's terms—than in significant social change. However, the persistence of traditional family forms based on contract rather than affection and embedded in extensive social and economic networks encourages mobilization at this level. In cultures where these traditional forms persist, the individual and the family are explicitly as well as implicitly connected to the larger society, and social rather than personal determinants form the basis of marriage, child custody, and the distribution of property. In some tribal societies, women were or are exchanged to maintain or extend men's property rights,[54] while in prerevolutionary China, "the family was at the center of a highly coherent and deeply rooted social philosophy that united all aspects of traditional society."[55]

Congruence between relationships within the family and relationships in the larger society provides a point of leverage from which revolutionary groups can challenge the state.[56] In addition, when the family is not simply a private affair but rather the locus of the socialization that produces cosmological beliefs and economic and political structures—and then becomes *part* of all of them—revolutionary transformation necessarily affects family life and women's roles as well as politics and the economy as a whole. When linkage between family relationships and those in the larger society is strong, it is "revolutionized" families or communities that, in producing the next generation, succeed or fail at preserving and extending what the revolution accomplished.

Structural differences between the privatized modern family and the socially organized traditional family underlie some of the differences between Huntington's Western and Eastern patterns of revolutionary transformation. Huntington identifies the focus of Western revolutions almost entirely with the structure of the state. This perspective reflects the liberalism embedded in his sociocultural perceptions but is also an outgrowth of the effects of privatization on the role of the family in Western society. Family structure, along with other structures within civil society, are irrelevant as causes of and are not substantially affected by Western revolutions. The minimal disruption of the social formation by revolutions of this type is a major reason why they appear to be less violent.

In contrast, Eastern revolutions have social causes and consequences and take place throughout the social formation. Where the mobilization of families and family members is a rational revolutionary strategy, it is likely to be pursued. The tactics of such mobilization will be shaped according to the role of women in the society. In Vietnam, women's legal and social position as a permanently inferior group created conditions under which they could be appealed to as a gender class. The Indochinese Communist Party, the Viet Minh, and the National Liberation Front all asked explicitly for women's support, promising that the postrevolutionary society would enhance their social role and social status. Where women have a separate but powerful status within complex kinship groupings, such as in the Philippines, appeals to women by revolutionary groups concentrate on their family role, recognizing their ability to deliver or withhold support for revolutionary activity on the part of their extended family groups.

Either of these tactics would be difficult to apply in a modernized society, where the family is privatized, atomized rather than autonomous, and dispersed through a political economy that is organized by class—which is an economically defined unit—rather than by kinship or community—which are socially defined units. Not only is there no direct linkage between the privatized family and the political economy, but the substitution of class for kinship and community as organizing principles of society means that the separate mobilization of women would simultaneously alienate men who would otherwise find their class interests coinciding with revolutionary goals. If it is true that Western revolutions proceed *from* rather than *to* a collapse of the state, then it is the absence of linkages between state and society and within civil society that underlies this pattern. Western revolutions depend for their success upon the collapse of the center, because effective mobilization at the periphery is unlikely.[57] This supports Huntington's assertion that revolutions do not occur in liberal democratic societies. His explanation, however, which relies on the democratic structure of the liberal state, is less compelling than would be an explanation that includes consideration of the extreme privatization characteristic of liberal societies.[58]

Women and Revolution

Although women have participated in revolutionary movements wherever they have occurred, few of these movements addressed directly the problems of women in prerevolutionary society or attempted to resolve these problems in postrevolutionary political and social constitutions and institutions. Women's liberation movements formed part of the English revolutions of the seventeenth century and the American and French revolutions at the end of the eighteenth, but in none of these did postrevolutionary regimes "remember the ladies" by defining their rights or protecting their interests independent of the interests of their male relations.[59] The obvious explanation for this is the Western, bourgeois, or political nature of revolutionary transformation in these cases.

The nominally socialist revolutions of the twentieth century are often contrasted favorably with the liberal revolutions of the past as models of women's as well as men's liberation,[60] but the evidence here is mixed at best. The Russian revolution at first liberated women rhetorically and in reality, but policies liberalizing marriage and access to abortion were soon reversed under Stalin. Women in the communist countries of Eastern Europe experienced a similar pattern of gender oppression, which also included the denial of nontraditional jobs to women.[61] The Nicaraguan revolution, which arguably featured a greater rate of military participation by women than any other, still resulted in the subordination of women's interests to state interests, even though a vast improvement in the autonomy and status of women took place.[62] Despite the rhetoric, communist women are still not equal to communist men and, ironically, the privatization of family life characteristic of modern capitalist societies continues under socialist regimes.[63]

The Chinese revolution resulted in substantial increases in female autonomy and political rights relative to those of men, and most of these have persisted through the upheavals in Chinese politics since 1949.[64] Indeed, some Chinese officials blame the decline in women's status during the 1980s on the liberalization that took place at that time: as a result of greater local and individual autonomy, state intervention in favor of women was curtailed.[65] Well before liberalization, however, the revolution itself sacrificed the full liberation of women in exchange for the political mobilization of the countryside through a patriarchally organized land reform strategy that virtually denied land ownership to women.[66] A biographer of Jiang Qing, the second wife of Mao Zedong and a leader of the "Gang of Four," points to female oppression both before and after the revolution as the primary source of her subject's authoritarianism.[67]

How then can we assess the interaction of women and revolutionary movements in order to evaluate the contribution of women and families to the success of a particular revolution and the success of that revolution in improving the situations of women and families? Three sets of related issues must be addressed in order to accomplish this.

Specifically, we need to examine: (1) the structure of the prerevolutionary society in terms of the status of women and the relationships among family, society, and the state; (2) the rhetorical and symbolic bases of legitimacy that develop in the revolutionary process; and (3) the symbolic and objective outcomes of the revolution. The structure of the prerevolutionary society should be analyzed with respect to two main points. One, the relative position of women with respect to men should be determined: Was gender a basis for discrimination under the old regime? In all prerevolutionary regimes up to the present day, gender has been a basis for discrimination. Gailey, like Peterson, argues that all states rest on a foundation consisting of gender hierarachy as well as class stratification, and that the "subordination of women . . . emerges as an integral part of the emergence of . . . the state."[68] If we accept this connection between the subordination of women and the social bases of states, all revolutions against state-based regimes have the potential to liberate women from men as well as to liberate men from one another but, because revolutions also result in the strengthening of state institutions, the continued subordination of women after revolutionary transformation is structurally favored.

In assessing the prerevolutionary context, we must also analyze the relationship between family, society, and the prerevolutionary state: What were the customs and laws affecting marriage and family life, including sexuality, reproduction, custody, property ownership, and inheritance, and how were they enforced? The answers to these questions allow us to see the degree of penetration by the state of social and kinship structures, and to determine whether and how the linkage between state and society enabled civil organization to challenge state power.

The relationship between family structure and the structure of the prerevolutionary political economy is relevant here. This point also requires us to examine the prerevolutionary situation in light of the differences between the privatized family and other family forms, and among various nonprivatized family types. Was it possible for women as a distinct social group to participate as agents of the revolution, or was female participation in the revolution subsumed politically as well as analytically under male participation organized on other social bases? Female participation as agents of revolution underlies the legitimacy of postrevolutionary demands for women's liberation. This notion goes back at least to the Renaissance and the writings of Bruni and Machiavelli, which idealized an army of citizen-soldiers:

> It is the possession of arms which makes a man a full citizen, capable of, and required to display, the multiple versatility and self-development which is the crown of citizenship.[69]

Mary Lou Kendrigan, for example, regards military service as a major avenue for the achievement of political equality by disadvantaged groups in society.[70] A parallel argument could be made about the legitimacy of group demands after a revolution. That is, what any group gets may be at least in part a function of what it is perceived to have earned by the blood of its members. Do women *as women* hold up half the sky, or does the individual woman hold up her man? If the latter, is it then only he and his group who are entitled to claim a share of the victory, or are she and hers entitled as well?[71]

The second set of questions deals with the rhetorical and symbolic bases of legitimacy. Are women's demands articulated as goals of the revolution? Do leaders acknowledge women's demands and treat them as legitimate? Are women's contributions to the revolution politically recognized and weighed with those of men by male leaders? Are there female leaders, women in positions of formal and real authority, within the revolutionary leadership? Are women's values incorporated into the values of the revolution and the postrevolutionary regime?[72] Rhetorical commitment to female equality is necessary to legitimate women's liberation in postrevolutionary society.[73] Such legitimacy, because it rests upon the perception that women as well as men have "paid the price" of victory, requires that the achievements of women be integrated with other revolutionary myths, and that women share ceremonial authority over them.

The third set of issues deals with symbolic and objective outcomes. After the revolution, do women as well as men have the liberty to participate in public life, the outcome that Hannah Arendt identifies as the primary aim of revolution? Does this participation result in the creation of institutions and the development of policies that protect women and children from subjugation to the wishes of individual men as well as the state? The connection between women's liberation and institutions that are responsive to the needs of women and families is evident from history: freedom for men alone has never been sufficient to protect the interests or the persons of women and children.[74] Consideration of this set of questions allows one to evaluate a revolution as a successful movement to liberate all persons as opposed to a successful movement to alter the social bases of political and economic power or the form and structure of support for a regime.

What We Can Learn by Studying Women and Revolution

The study of women and revolution is interesting and important from both normative and analytical standpoints. Normatively, since the social role of women as a class is always defined at least in part by their reproductive capabilities, women will almost inevitably experience revolution and its outcomes in a different way from men. Classifying revolutions so that social impacts may be ignored in the analysis of paradigm cases reflects a modern

Western philosophical bias that is not simply sexist but also rigidly masculinist and ahistorical. Huntington is correct in defining revolution as "a rapid, fundamental, and violent domestic change in the . . . social structure . . ." but he is incorrect in his concentration on new men at the expense of excluded women and families.

Scholars from the right as well as the left commonly treat interest groups—groups with a professional or class connection to the political economy—as units of analysis in the study of both Western and Eastern patterns of revolution. However, the impact of community on revolutionary movements is less frequently pursued in studies of revolutions that follow the Western pattern, and connections between women's roles, family structure, and revolutions of either pattern are rarely explored.[75] The members of revolutionary groups who are consumers and sometimes even producers of this literature, and who use it to envision concrete possibilities for themselves, encourage women to subordinate their interests *as women* to their interests as members of an economic class or professional group in the course of their participation in revolutionary movements. Encouraging class interests over female gender interests is a risky strategy in revolutions in societies where there is a strong middle class because it could backfire: middle-class women are often strong counterrevolutionaries. This pattern is especially strong in bureaucratic authoritarian states in Latin America, where privatization and atomization of civil society is a strategy consciously applied by state elites to ensure their continuation in power. While the privatization of the family, a major arena in the life of nearly every woman in every society, continues, the interplay between family, society, and political economy remains underexamined.

This heightens the analytical importance of studying women and revolution. Huntington rigorously defines revolution as a rapid and fundamental change at every level of a society—mythic, social, and political. This definition, along with his distinction between Western and Eastern revolutionary patterns, poses at least the possibility that revolution in modernized societies might be structurally constrained, a possibility Huntington explores very briefly in the context of democratic and communist states. The relationship between modernization and revolution is discussed at greater length by Moore, who attributes some of the differences in the outcomes of liberal, fascist, and communist revolutions to the stage of modernization reached by a particular society.[76] Skoçpol, writing about "social revolutions" in France, Russia, and China, nominates the peasantry as the key group in these countries who advanced "social-revolutionary situations," pushing these revolutions beyond simple "interregnums of intraelite squabbling leading to the break-up of the existing polity or the reconstitution of a similar regime on a more or less liberal basis."[77] Such observations reinforce Karl Polanyi's notion that modernization is a social and economic process that takes place at the level of the family and the community as well as of the nation.[78] The privatization of the family, like the spread of capitalism to members of formerly feudal economic classes, breaks the integral connection of unit to society and reduces the role of family and community as structural constraints on the power of political and economic regimes.

Yet another connection between women, families, and political transformation that should be systematically explored is a hypothesis already noted, that state formation necessarily results in the repression of women. If this is correct, revolutionary transformation cannot liberate women unless it also eliminates or constrains state power. This relationship between state power and the oppression of women is often construed from another perspective: Charles Fourier once wrote that the "extension of *privileges* to women is the general principle of all social progress."[79] Both constructions imply that the state is an extension of the power of men and posit a direct connection between the level of women's liberation and the effectiveness of constitutional restraints on state power.

The revolutionary potential of the bourgeois family should also be an object of research and analysis. Despite Zaretsky's concern that privatization has divorced the family from society and made it irrelevant to social transformation, I believe that the role of women and the structure of the family remain potential keys that could open an entirely new way to conceive of and to achieve revolutionary transformation in the modern world. The privatization that isolates the state from responsibility for the family may be turned to advantage if it also insulates the family from state manipulation and control and preserves it as a unit that can challenge state power. This can occur in two ways. Families may form the units of a newly constituted civil structure capable of challenging the state directly. Christian base communities in Latin America and the domestic organization of the Palestinian intifada are made up of family units joining into communities, which in turn serve as bases for defense against and attacks upon repressive states.

The second way that families may challenge state power is less direct. It rests upon the congruence between theories and the social structures that form their problematiques. Change in any one introduces new terms of discourse that may also be applied to change the others. Stone described how the state used this congruence to support growing absolutism by fostering the development of the patriarchal family as a mirror image of itself. Modern macrostructures such as the international system and the nation-state are based firmly on this pattern of dominance and submission, and are supported by the illusion that "dominance rests on values [that are] universal, eternal, and exclusive."[80] The hegemony of this value system is challenged when it becomes possible to see that dominance is none of these things. Egalitarian family forms that subjugate neither women nor children refute the claim to universality underpinning dominance at other levels of society.

Transformation of the family from an authoritarian to an egalitarian unit promises to cut new paths toward multiple patterns of autonomy and community, increasing the number of "vulnerable points" at which critics can challenge the status quo.[81] Attacks on egalitarian families by statists also demonstrate that the state and other structures of dominance are vulnerable to this indirect challenge.[82]

Conclusions

The normative and analytical concerns reflected in feminist theory and research are not confined to "women's issues" as these are defined by the political and scholarly "mainstream." Feminism as a philosophical and intellectual framework challenges the Western tradition insofar as it relegates women and families to the realm of "nature" that exists to be subjugated and exploited. Feminists, along with other postmodern analysts, are engaged in the search for "alternative conceptualizations of human community at levels both below and beyond that of the modern state."[83]

The examination of the role of women in revolution is directly concerned with enlarging our understanding of human community in the context of the modern or modernizing state. As such, it is a subject whose pursuit can expand the terms of political discourse beyond the trap of perpetual conflict to include possibilities for the recreation of international as well as domestic society.

Notes

1. Samuel Huntington, *Political Order in Changing Societies* (New Haven: Yale University Press, 1968), 264.

2. For examples, see Huntington, *Political Order*; Hannah Arendt, *On Revolution* (New York: Viking Press, 1963); Barrington Moore, Jr., *Social Origins of Dictatorship and Democracy: Lord and Peasant in the Making of the Modern World* (Boston: Beacon Press, 1966); Theda Skoçpol, *States and Social Revolutions* (New York: Cambridge University Press, 1979); J. G. A. Pocock, ed., *Three British Revolutions: 1641, 1688, 1776* (Princeton, NJ: Princeton University Press, 1980); Ted Robert Gurr, *Why Men Rebel* (Princeton, NJ: Princeton University Press, 1970).

3. See, for example, Aristotle, *Politics*, trans. Hippocrates G. Apostle and Lloyd P. Gerson (Grinnell, IA: Peripatetic Press, 1986), especially Book Eta.

4. Elaine Pagels, *Adam, Eve, and the Serpent* (New York: Random House, 1988); Peter Brown, *The Body and Society: Men, Women and Sexual Renunciation in Early Christianity* (New York: Columbia University Press, 1988).

5. See, for examples, Huntington, *Political Order*; Moore, *Social Origins*; Skoçpol, *States and Social Revolutions*; Walt W. Rostow, *Politics and the Stages*

of Growth (Cambridge: Cambridge University Press, 1971). Karl Polanyi's analysis of modernization in the West, *The Great Transformation* (New York: Farrar and Rinehart, 1944), sees domestic political conflict as the inevitable outcome of global capitalism, but he does not deal with revolutions as such in his analysis.

6. Lynn Hunt, *Politics, Culture, and Class in the French Revolution* (Berkeley: University of California Press, 1985).

7. Huntington, *Political Order*.

8. Moore, *Social Origins*.

9. Skoçpol, *States and Social Revolutions*.

10. An example of an individual-level theory of revolution is Gurr's *Why Men Rebel*, which uses the theory of relative deprivation to explain the origins of revolution. Farideh Farhi, in "Sexuality and the Politics of Revolution in Iran" (paper presented at the annual meeting of the American Political Science Association, San Francisco, September 1990), criticizes the omission of consideration of what she calls "the revolutionary culture" in structural studies of revolution, a phenomenon that operates at the individual level of analysis. Skoçpol discounts this dimension of revolution as an explanatory variable when structural variables are available: "Even after great loss of legitimacy has occurred, a state can remain quite stable—and certainly invulnerable to internal mass-based revolts—especially if its coercive organizations remain coherent and effective" (*States and Social Revolutions*, 32).

11. Alexis de Tocqueville, *The Old Regime and the French Revolution*, trans. Stuart Gilbert (Garden City, NY: Doubleday, 1955).

12. Hunt, *Politics, Culture, and Class in the French Revolution*; also Farhi, "Sexuality and the Politics of Revolution in Iran."

13. The harmonization of normative and positive theory to conform to a dominant ideology is discussed explicitly in many works, especially on natural science. Among them are: Cynthia Eagle Russett, *Darwin in America: The Intellectual Response, 1865–1912* (San Francisco, CA: W.H. Freeman, 1976); Stephen Jay Gould, *The Mismeasure of Man* (New York: Norton, 1981). Jean Bethke Elshtain has also noted this tendency in political theory. See "Prolegomenon to a (Real) Paper on Sovereignty," draft manuscript, 1990.

14. Louis Althusser, "Ideology and Ideological State Apparatuses: (Notes toward an investigation)," in *Lenin and Philosophy and Other Essays*, trans. Ben Brewster (New York: Monthly Review Press, 1971).

15. Robert W. Cox, "Social Forces, States, and World Orders."

16. This is not meant to imply that all women actually mother nor that men are not also biologically bound to reproduction.

17. Susan Moller Okin, *Women in Western Political Thought*; also Okin, *Justice, Gender, and the Family* (New York: Basic Books, 1989); and Jill K. Conway, Susan C. Bourque, and Joan W. Scott, "Introduction: The Concept of Gender," *Daedalus* 116 (Fall 1987).

18. Claude Levi-Strauss, *The Elementary Structures of Kinship*, rev. ed., (Boston: Beacon Press, 1969).

19. See the essays by Fran Sanders, Abbey Lincoln, Kay Lindsey, Toni Cade, Gail Stokes, and Jean Carey Bond and Pat Peery in *The Black Woman*, ed. Toni Cade (New York: Signet, 1970). And recall the famous words of Stokely Carmichael, when asked about the position of women in the civil rights movement: "The position of women in the movement is prone [sic]." This is only one of many possible examples of men as a class working to dilute or destroy the sense of women as a class.

20. See, for example, Lawrence Stone, *The Family, Sex, and Marriage in*

England 1500–1800 (New York: Harper and Row, 1977); or Christine Gailey's *Kinship to Kingship.*

21. Abigail Adams, "Remember the Ladies . . ." in *The Feminist Papers: From Adams to de Beauvoir*, ed. Alice S. Rossi (New York: Columbia University Press, 1973).

22. Betty Friedan, *The Feminine Mystique* (New York: Dell, 1963).

23. Ruth Benedict, *The Chrysanthemum and the Sword: Patterns of Japanese Culture* (New York: Meridian, 1946).

24. Interviews by the author with Japanese families in Kitakyushu, Japan, June 1989.

25. Joseph Campbell believes that the Genesis myth is unique among creation myths in defining woman as sinner and thus separating life from goodness. Joseph Campbell with Bill Moyers, *The Power of Myth* (New York: Doubleday, 1988), 45–48. A discussion of the considerable literature on creation myths and their transformation at that point when state formation replaces kinship structures can be found in V. Spike Peterson, "An Archeology of Domination."

26. Most of Rousseau's discussion of the development of the family can be found in *A Dissertation on the Origin and Foundation of the Inequality of Mankind*, trans. G. D. H. Cole, in *Great Books of the Western World*, vol. 38 (Chicago: Encyclopedia Brittanica, 1952) and in *Emile*, trans. Barbara Goxley (London: Everyman's Library, 1984), Rousseau's novel about a "natural" man in the civilized world. His assumptions regarding the ideal pattern of sexual roles within the family are analyzed by Susan Moller Okin in "Rousseau's Natural Woman," *Journal of Politics* 41 (May 1979) and in *Women in Western Political Thought*, especially chapters 5–8.

27. Okin, "Rousseau's Natural Woman," 398.

28. Okin, "Rousseau's Natural Woman," 402.

29. Friedrich Engels, *The Origin of the Family, Private Property, and the State* (New York: Penguin Books, 1884/1985).

30. Engels, *Origin of the Family*, 78–83.

31. Engels, *Origin of the Family*, 131.

32. Engels, *Origin of the Family*, 141.

33. Peterson, "An Archeology of Domination."

34. Stone, *The Family, Sex, and Marriage in England 1500–1800*, 7, 123–40; quote on p. 7.

35. Stone, *The Family, Sex, and Marriage in England 1500–1800*, 7.

36. Stone's discussion of the impact of temperament can be found in *The Family, Sex, and Marriage*, chapter 11. Stone organizes his work into comparative analyses of dominant family forms within several social classes through each section of his book.

37. Zaretsky, *Capitalism, the Family, and Personal Life.*

38. Hannah Arendt, *The Human Condition: A Study of the Central Dilemmas Facing Modern Man* (Garden City: Doubleday Anchor, 1959), 46, 188.

39. Zaretsky, *Capitalism, the Family, and Personal Life*, 23.

40. Stone, *The Family, Sex and Marriage*, chapters 5–6; Witold Rybczynski, *A Short History of an Idea: Home* (New York: Viking, 1986), chapter 3.

41. Peterson, "An Archeology of Domination," 180–85.

42. Elizabeth Janeway, *Man's World, Woman's Place: A Study in Social Mythology* (New York: Delta Books, 1971). Even the great liberal feminist John Stuart Mill idealized the bourgeois family and the sequestering of women within it

as "essential for humanity." (Cited in Okin, *Women in Western Political Thought*, 226.)

43. Hanna Fenichel Pitkin, *Fortune Is a Woman*, 19–22.

44. John Gerard Ruggie, "Continuity and Transformation in the World Polity: Toward a Neorealist Synthesis," in *Neorealism and Its Critics*, ed. Robert O. Keohane (New York: Columbia University Press, 1986).

45. Pitkin, *Fortune Is a Woman*. Although his analysis does not examine gender relations, Ruggie, like Pitkin, looks at the substitution of possessive individualism at the individual and state levels for the communitarian ethic of the medieval period as congruent belief systems underlying the operation of the modern world system of competitive nation-states. Ruggie, "Continuity and Transformation in the World Polity," 142–45.

46. Stone, *The Family, Sex, and Marriage*, chapter 6; Peter Gay, *The Bourgeois Experience: Victoria to Freud* (New York: Oxford University Press, 1984), vol. 1, *Education of the Senses*, chap. 6.

47. Page Smith, *Daughters of the Promised Land* (Boston: Little Brown, 1971), 41–47; Peter Gay, *The Tender Passion*, in *The Bourgeois Experience: Victoria to Freud*, vol. 2 (New York: Oxford University Press, 1986), 100–106.

48. Carroll Smith-Rosenberg, *Disorderly Conduct: Visions of Gender in Victorian America* (New York: Oxford University Press, 1985), 51.

49. See, for example, George Gilder's *Sexual Suicide* (New York: Quadrangle Books, 1973). This perspective is analyzed in Kenneth Clatterbaugh, *Contemporary Perspectives on Masculinity: Men, Women, and Politics in Modern Society* (Boulder, CO: Westview, 1990), chapter 2.

50. Zaretsky, *Capitalism, the Family, and Personal Life*, 90–94.

51. This is evident in the most successful national movement in the United States to attack family pathologies that express themselves as substance abuse, Alcoholics Anonymous and such related organizations as Alanon, Alateen, and Narcotics Anonymous. For a defense of this private attack on family pathology expressed as substance abuse see A. Lawrence Chickering, "Denial Hardens the Drug Crisis," *Wall Street Journal*, 25 July 1988, 16. Although Chickering is criticizing statist attacks on the "drug problem," he dismisses the connection between substance abuse and the political economy as less important and less susceptible to change than individual attitudes.

52. This point is emphasized by both Peterson and Stone.

53. Alfred Stepan, "State Power and the Strength of Civil Society in the Southern Cone of Latin America," in *Bringing the State Back In*, ed. Peter B. Evans, Deitrich Rueschemeyer, and Theda Skoçpol (New York: Cambridge University Press, 1979).

54. Levi-Strauss, *The Elementary Structures of Kinship*; George Duby, *The Knight, the Lady, and the Priest: The Making of Modern Marriage in Medieval France*, trans. Barbara Bray (New York: Pantheon, 1983); Clifford Geertz, *Negara: The Theatre State in Nineteenth-Century Bali* (Princeton, NJ: Princeton University Press, 1980), 35–36, 40 . The notion of women as counters in men's power games is criticized by Marxist feminist anthropologists who see this view as the result of the sexism of field observers which leads them both to constrict their sources of information to what appear to be members of male elites, and to interpret what they learn to conform to their Western sexist biases. See, for example, Gailey, *Kinship to Kingship*, 3–6.

55. Zaretsky, *Capitalism, the Family, and Personal Life*, p. 79; also Frances Fitzgerald, *Fire in the Lake* (Boston: Little Brown, 1972). The integration of private and public life in traditional Western society is implied in the work of J.

G. A. Pocock, *The Machiavellian Moment: Florentine Political Thought and the Atlantic Republican Tradition* (Princeton, NJ: Princeton University Press, 1975), 42–43; and Pagels, *Adam, Eve, and the Serpent*, chapter 5.

56. This congruence is outlined for Vietnam by Fitzgerald in *Fire in the Lake*, 19–24.

57. The uses of the privatization of social life to decrease challenges to oppressive regimes can be seen in the case of Chile and what Alfred Stepan calls "the Santiago boys." See "State Power and the Strength of Civil Society," 322–23.

58. Huntington, *Political Order*, 275. The argument I make here is foreshadowed in Walter Dean Burnham, *Critical Elections and the Mainsprings of American Politics* (New York: Norton, 1970). Burnham denies that the paradigm of the liberal state, the United States, adjusts smoothly to demands for inclusion by new groups, the argument that Huntington uses to explain the absence of revolution in democratic states. Burnham finds repeated attempts by excluded groups to mount social revolutions in the United States, and argues that it is the successful atomization of such groups through the electoral process that prevents their achieving their programmatic goals. The judgment that liberalism as practiced in the United States has strangled American democracy can also be found in Mary G. Dietz, "Context is All: Feminism and Theories of Citizenship," *Daedalus* 116 (Fall 1987): 16.

59. The letter of Abigail Adams to her husband John, written during the deliberations on the constitution, asks that he "remember the ladies" by denying their husbands "unlimited power" over them—see Rossi, *The Feminist Papers*, 10–11. Lawrence Stone remarks that English feminists took the rhetoric of the English revolutions, specifically the rejection of Divine Right of Kings and the doctrine of passive obedience to the state, as bases for their arguments supporting women's liberation. ("The Results of the English Revolutions of the Seventeenth Century," in *Three British Revolutions*, ed. Pocock, 71. One of the most famous contemporary analyses supporting women's liberation, Mary Wollstonecraft's *Vindication of the Rights of Women*, is another example of women's desires to see revolutionary outcomes be extended to women—and the lack of any such desires on the part of male revolutionaries.

60. Valentine M. Moghadam, "Revolution, Culture, and Gender: Notes on 'The Woman Question' in Revolutions," paper presented at the 12th World Congress of Sociology, Madrid, 1990.

61. Hilda Scott, *Does Socialism Liberate Women?* (Boston, MA: Beacon Press, 1974); Maxine Molyneux, "Mobilization Without Emancipation? Women's Interests, the State, and Revolution in Nicaragua," *Feminist Studies* 11 (Summer 1985): 229.

62. Molyneux, "Mobilization Without Emancipation?"

63. For example, see Scott, *Does Socialism Liberate Women?* especially chapter 9.

64. Edgar Snow, *Red Star Over China*, rev. ed. (New York: Modern Library, 1944), 272–73; Harrison Forman, *Report from Red China* (New York: Henry Holt, 1945), 70, 154–57, 193–94; Theodore H. White and Annalee Jacoby, *Thunder Out of China* (New York: William Sloane, 1946), 204–205; Tao Gia, "Women in China," public lecture given at Old Dominion University, Norfolk, VA, 21 August 1987.

65. Interview with Wang Li, Counsellor, Department of American and Occidental Affairs, Foreign Ministry, Beijing, 13 May 1989.

66. Judith Stacey, *Patriarchy and Socialist Revolution in China* (Berkeley, CA: University of California Press, 1983).

67. Ross Terrill, *The White-Boned Demon: A Biography of Madame Mao Zedong* (New York: William Morrow and Company, 1984).

68. Gailey, *Kinship to Kingship*, xi. See also Peterson, "An Archeology of Domination."

69. Pocock, *The Machiavellian Moment*, 90.

70. Mary Lou Kendrigan, "Citizenship, Gender Roles, and Military Service," paper presented at the annual meeting of the Midwest Political Science Association, Chicago, April 1986.

71. Kendrigan's argument is based on the notion that blood sacrifice is the only valid ticket entitling a group to admission to power. This argument is rejected in Gailey's concept of "gender hierarchy," which asserts not simply the social oppression of women as a class but also the ideological suppression of values associated with women and the association of values attributed to "maleness" with social power. The argument I make in this chapter takes the androcentric perspective that women's blood payments are entitlements to power, but I do not believe that this is normatively preferable to a gender-neutral entitlement to liberty as the result of revolutionary transformation.

72. Gailey argues that states create gender hierarchy, the elevation of men and masculine values above women and feminine values, and that masculine dominance can be read from the value structure alone, even if political rhetoric and legal frameworks assert that women are equal to men. *Kinship to Kingship*, xi.

73. See the discussion by Lynn Hunt on the importance of rhetoric in reconstituting regimes after revolutions in *Politics, Culture, and Class in the French Revolution*, 20–24; also Molyneux, "Mobilization Without Emancipation?" 229.

74. John Stuart Mill and Harriet Taylor Mill, *On the Subjection of Women* (New York: Fawcett Books, 1869/1971); Okin, *Women in Western Political Thought*.

75. In two notable exceptions, Barrington Moore looked at communal relations and community structures in his analysis of revolutions that followed both "Western" and "Eastern" patterns. For example, he considered the structure and role of the family farm in the midwestern United States as an element in the development of the Civil War, which he saw as the real American revolution. Lynn Hunt looked at kinship and community networks in her structural and motivational analyses of the new men of the French revolution and their role in political and social transformation.

76. Moore, *Social Origins*, 472–81.

77. Skoçpol, *States and Social Revolutions*, 112.

78. Polanyi, *The Great Transformation*.

79. Quoted in Zaretsky, *Capitalism, the Family, and Personal Life*, 67, emphasis added.

80. Lester Edwin J. Ruiz, "Theology, Politics, and the Discourse of Transformation," *Alternatives* 13 (April 1988):161.

81. Bradley Klein, "After Strategy: The Search for a Post-Modern Politics of Peace," *Alternatives* 13 (July 1988): 312–13.

82. Michael Rogin, *Ronald Reagan, the Movie, and Other Episodes in Political Demonology* (Berkeley, CA: University of California Press, 1987), 200–205, 240–245, 293–295.

83. Klein, "After Strategy," 313.

5

The "State" of Nature:
A Garden Unfit
for Women and Other Living Things

Anne Sisson Runyan

With the rise of modern science, capitalism, and the Enlightenment, organic views of relationships among the natural world, political authority, and social organization gave way to more mechanistic renderings of relationships among nature, state, and society. The ideology of a natural order was replaced by the Hobbesian notion of an artificial order imposed by the sovereign state upon its atomistic, competitive, and avaricious subjects, who consented to this imposition of order out of fear of the perpetual conflict in the "state of nature." Thus, as nature came to be viewed as a site, not of order, but of disorder, the artifice of the sovereign state gained ascendancy to reimpose the balance that nature was once seen to provide. In this sense, the state was both contrasted with nature and also an heir to the functions previously assigned to nature. As William Chaloupka and R. McGreggor Cawley have observed:

> Nature has continually been the preferred sign (symbol, code) for the justification of authority. This is a pattern established for modernity by Hobbes—the nature of the human organism, properly understood, justified coercive political authority. Once that pattern was established, variations on it soon became a central basis for developments in western political thought. In other words, once the link between the terms of nature and the justification of authority became evident, nature quickly and effortlessly entered political discourse. To put it another way, it is remarkably post hoc to ask "should trees have standing?" Elements of nature, including trees, have occupied a privileged position for nearly as long as there have been people around to observe them, to appeal to them as a source of authority in political discourse, to hear them fall in the forest.[1]

Like nature, women, too, have served as central and omnipresent symbols underpinning justifications for political authority. In particular, it is women's long association with nature in Western political discourse that has given them a "privileged" position in the construction of not only the political, but also the patriarchal authority of the state. As Donna Haraway has pointed out, by writing "the themes of race, sexuality, gender, nation, family, and class . . . into the body of nature,"[2] Western political and scientific thought can be seen as a story about "the construction of the self from the raw material of the other, the appropriation of nature in the production of culture, the ripening of the human from the soil of the animal, the clarity of white from the obscurity of color, the issue of man from the body of woman, the elaboration of gender from the resource of sex, the emergence of mind by the activation of body."[3] In Western political thought, the state becomes both representative of and a mediator for the production of white, Western, patriarchal culture from nature. By taking on the perceived role of nature as orderer and balancer, the state has made women, people of color, and the natural world with which they have become associated the objects of its taming function.

Given this dialectical relationship between those things deemed "natural" and the political authority of the state, it is contended here that anthropomorphic, androcentric, and racist metaphors of "nature" have been instrumental in the construction of the metaphysics of the modern, Western state. Whether the state has been viewed as continuous with nature (as in pre-Enlightenment ideologies) or juxtaposed to nature (as in Enlightenment ideologies), its metaphysics has read order, unity, and an intolerance of difference into both nature and the body politic. This has led to a suppression and exploitation of all those things that are defined as "natural" (including, for example, animals, women, and people of color) and that do not fit into the designs of the white, Western man and his state.

It is also argued that more ecocentric and gynocentric conceptions of nature, designed to counter the repressive characteristics of modern state control over the "natural," are also problematic, for they, too, assume that nature is a source of order, unity, and harmony. There are, however, some ecofeminist perspectives that resist unified metaphors of nature, *choosing* to exit from the cultivated "garden" of white, Western man and his state and to enter into a more "fractious" and just politics through which people's relationships with each other and with nature can be redefined.

Nature as the State

Before discussing the contemporary terrain of environmentalist, and, in particular, ecofeminist resistance to modern state mastery over the "natural world" and those associated with it, it is necessary to review the historical currents that gave rise to the competing paradigms of nature/woman as nurturer vs. nature/woman as resource. Pre-Enlightenment organicism, ranging from ancient Greek to Renaissance thought, took several forms over time and varied according to the social strata and material contexts out of which these perspectives arose. Renaissance belief that the world was alive was derived from both Platonic and Aristotelian portrayals of nature as a passive female/mother, which needed to be impregnated either by the "Ideas" of the father or the seed of the male principle to enliven matter.[4] This conception of matter as a passive female awaiting the generative qualities of the male also informed Renaissance cosmology, which saw the male heavens raining down semen on the female earth to set the workings of nature in motion.[5] Organicist thought was thus based on animist conceptions of nature as "a person-writ-large"[6] and on a general reverence for the earth as the nurturing womb from which life sprang. While this world view restrained use of the environment through the Renaissance, the notion that matter as female was passive and inert nonetheless set the stage for a different kind of ideology that would sanction the exploitation of both women and the natural world.[7]

There were also other contradictions in pre-Enlightenment organicist thought that paved the way for a move from nature/woman as nurturer to nature/woman as resource. As Carolyn Merchant explains, hierarchical organicism read the prevailing feudal order into nature, likening each part of the human body to a part of the hierarchical body politic.

> Reflecting the cultural perspective of feudal lords and territorial princes, it conceived of the commonwealth as a "person-writ-large." Its body was endowed with life and ruled by reason in the form of the prince, who, together with the clergy, functioned as its soul. Judges and governors, who communicated its dictates to the provinces, represented its sense organs—the eyes, ears, and tongue. The good of the commonwealth was invested in its senate, which occupied the position of the heart. Of the hands, one was armed and protected the citizenry from outside attack, while the other, unarmed, disciplined them from within. Both were restrained by the reason and justice of the prince. Keepers of the state's finances were confined to the stomach and intestines, who for the body's health must avoid anal retention and congestion of their holdings. The feet were farmers, craftspeople, and menial workers, so numerous as to cause the organism to resemble a centipede, rather than a human.[8]

Thus, organicism served to naturalize monarchy and hierarchy in political organization. Moreover, by appropriating nature in such a way that privileged the whole over the parts, the "interest of the state assumed central importance in comparison to the individual parts," so that "the interest and happiness of the state could be different from the interests and happinesses of the individual members or their sum."[9]

Merchant notes that this paternalistic organicism gave way to an even more virulent patriarchal organicism when James I of England sought greater authority for the head of state by likening the king and his subjects to a father and his children. Armed with such absolute patriarchal authority, "if disease in one part of the body affected the other organs, the head might be forced to 'cut off some rotten members . . . to keep the rest of the body in integrity.'"[10] As Merchant goes on to point out, this exaggerated role for the head of state eventually undermined the interconnected, even if hierarchical, vision of organicism, leading to the Hobbesian notion of the state as an artificial person-writ-large.

> Whereas in Salisbury's *Policraticus* the body was endowed by life and ruled by the prince who together with the clergy constituted its soul, the great Leviathan is "but an artificial man . . . in which the sovereignty is an artificial soul" giving not vital life but artificial motion. In Salisbury's organism, the judges and governors who communicated with the people represented its sense organs; in Hobbes' machine state the magistrates and judges were, instead, its artificial joints. For Salisbury, the senate held the position of the heart and represented the good of the commonwealth; Hobbes assigned the heart (a spring) no human function whatever and dispensed rewards and punishment through the nerves. For Salisbury, the prince embodied wisdom and used it to restrain the arms of the organism; for Hobbes, equity and laws, formed an artificial reason. In *Policraticus*, the financiers in the intestinal tract dispensed the state's finances being wary of anal hoarding; in *Leviathan*, the accumulation of wealth and riches of all members constituted the strength of the artificial man while business assured its safety. The feet, which were the multitudes of common people for Salisbury, having no riches to contribute were not even mentioned by Hobbes. The Hobbesian metaphor thus not only became completely mechanical but was also fully consistent with a description of a market economy, the strength and operation of which depended on money exchanges and quantitative calculations.[11]

Maternalistic views of nature and paternalistic views of the state gave way to mechanistic renderings of nature and the state, in which nature was stripped of any nurturing or benign qualities, leaving the heartless state, therefore, to order the body politic according to the logic of the "state" of nature as machine.

Despite this transition from what Jane Bennett calls holistic "Faith" in the interconnectedness of nature—which "speaks and says that it coheres through relations of resemblance"[12]—to the Enlightenment world view— "conceiving everything in the world as the secure and eminently knowable creation of consciousness"[13]—the modern state is no more tolerant than the hierarchical organicist state of deviance within the body politic. In fact, as nature lost its benign and mystical qualities in the face of the rise of the market economy and the scientific revolution, it began to represent a site of disorder, a hostile wilderness that would have to yield its secrets and its unpredictability to the new authority of Enlightenment man. While women did not fare particularly well in ancient and medieval hierarchical societies even when associated with more benign characteristics of nature, their symbolic association with nature's dark and disorderly side made them the special targets of the sixteenth- and seventeenth-century witchhunts. The witchhunts were designed to suppress animism in the wake of the Scientific

Revolution and the Reformation, finding advocates among such men as the father of the principle of state sovereignty, Jean Bodin, and the father of modern science, Francis Bacon. Women, like nature, were now to conform to "a new synthesis of the cosmos, society, and the human being, construed as an ordered system of mechanical parts subject to governance by law and to predictability through deductive reasoning."[14] Of course, women could not presume to have access to rationality, but if kept in their proper places under patriarchal authority, they could at least be adequately controlled.

The State as Nature

Bennett argues that the modern state's obsession with a coherent order even in the absence of an organicist world view lies in the dialectic between Faith and Enlightenment. Despite the Enlightenment critique of Faith as irrational, Faith continues to be present, even if subsumed, in the Enlightenment project to recreate "home"—"to find a relation with the social and physical environment that is again comfortable, unified, and meaningful."[15] If an immanent God and universe cannot provide this, then the exercise of mastery over the "outside" world and the suppression of individual particularistic wills must do so. In Hegel's words, as Bennett tells us, the project to recreate "home" is achieved when the world is made to "'exhibit the same Reason which the Subject possesses'" and when the Suppression of individual particularistic wills creates a harmonious universal will—embodied by the State.[16]

Thus, in this dialectical process, the state is reunified with nature through the transcendence of the state over nature. This process has been and continues to be aided by the practices of modern science, which generate "simultaneously the technological and imaginative projects, fears, and desires both for reclosing the broken globe in a recreation of the garden and for escaping finally from her gravity into a purely abstract space."[17] As Haraway notes, until the late twentieth century, "the knower had to be socially male in his relations to the earth and to the natural-technical objects of knowledge which his fertile mind and hands generated from her raw materials."[18] Moreover, since the advent of modern science, the midwife between nature and man's statist projections has had to be white.

In Haraway's genealogy of the study of primatology during the nineteenth and twentieth centuries, it is the white man who has excluded himself from "'nature' by both history and a Greek-Judeo Christian myth system."[19] Thus, it is he who must effect the return to it. This project has become increasingly important in the late twentieth century as the white man "is being thrown out of the garden by decolonization and perhaps off the planet by its destruction in ecological devastation and nuclear holocaust."[20] Not surprisingly, the white woman, as nurturer, re-enters as white man's "surrogate," in the guises of such white woman primatologists as Jane Goodall and Dian Fossey, to "negotiate the discourses of exterminism and extinction in space and the jungle"[21] by touching the beasts who stand as "(colored) surrogates for all who have been colonized in the name of nature and whose judgment can no longer be repressed."[22] Haraway goes on to explain that white women are perceived as close enough to nature to "mediate the required touch with nature that could reassure 'man'"[23] of a benign relationship with the natural world. She notes that both women and men of color are still perceived as so coterminous with nature that their touch would not bring about a healing between white man and nature, but rather would expose the racist and sexist dominion over "the natural" that the white man sustains.

The Enlightenment attempt to recreate home, particularly in the face of ecological, technological, and political crisis, haunts not only modern science but also contemporary state policies that favor "environmental management." Late twentieth-century environmental management strategies recognize some limits to the carrying capacity of the biosphere and to some extent acknowledge the threat these limits pose to the white man's garden cultivated by the modern, Western state. Nevertheless, these strategies continue to reject "the premodern faith that nature is designed to harmonize with human projects. So human needs, purposes, and aims must be imposed on it."[24]

Indeed, there are those who argue that, as a result of state-sponsored environmental management practices, we are living in a "postnatural" world. As Mark Weaver points out,[25] this is the position taken by Bill McKibben in *The End of Nature*.[26] For McKibben, the natural world has been so thoroughly "touched" by the human hand that there is nothing "natural" left. There is no aspect of "nature" outside of human design and no "wilderness" to which we can retreat. Weaver argues that Donna Haraway makes a similar case in her writings.[27] Although both Haraway and McKibben sketch a world in which there is no longer any plausible distinction between nature and artifice, McKibben advocates a retreat back to a reverence for nature, recreating a garden for man, while Haraway sees this project as thoroughly suspect, given that this conception of nature resurrects the boundaries between white, Western man and nature that allow him to define it and mold it for his purposes.

Reclaiming Nature from the State

As can be seen from McKibben's and other current ecologists' writings, a contemporary resurrection of ideologies of Faith is now countering the Enlightenment-inspired project of state-orchestrated environmental management. The "natural holists," as Bennett would call them, are heir to the communal and utopian variants of medieval organicism identified by Merchant. Both variants arose out of the peasant experience. Communal organicism emphasized "the primacy of community, the collective will of the people, and the idea of self-regulation and consent"[28] that characterized village politics and medieval agricultural practices before manorial taxation, increased population pressures, and increased disease undermined the subsistence economy.[29] Utopian organicism, as expressed by Christian millenarians and utopian writers from the twelfth to the seventeenth centuries, "articulated a philosophy of communal sharing that responded to the interests of artisans and the poor for more egalitarian distribution of wealth based on an original harmony between people and nature."[30] As Merchant observes, the "communal and utopian variants of the organic model are compatible with the ecology movement's emphasis on the integrative aspects of small communities in which people observe the limits of the ecosystem resources."[31]

This attempt to return home in order to counter the instrumentalist project of trying to recreate home by defining "nature" (and all those creatures associated with it such as women, people of color, animals, etc.) "as a standing reserve" is fraught with problems of its own. Even though natural holists effectively critique environmental managers for their thoroughgoing anthropomorphism—which leads to a logic of mastery over nature at any cost—anthropomorphism also lurks in the heart of natural holism. This is most obvious in attempts to extend human rights to animals, insects, plants, and rocks. Not only does this impose human purpose upon nonhuman life, but it also continues to construe nature's "rights as human conveniences."[32] The anthropomorphism of natural holists may check the Promethean urge towards mastery, but it does not eradicate it. Moreover, as philosopher of science Kristin Shrader-Frechette has observed, where all have the same rights, there is no way to adjudicate whose take priority when these rights come into conflict.[33]

This question becomes particularly problematic when we see how women's rights have become juxtaposed to nature's rights, both despite and because of women's continual association with nature. As Lin Nelson points out, "the bleak, sometimes horrific, conditions that oppress us are created not only by polluters, but also by the architects of policy, science, and health care who at best patch things up with distracting, ineffective, and sometimes dangerous 'solutions.'"[34] These solutions entail ever greater control over women's bodies and lives. Construed as more vulnerable to contaminants, women's bodies become sites of inspection to determine ecological health or illness. As Nelson notes, "many of us would applaud the undertakings of selective researchers, provided that we are guaranteed our rights as research subjects, or, better yet that we are involved in initiating and guiding research. But all too often it doesn't happen that way."[35] Moreover, women's reproduction is closely monitored by state policymakers and scientists, because female fecundity represents the danger of overpopulation, particularly in the Third World. Finally, for the good of their own "reproductive environment" and the "rights of the fetus," women workers are treated as a special protected class, denied jobs in the swiftly proliferating polluted workplaces of the world economy.

Even when the anthropomorphic (and androcentric) extension of human rights strategy is elided into a more ecocentric or biocentric view commonly espoused by deep ecologists and many ecofeminists, there still lurks a logic that "nature is designed for us and we designed to fit it."[36] J. Baird Callicott, for example, acknowledges that the notion that human beings "are only 'plain members and citizens' of the biotic community" can lead to an "environmental fascism," wherein human beings, who put the greatest pressure on the environment's carrying capacity, would be required to cut back their numbers.[37] The lack of any gender analysis in this context, once again, places special burdens and controls on women, particularly women of color.

Moreover, in Callicott's defense of the land ethic, the state is no longer an artificial extension of the natural community; rather, the natural community becomes an extension of the model of the state.

> Being citizens of the United States, or the United Kingdom, or the Soviet Union, or Venezuela, or some other nation-state, and therefore having national obligations and patriotic duties, does not mean that we are not also members of smaller communities or social groups—cities or townships, neighborhoods, and families—or that we are relieved of the peculiar moral responsibilities attendant upon and correlative to these memberships as well. Similarly our recognition of the biotic community and our immersion in it does not imply we do not also remain members of the human community—the "family of man" or "global village"—or that we are relieved of the attendant and correlative moral responsibilities of that membership, among them to respect universal human rights and uphold the principles of individual human worth and dignity. The biosocial development of morality does not grow in extent like an expanding balloon, leaving no trace of its previous boundaries, so much as like the circumference of a tree. Each emergent, and larger, social unit is layered over the more primitive, and intimate, ones.[38]

This implies that the rights, obligations, and duties we have with respect to the Enlightenment state are somehow compatible with the Faith ethic of natural holism. It also suggests that we freely choose membership in our "communities" and enjoy equality of rights and obligations within them. Finally, it assumes that the only chauvinism left is the one humans feel toward nature. Indeed, George Bradford, in his study of the "deep ecology" movement, finds the ecocentric perspective, which sees "the pathological operationalism of industrial civilization as a species-generated problem,"[39] extremely worrisome:

> Concealing socially generated conflicts behind an ideology of "natural
> law," they contradictorily insist on and deny a unique position for
> human beings while neglecting the centrality of the social in
> environmental devastation. Consequently, they have no really "deep"
> critique of the state, empire, technology, or capital, reducing the
> complex web of human relations to a simplistic, abstract, and
> scientistic caricature.[40]

Interestingly, too, the evocation of "the family of man" in Callicott's
passage, as well as its appeal to the principles of liberal internationalism
arising from the building blocks of "primitive" associations, has a very
distinctive and unhappy origin. Haraway tells us that it was the paradigm of
Man the Hunter, originating among physical anthropologists in the 1950s,
that provided the scientific grounding for the construction of "universal man"
and "universal human rights" in the documents of the postwar United
Nations.

> The fundamental social consequence of hunting was a new kind of social
> cooperation—1) among males, and 2) from males to the group in food
> sharing. Economic interdependence followed from hunting. . . . The
> contradictory creature produced through the hominizing behavior of
> hunting was a natural global citizen, as well as a natural neo-imperialist;
> a natural political man, as well as a natural sadist; a natural providential
> father and reliable colleague, as well as a natural male supremacist. . . .
> At the origin, man was made as his own creator and destroyer, fully free,
> constrained only by a nature that made him equal to his brothers and
> responsible for his fate. Hunting is the act of human procreation,
> founding at once the nuclear family and the family of man—and laying
> the foundation for the uneasy technological-family discourses of the
> nuclear age.[41]

Thus, the UN doctrine of equality and cooperation among men of different
races and nationalities, designed to establish a new postwar world order of
liberal democracy and peaceful relations among states, was founded upon a
masculinist and sexist construction of man's nature—a nature which required
violent mastery over the environment, in the form of the hunt, for its
fulfillment. Of course, the paradigm of Man the Hunter has not survived
feminist critiques, which have displaced its hegemony by positing Woman
the Gatherer as a more likely motor of human cooperation. Woman the
Gatherer also provided a far more potent symbol for women's agency and for
their liberation from male domination during the UN Decade for Women than
did the male-based model for universality. Furthermore, "the biological
characterization of universal man, grounding a shared human nature
promising a permanent break between race and culture at the cost of heeding
the constraints on the obsolescent hunter-gatherer in nuclear society, looked
like a denial of cultural reinvention and post-colonial difference"[42] to those
currently engaged in antiracist and anti-imperialist struggles.

In short, ecologists like Callicott have not attended sufficiently either to social, economic, and political relations or to the problematic connections among the Enlightenment principles of individual freedom, human universality, and mastery over nature. Of course, some environmentalists do recognize that both individualist and collectivist states in the modern era, which either sacrifice universal human rights for individual rights or individual rights for universal ones, engage in the Promethean urge to control human beings and nature. In fact, it is correctly noted in *The State of the Earth Atlas* that "Dividing the world into communist and capitalist states, or free market and state-controlled economies, is of limited value in explaining the environmental state of the earth . . . the biggest blocs of environmental alliance are among rich and industrial nations and among poor and non-industrial ones."[43] Thus, for some ecologists, the only alternative for saving the planet from the excesses of industrialization, practiced most by rich, but increasingly by poor, states, is the development of a more "attuned" state "which acknowledges the limits to social order and human mastery and then advocates a modest, decentralized steady state where humans need not try to be in full charge."[44]

Paul Taylor, a philosopher of the school that Bennett names "expressivism" and an advocate of the attuned, steady state, recommends "objectivity" and a "wholeness of vision" as the basis for recognizing all organisms as "teleological centers of life."[45] Objectivity is achieved through a "heightened state of reality-awareness" wherein "we are ready to let the individuality of the organism come before us, undistorted by our likes and dislikes, our hopes and fears, our interests, wants, and needs."[46] Wholeness of vision entails the acknowledgement that "our true relation to other forms of life, even those that might do us harm, is a relation among beings of 'equal' inherent worth and not a relation between superior, higher beings and inferior, lower ones."[47] Such relations seem to bode well for women, people of color, and nature insofar as this model implies that previously subordinated and exploited living organisms have purposes of their own that are not amenable to the designs of the white man and the state. As Bennett points out, however, Taylor also believes that this "recalcitrant nature need not remain alien, for it is in truth an amicable companion for humans if only we give it its due."[48] Given this continued desire for home and a happy reunion of self and nature, natural holism, even in its most radical variant, utimately "can bear the burden of accommodating nature only on the condition that it is a garden planted for humans."[49]

Nature as Garden

This notion that nature, by its nature, must be a safe and accommodating "environment" for human beings haunts calls for ecological security to overcome the excesses of state sovereignty, and is also implicit in ecofeminist faith in the nurturing power of the earth and in whole earth representations. For example, Patricia Mische, in "Ecological Security and the Need to Reconceptualize Sovereignty," claims that the

> Earth does not recognize sovereignty as we know it. The sovereignty of the Earth preceded and still supercedes human sovereignties. The sovereignty of the earth is not a static or finished state in which power is held within one entity or system. Rather, it is an interactive and dynamic process in which power and energy and authority are shared within a total system in ways that enhance the prospects for the continuance of life.[50]

Thus, at one and the same time the "Earth" is both alien to human projects and also a fundamentally hospitable home for human life. We also see in numerous ecofeminist writings[51] a tendency to represent nature as an orderly, nurturing female who tries to take care of all her children despite abuses she might suffer. While many ecofeminist tracts also represent nature as a powerful female force, typically a goddess, that will fight back, implicit in these narratives is the idea that ecological and gender balance once prevailed and that it can be restored once we begin to live in harmony with nature.

Nevertheless, there are a growing number of ecofeminist writers who eschew such essentializing and harmonious images. For example, Yaakov Jerome Garb offers a very cogent critique of the insidiousness of whole earth representations for both nature and women. However useful the whole earth image has been in giving us a picture of a borderless, global community, Garb warns that this image simply reinforces the will to transcendence, unity, and purity inherent in the Enlightenment project of modernity and in Western patriarchal thought. The image of the whole earth denies the underside of holism—the "entrapping web" of global social, economic, political, and ecological crises born of the unifying project of modernity and the "'dis'integration of the systems that maintain our air, our water, our food."[52] Moreover, it is significant that this image was photographed from our modern technological spaceships and that it appeals only to our visual senses. That is, it offers us a sterile and harmonious picture of Mother Earth by denying man-made disasters and natural forces of death and decay; at the same time, it encourages us to seek heroic extraterrestrial escape from the mundaneness of life on earth. Finally, the "whole Earth perspective provides us with a small, comprehensible, manageable icon—an easily manipulable token Earth that we can use to replace the unfathomably immense and overwhelmingly complex reality of the world that surrounds us."[53] Questioning the embrace of this whole earth image by New Age types, deep ecologists, and many ecofeminists, Garb asks:

Isn't this impulse for a single true image a manifestation of modernity's obsolete quest for a single privileged viewpoint that gives us the whole picture, the one true representation? Isn't this urge a product of the same monotheistic and centralizing tendencies that have gotten us into so much trouble in the first place? Isn't the fantasy that we can somehow contain the Earth with our imagination, bind it with a single metaphor, the most mistaken presumption of all? What would it be to live with multiple images of the Earth—fragmented, partial, and local representations that must always be less than the Earth we try to capture through them?[54]

This passage is reminiscent of Donna Haraway's work, ranging from her articles, "A Manifesto for Cyborgs: Science, Technology, and Socialist Feminism in the 1980s" (1985) and "Situated Knowledges: The Science Question in Feminism and the Privilege of Partial Perspective" (1988), to her book, *Primate Visions: Gender, Race, and Nature in the World of Modern Science* (1989). Throughout these writings, Haraway insists that feminists resist the seduction of "Frankenstein's monster" who expects "its father to save it through a restoration of the garden; i.e., through the fabrication of a heterosexual mate, through its completion in a finished whole, a city and cosmos" or the finished whole of the "community on the model of the organic family."[55] But just as feminists must resist this "god trick" of transcendence, so, too, must they resist the goddess trick of innocence. As Haraway puts it:

Feminists don't need a doctrine of objectivity that promises transcendence, a story that loses track of its mediations just where someone might be held responsible for something, and unlimited instrumental power. We don't want a theory of innocent powers to represent the world, where language and bodies both fall into the bliss of organic symbiosis. We also don't want to theorize the world, much less act within in it, in terms of Global Systems, but we do need an earth-wide network of connections . . . in order to build meanings and bodies that have a chance for life.[56]

Recognizing that "meanings and bodies" are not given, but "get made," Haraway proposes alternative readings of both humans and nature that might serve a more liberatory politics. As noted earlier, she argues that there is no plausible distinction between nature and artifice. Similarly, she contends that there is no way to separate humans from machines—hence her term, "cyborg," which she suggests is the most potentially emancipatory description of or metaphor for political beings in late capitalist, post-industrial, postmodern society. By seeing ourselves as cyborgs, she contends, we explode the dualism between nature and culture, thereby disenthralling ourselves from a politics of either innocence, which shuns culture and technology, or transcendence, which appropriates and exploits the "natural." Moreover, when the distinctions of nature and culture are blurred, nature can no longer be viewed as an inert resource or a benign nurturer. Instead, for Haraway, a more apt metaphor is nature as "Coyote or Trickster,"[57] a symbol that "suggests the situation we are in when we give up mastery but keep searching for fidelity, knowing all the while that we will be hoodwinked."[58]

In short, Haraway seeks a politics that does not rest on the problematic claim that women and people of color are "closer to nature." Cyborg feminism "skips the step of original unity, of identification with nature in the Western sense,"[59] and, instead, posits women, people of color, and nature as active agents in the necessarily political production of knowledge. These agents are not from the "Garden" of the "liberal 'west,'" where "competition, mobility, sexuality, and energy . . . are the marks of individuality, of value, and of first or primate citizenship."[60] Rather, agency, in Haraway's view, refers to actors not reducible to "a screen or a ground or a resource, never finally as slave to the master that closes off the dialectic in his unique agency and his authorship of 'objective' knowledge."[61]

As noted earlier, this paradigm of scientific objectivity and control has been instrumental in state mastery over nature. In particular, Newtonian and Darwinian metaphysics, dominating scientific inquiry well into the twentieth century, have been consonant with and productive of the search for coherence in and control of the "natural" and political worlds. Contemporary science, however, is representative of a more contested terrain. While a great deal of scientific research is funded and appropriated by the state, usually in service to military and corporate ends, scientific investigation, to the degree that it is not exclusively dominated by state interests, white Western males, and pure positivists, is less anchored in the metaphysics of coherence and control, thus opening the way for deriving different and more valid scientific methods and conclusions.[62] If contemporary science is correct in its findings so far that nature has no inherently predictable or harmonious nature, that irregularities are as common as regularities, that "nature is a field of chance rather than a composite of stable, rationally ordered substances,"[63] then we must resist reading an order into it that can feed into the fatal flaw of both Faith and Enlightenment, natural holism and environmental management—the intolerance of deviance and difference.

Exiting the Garden of State and Nature

The more appropriate response to a less ordered world than supposed, according to Jane Bennett, is to adopt an ethic and a politics of "fractious holism," which can inform not only our relationships with nature, but also with each other. Those committed to social change should not abandon their critique of the Promethian hubris that has been so harmful to the natural world, human beings that are a part of it, and women and people of color in particular. Nor should we abandon the project of moving toward a more steady state that creates greater possibilities for justice, even if not total harmony. Bennett insists, however, that steady-state projects must not be based on either a reverence for nature or the longings for a harmonious home. The problem with these positions is that they do not allow the existence of "other." They insist either on the "assimilation" of otherness through the reconcilation of the human self and nature or the "normalization" and marginalization of otherness to ensure an ordered natural and political community.[64]

As we have seen, such programs ultimately have very negative consequences for those who, through the lens of the white man's state, have been deemed unruly, unpredictable, disorderly "others" in need of control, such as women, minorities, Third World peoples, and the natural world. Fractious holism, instead, encourages space for otherness, recognizing that every human project by definition imposes some form of order on the world, and therefore generates "that which does not fit," that which "resists our designs."[65] Rather than replicating yet again the modern state's repeated attempts to submerge that otherness, that particularity, that dissent, by mastery or assimilation in the name of unity and harmony, fractious holism offers a politics of difference and deviation. Such a politics refuses to see the natural world as organized either around human ends or around the needs of the state, and refuses to see women's bodies and lives organized around the needs of the white man's state or as subsumed by the images and claims of an anthropomorphized, state-centric "environment." As Haraway notes, when nature and culture are "reworked," seen as hybrids of each other, disallowing claims of either innocence or transcendence, "one can no longer be the resource for appropriation or incorporation for the other."[66]

Moreover, it is precisely because the reality of ecological and biological interdependence ensures neither equality nor harmony that tolerance for difference and dissent needs to be the basis for a more just politics. An ecofeminist politics informed by fractious holism would entail resisting the ideal of harmony and stability even as feminists struggle to create more hospitable and just, though always tentative, homes within our overlapping organic, technical, and social environments. As Haraway puts it:

> Cyborgs are not reverent; they do not re-member the cosmos. They are wary of holism, but needy of connection—they seem to have a natural [sic] feel for united front politics, but without the vanguard party. The main trouble with cyborgs, of course, is that they are the illegitimate offspring of militarism and patriarchal capitalism, not to mention state socialism. But illegitimate offspring are often exceedingly unfaithful to their origins. Their fathers, after all, are inessential.[67]

Since science or speculative fiction, as Haraway argues, can give us glimpses of worlds unanchored by the dualisms and dialectics of nature/culture, human/machine, woman/man, black/white, and organic holism/state mastery, it might be useful to turn to Ursula LeGuin's *The Dispossessed: An Ambiguous Utopia*[68] as an example of refusing holism while still seeking connection. This story is about a male physicist, Shevek, who is neither at home in his anarcha-feminist world (a world of Faith), where abstract science is suspect, nor in the patriarchal, state-centric world (an Enlightenment world) to which he goes, where science serves "'society, not mankind, not the truth, but the state.'"[69] According to Patrocino Schweickart, the central theme of this story is that the nowhere-at-home Shevek has fashioned a science and an identity that is not dependent upon the domination of nature or women. He rejects the notion of oneness with nature, but also refuses to exploit nature for the purposes of domination. Moreover, he recognizes women as autonomous yet fellow human beings who are "bound to him by relations of 'identity in difference.'"[70] Shevek's response to the knowledge that women and nature are not coterminous with his being is not to relegate them to "other" for the purpose of mastery or assimilation, but rather to cultivate an understanding of that which is different from his experience. Thus, LeGuin sustains a tension between people and nature, men and women, and science and nature, yet suggests these differences "need not imply reciprocal alienation."[71] By privileging ambiguity over certainty, partiality over wholeness, she offers us a vision of more just social, political, and scientific relations that do not rely on a quest for unity and harmony. Such relations do not rest on melding human consciousness with nature, but on recognizing that humans are in relation to nature in a way that neither denies nor attempts to control this relation. Nature, thus, becomes something with us, in us, and yet not like us. Such a conception allows for connections between people and nature, and men and women, as well as among peoples, that need not rest on hierarchy or harmony.

When we begin to refashion political community on relations of "identity in difference," which eschew the dominating, unifying, and harmonizing impulses of the modern state, we are faced with the central task of rethinking who and what constitutes "we" in our conceptions of political community. This process involves rejecting not only the idea of nature, and those associated with it, as a screen, ground, or resource, but also anthropomorphic and androcentric notions of agency, either projected on nature or used as the standard to which all actors are supposed to conform for membership in a political community. Broadening notions of agency, beyond the "man-self," his consciousness, his interests, and his actions, broadens the number and heterogeneity of actors in the world that constitutes "our" community.

When these other actors from the "natural" world are included in the calculus, not on "man's" terms or on the basis of equally problematic romantic and transcendental projections, the boundaries and purposes of political community become more ambiguous and, thus, less intolerant and hubristic. Haraway refers to this project as shifting from "survivalist" communities, which are characteristic of modern states, to "survivable" communities, which are committed to making the world livable on a daily basis for all its inhabitants.[72] There is no certainty as to how to best determine, much less negotiate, the needs of different inhabitants in order to make the world more livable for all of "us." The very process, however, of constantly reconfiguring who and what is involved in "our" communities, under this condition of uncertainty, can give rise to more chastened, yet radically different political identities, practices, and formations that might be far more survivable for women and other living things than the ruthlessly cultivated garden of the modern state.

Notes

1. William Chaloupka and R. McGreggor Cawley, "The Great Wild Hope: Nature, Environmentalism, and the Open Secret," paper presented at the annual meeting of the Southern Political Science Association, Atlanta, Georgia, November 1990, 2.

2. Haraway, *Primate Visions*, 1.

3. Haraway, *Primate Visions*, 11.

4. Allen G. Debus, *Man and Nature in the Renaissance* (Cambridge: Cambridge University Press, 1978), 34; see also Merchant, *The Death of Nature*.

5. Merchant, *The Death of Nature*, 16.

6. Merchant, *The Death of Nature*, 28.

7. Merchant, *The Death of Nature*, 20.

8. Merchant, *The Death of Nature*, 70.

9. Merchant, *The Death of Nature*, 73.

10. Merchant, *The Death of Nature*, 75.

11. Merchant, *The Death of Nature*, 212.

12. Bennett, *Unthinking Faith and Enlightenment*, 9.

13. Bennett, *Unthinking Faith and Enlightenment*, 23.

14. Merchant, *The Death of Nature*, 214.

15. Bennett, *Unthinking Faith*, 23.

16. Bennett, *Unthinking Faith*, 38.

17. Haraway, *Primate Visions*, 136.

18. Haraway, *Primate Visions*, 136.

19. Haraway, *Primate Visions*, 159.

20. Haraway, *Primate Visions*, 152.

21. Haraway, *Primate Visions*, 152.

22. Haraway, *Primate Visions*, 152.

23. Haraway, *Primate Visions*, 153.

24. Bennett, *Unthinking Faith*, 46.

25. Mark R. Weaver, "Nature Without Transcendence or Innocence: An Ecological Politics for Cyborgs," paper presented at the annual meeting of the Southern Political Science Association, Atlanta, Georgia, November 1990.

26. Bill McKibben, *The End of Nature* (New York: Doubleday Dell, 1989).

27. Weaver particularly refers to Haraway's "A Manifesto for Cyborgs."

28. Merchant, *The Death of Nature*, 76.

29. Merchant, *The Death of Nature*, 47–48.

30. Merchant, *The Death of Nature*, 79–80.

31. Merchant, *The Death of Nature*, 95.

32. Bennett, *Unthinking Faith*, 54.

33. This was an argument made by Kristen Schrader-Frechette in her lecture series given for a National Endowment for the Humanities Summer Seminar, "Seventeenth-Century Ideas about Progress and Their Twenty-first-Century Implications," at Potsdam College of SUNY, Potsdam, NY, June 1990.

34. Lin Nelson, "The Place of Women in Polluted Places," in *Reweaving the World*, ed. Diamond and Orenstein, 185.

35. Nelson, "The Place of Women," 180.

36. Bennett, *Unthinking Faith*, 139.

37. J. Baird Callicott, *In Defense of the Land Ethic* (Albany: State University of New York Press, 1989), 92.

38. Callicott, *In Defense of the Land Ethic*, 93.

39. George Bradford, *How Deep is Deep Ecology?* (Ojai, CA: Times Change Press, 1989), 10.

40. Bradford, *How Deep is Deep Ecology?* 10.

41. Haraway, *Primate Visions*, 216.

42. Haraway, *Primate Visions*, 229.

43. Joni Seager, ed., *The State of the Earth Atlas* (New York: Touchstone/Simon and Schuster, 1990), 12.

44. Bennett, *Unthinking Faith*, 91.

45. Paul W. Taylor, *Respect for Nature* (Princeton, NJ: Princeton University Press, 1986), 125.

46. Taylor, *Respect for Nature*, 126.

47. Taylor, *Respect for Nature*, 133–134.

48. Bennett, *Unthinking Faith*, 130.

49. Bennett, *Unthinking Faith*, 139.

50. Patricia Mische, "Ecological Security and the Need to Reconceptualize Sovereignty," *Alternatives* 14 (1989), 424.

51. See, for example, Elizabeth Dodson Gray, *Why the Green Nigger? Remything Genesis* (Wellesley, MA: Roundtable Press, 1979); Leonie Caldecott and Stephanie Leland, eds., *Reclaim the Earth: Women Speak Out for Life on Earth* (London: The Woman's Press, 1983); Judith Plant, ed., *Healing the Wounds: The Promise of Ecofeminism* (Philadelphia, PA: New Society Publishers, 1989); and Diamond and Orenstein, *Reweaving the World*.

52. Yaakov Jerome Garb, "Perspective or Escape? Ecofeminist Musings on Contemporary Earth Imagery," in *Reweaving the World*, ed. Diamond and Orenstein, 270.

53. Garb, "Perspective or Escape?" 270.

54. Garb, "Perspective or Escape?" 277–278.

55. Haraway, "A Manifesto for Cyborgs," 67.

56. Haraway, "Situated Knowledges," 580–581.

57. Ecofeminists like Sharon Doubiago in her article, "Mama Coyote Talks to the Boys," in *Healing the Wounds*, ed. Plant, 40–44, are more wary of the "figure of Coyote, that skinny, immoral, overly masculine cartoon trickster" (43).

58. Haraway, *Primate Visions*, 594–595.

59. Haraway, "A Manifesto for Cyborgs," 67.

60. Haraway, *Primate Visions*, 292.

61. Haraway, "Situated Knowledges," 592.

62. See, in particular, Helen E. Longino, *Science as Social Knowledge: Value and Objectivity in Scientific Inquiry* (Princeton, NJ: Princeton University Press, 1990).

63. Bennett, *Unthinking Faith*, 59. This was also an argument made by Schrader-Frechette in "Seventeenth-Century Ideas" (see note 33).

64. Bennett, *Unthinking Faith*, 156–157.

65. Bennett, *Unthinking Faith*, 152.

66. Haraway, "A Manifesto for Cyborgs," 67.

67. Haraway, "A Manifesto for Cyborgs," 68.

68. Ursula LeGuin, *The Dispossessed: An Ambiguous Utopia* (New York: Avon Books, 1974).

69. Patrocinio Schweickart, "What If . . . Science and Technology in Feminist Utopias," in *Machine Ex Dea: Feminist Perspectives on Technology*, ed. Joan Rothschild (New York: Pergamon Press, 1983), 208.

70. Schweickart, "What If?" 209.

71. Schweickart, "What If?" 209.

72. Remarks made by Donna Haraway, panel on "Political Theory/Primate Visions: Reflections on Donna Haraway," annual meeting of the American Political Science Association, Washington, DC, August 1991. I am indebted to Professor Haraway for her thoughts during and after this panel on the notion of rethinking political community.

6

Sovereignty, Identity, Sacrifice

Jean Bethke Elshtain

But we are coming to the sacrifice.

Edmund Blunden
"Vlamertinghe: Passing the Chateau, July 1917"
from *Poems of Many Years*

The sacrifice you make will never be forgotten.

President George Bush
Christmas Eve Message to
US Troops, 1990

Sacrifice ME [a. F, ad. L]
1. Primarily, the slaughter of an animal as an offering to God or a deity. Hence the surrender to God or a deity, for the purpose of propitiation or homage, of some object or possession. Also *fig.* the offering of prayer, thanksgiving, penitence, submission, etc.
2. That which is offered in sacrifice; a victim immolated on the altar; anything offered to God or a deity as an act of propitiation or homage.
3. *Theol.* The offering by Christ of himself to the Father as a propitiary victim in his voluntary immolation upon the cross. b. Applied to the Eucharistic celebration regarded as a propitiary offering of the body and blood of Christ in perpetual memory of the sacrifice offered by him in his crucifixion.
4. The destruction or surrender of something valued or desired for the sake of something having a higher or more pressing claim; the loss entailed by devotion to some other interest. b. a victim.

From the *Oxford English Dictionary*

When I was at work on my book, *Women and War*, a realization slowly but irrevocably grew on me. It was, in some respects, a happy dawning; in other ways, my crystallizing convictions troubled, vexed, and haunted; for one incessant and insistent theme emerged from the several hundred "war stories" I encountered—the theme of sacrifice. The young man goes to war not so much to kill as to die, to forfeit his particular body for that of the larger body, the body politic, a body most often presented and re-presented as feminine: a mother country bound by citizens speaking the mother tongue.

The reason that this realization was, in some sense, a relief lay in the fact that the many—I can only call them "Manichean"—texts, some but not all by feminists, which laid the blame for war, as well as the causal explanation *of* war, on the doorstep of male aggressivity, came under compelling pressure and grew less and less believable the more I read, pondered, and studied. Some aggressive drive peculiar to the male sex did not surface as the most potent theme that drove men to their deaths in time of war. A relief, then, that my own young son was probably not a beast lurking and awaiting the chance to bare his fangs and shed some blood, not his own. But a terrible sadness, too, a foreboding recognition that Plutarch's *Sayings of Spartan Mothers*, repeated by Jean-Jacques Rousseau, might linger yet, just beneath the surface of everyday, conscious recognition, poised, ready to emerge full-force should this country ever again find itself in a full-fledged war. We just passed through a war and the sacrificial theme indeed resurfaced: it is in full flower as of this writing.

But, first, consider the Rousseau I have in mind, he who honors Spartan mothers whose sayings Plutarch detailed in Volume III of his *Moralia*, reproducing tales, anecdotes, and epigrams that constructed the Spartan woman as a mother who reared her sons to be sacrificed on the altar of civic necessity. Such a martial mother was more pleased to hear that her son died "in a manner worthy of [her] self, his country, and his ancestors than if he had lived for all time a coward." Sons who failed to measure up were reviled. One woman, whose son was the sole survivor of a disastrous battle, killed him with a tile, the appropriate punishment for his obvious cowardice. Spartan women shook off expressions of sympathy in words that bespeak an unshakable civic identity. Plutarch recounts a woman, as she buried her son, telling a would-be sympathizer that she had had "good luck," not bad: "I bore him that he might die for Sparta, and this is the very thing that has come to pass for me."[1]

Mother and mother's milk serve as a foundation for civic-spiritedness and willingness to die. Just as the adult man who lacks respect for his mother is a wretch, "a monster unworthy of seeing the light of day," so the citizen who does not love and adore his country, and everyday "feel the eyes of his fellow-countrymen upon him every moment" is no real citizen. The authentic citizen is "so completely dependent upon public esteem as to be unable to do anything, acquire anything, or achieve anything without it."[2] And creating such citizens is the primal and primary female civic task. Rousseau describes the female "citizen" as follows: "A Spartan woman had five sons in the army and was awaiting news of the battle. A Helot arrives; trembling, she asks him for news. 'Your five sons were killed.' 'Base slave, did I ask you that?'

'We won the victory.' The mother runs to the temple and gives thanks to the gods. This is the female citizen."[3]

The potent love of mother country, and willingness to serve and protect her, will shrivel on the civic vine if mothers no longer figure overpoweringly in the affections and upbringings of their children. This was Rousseau's conviction and it is one repeated, deeply inscribed, in the political thought and consciousness of the West, nowhere receiving a more grandiose elaboration than in the philosophy of Hegel and in his theory of the triumphant *Kriegstaat*.[4] We all know, in broad strokes, the story Hegel tells. Hegel as a young man celebrated the national ideal to which the French Revolution gave birth with its *levée en masse*, the first mass mobilization of men, women, and children for all-out war. His vision of the family, civil society, and the state is densely textured and impossible to characterize simply. What follows is radical surgery, but I don't think I've amputated any essential body part. As a state-identified being, the *self* of the male citizen is fully unfolded and made complete. The state is the arena that calls upon and sustains the individual's commitment to universal ethical life, satisfying expansive yearnings through the opportunity to sacrifice "in behalf of the individuality of the state." For with the state comes not simply the possibility but the inevitability of war.

War transcends material values. The individual reaches for a common end. War-constituted solidarity is immanent within the state form. But the state, hence the nation, comes fully to life only with war. Peace poses the specific danger of sanctioning the view that the atomized world of civil society is absolute. In war, however, the state as a collective being is tested, and the citizen comes to recognize the state as the source of all rights. Just as the individual emerges to self-conscious identity only through a struggle, so each state must struggle to attain recognition. The state's proclamation of its own sovereignty is not enough: that sovereignty must be recognized. War is the means to attain recognition, to pass, in a sense, the definitive test of political manhood. The state is free that can defend itself, gain the recognition of others, and shore up an acknowledged identity. The freedom of individuals and states is not given as such but must be achieved through conflict. It is in war that the strength of the state is tested, and only through that test can it be shown whether individuals can overcome selfishness and are prepared to work for the whole and to sacrifice in service to the more inclusive good. The man becomes what he in some sense is meant to be by being absorbed in the larger stream of life: war and the state. To preserve the larger civic body, which must be "as one," particular bodies must be sacrificed.[5]

That is the great and terrible story. For many who yearn for a transformed world, these formulations no doubt sound pretty awful; they might insist, furthermore, that we've put sure and certain distance between ourselves and the Hegelian state in this matter. I am not so sanguine. To expose the doubts I harbor, I will move backward—to pre-Hegelian moments and traces of sacrificial civic identity—and then forward, to post-Hegelian signs. I am taking to heart here Foucault's insistence that the task of political criticism is to follow lines of fragility in the present, to manage to grasp why and how that which is might be construed differently. This is another way of restating Hannah Arendt's dictum that the task of political theory is to "think what we are doing."

The *is* is states and the entanglement of our identities with them, so much so that a will-to-sacrifice may be inscribed in and through, indeed be constitutive of, our selfhood, male and female. This is a strong claim. Let me try to back it up. Before Rousseau, before Hegel, before the modern nation-state, the idea and ideal of sacrificial political identity had been forged in the hoplite warfare of the Greek phalanx where the will-to-sacrifice was also a triumph of the will—what B. H. Liddell Hart calls the "chief incalculable" in warfare. Writes Victor Hanson: "Along with regimental spirit, an even better incentive for hoplites to stand firm was the sight of their own commanding officer, the *strategos*, fighting alongside them in the very front ranks of the army."[6] This preparedness to die was much enhanced by the sight of gray-bearded grandfathers fighting alongside smooth-faced grandsons. The affair was overwhelmingly familial and tribal. The Spartans, the model for later civic republicans and early modern state builders, honored but two identities with inscriptions on tombstones—men who had died in war and women who had succumbed in childbirth: both embodied the sacrificial moment of civic identity. In Athens, too, death was anonymous on the funerary *relievos* with the exception of the soldier and the childbearing woman.

Ernst Kantorowicz, in his classic, *The King's Two Bodies*, traces the ideal of "pro patria mori." He begins by reminding us that the word *patria* referred initially to a hamlet, village, township. The warrior died for loyalty to his lord rather than some abstract juridical ideal or territory. But around the twelfth and thirteenth centuries the concept underwent a transformation and began to refer to kingdoms and nations, and to have deep emotional and symbolic content. He writes: "Neither from the idea of polity-centered kingship nor from that of the state as *corpus morale, politicum, mysticum* can there easily be separated another notion which came to new life independently of, though simultaneously with, the organological and corporational doctrines: the *regnum* as *patria*, as an object of political devotion and semi-religious emotion."[7] The community having been endowed with a "mystical" character—the *corpus republicae mysticum*—sacrifice in her name grew more exigent, not only defensible but obligatory. The Christian martyr who had sacrificed for an "invisible polity" becomes the soldier who remained faithful unto death—the model of "civic self-sacrifice." Christian doctrine, then, having transferred the political notion of the *polis* to the city of God, and honoring those who died in her name, is now transmuted to underwrite (not without tension) the "new territorial concept of *patria*."[8] Kantorowicz speculates that much of the force of this new patriotism derived from "ethical values transferred back from the *patria* in heaven to polities on earth."

The death of the warrior *pro patria* was interpreted as self-sacrifice for others, a "work of *caritas*." (Greater love hath no man than this . . .) The theme of brotherly love was struck again and again. Men who were killed in a campaign (the example is the crusades) died "for the love of God *and his brothers*" and received "eternal beatitude according to the mercy of God."[9] In the thirteenth century, Kantorowicz continues, "the Christian virtue of *caritas* became unmistakably political" and was "activated to sanctify and justify, ethically and morally, the death for the political 'fatherland.'"[10] This love for the wider body is declared by St. Thomas to be founded "in the root of charity which puts, not the private things before those common, but the common things before the private . . . the *amor patriae* deserves a rank of honor above all other virtues." The magnanimity of the soldier's sacrifice is celebrated in verse and song for, to the soldier, his brothers and his "fatherland" are dearer than his life. "Thus it happened that in the thirteenth century the crown of martyrdom began to descend on the war victims of the secular state."[11]

Now, a breathless and rapid leap to the twentieth century: J. Glenn Gray, in *The Warriors*, examines the impulse to self-sacrifice characteristic of warriors who, from compassion, would rather die than kill. He calls the freedom of wartime a communal freedom as the "I" passes into a "we," and as human longings for community with others find a field for realization. Communal ecstasy explains a willingness to sacrifice and gives dying for others a mystical quality; in this sense, Grey finds a similarity between the self-sacrifice of soldiers and the willingness of martyrs to die for their faith. "Such sacrifice seems hard and heroic to those who have never felt communal ecstasy," writes Gray. "In fact, it is not nearly so difficult as many less absolute acts in peacetime and civilian life. . . . It is hardly surprising that men are capable of self-sacrifice in wartime."[12] Nor are the women exempt from a sacralizing of sacrifice. There are hundreds of hair-raising tales of bellicose mothers, wives, and girlfriends writing the combat soldier and requesting the sacrifice of the enemy as a tribute, or gift, to her.

But I am more interested in the construction of the noncombatant female's will to sacrifice her own loved ones. Just one example, taken from my book, *Women and War*: Vera Brittain's voice is lodged securely in the ranks of woman pacifists and antimilitarists, and she has become a heroine to contemporary feminist antiwar activists and thinkers—not, however, without some ambiguity. In *Testament of Youth*, Brittain hankers after her wartime months in Malta (during the Great War), because Malta had come to seem a "shrine, the object of a pilgrimage, a fairy country which I knew I must see again before I die . . . Come back, magic days! I was sorrowful, anxious, frustrated, lonely—but yet how vividly alive!" But it is Brittain's wartime diaries for 1913–1917, published as *Chronicle of Youth*, with which I am here concerned. Brittain believed England must enter the war and could not remain neutral. Not to come to the aid of France would make England guilty of the "grossest treachery." Feeling much of the time as if she were dreaming, Brittain logged entries of how her father raved at her brother not to volunteer, while brother Edward, with a bit of class snobbism, told "Daddy" that, "'not being a public school man or having any training,' he would not possibly understand how impossible it was for others to remain in inglorious inaction."

Brittain understood the action required of war fighters in sacrificial terms. Disdaining her father's lack of courage in behalf of her brother, she noted the "agony of Belgium," remarking, bitterly, on "the unmanliness of it, especially after we read in the *Times* of a mother who said to her hesitating son, 'My boy, I don't want you to go but if I were you I should!'" Brittain's beloved, Roland, longed to take part in the war, finding in the possibility of sacrifice something "ennobling and very beautiful." After Roland died, Brittain capitalized the personal pronoun—"Him"—transfiguring Roland into a latter-day Christ in her entries about him. He died and became, in "His" sacrifice, a beatific figure for her. "On Sunday night at 11:00—the day of the month and hour of His Death—I knelt before the window in my ward and prayed, not to God but to him. . . . Always at that hour I will turn to Him, just as Mohammedans always turn to Mecca at sunrise." Apotheosized in death, Roland lives on. The life of the individual is a fit and worthy sacrifice so that the body politic may live.[13]

Whence this identity, this identification of self and nation? A caveat: the identification and the will-to-sacrifice of which I write is not a single phenomenon but many. There is a contrast between *publica caritas* of the medieval sort and the overheated nationalism or civic blood lust characteristic of classical civic humanists and twentieth-century dictators alike. As an instance of the former, I have in mind Caluccion Salutati's exclamations that the sweetness of one's love for the *patria* is such that one must not cavil at crushing one's brothers or delivering "from the womb of one's wife the premature child with the sword."[14] Salutati was extreme but that sort of extremism has, alas, been the norm in many of the great and horrible events of our own century.

A question and a caveat: How did it come about that war for the king, then for country, then for more abstract ideals and demands for the 'imagined community,' got intermingled and served to frame the horizon within which the will-to-sacrifice was, and is, ongoingly forged? Max Weber writes of the "consecrated meaning" of death for the warrior, the conviction that his death alone provides the needed support for the "autonomous dignity of the polity resting on force."[15] Only a preparedness to forfeit one's own life rounds out, or instantiates in all its fullness, devotion to the political community, and only such devotion affords any dignity to a politics that would otherwise turn on brute force. Although a state cannot survive if it attempts to embody a universalistic ethic of *caritas*, without *some* such ethic, coercion alone reigns. Hence the importance of the "consecrated meaning" of the warrior's death. But many of the deaths, the civic sacrifices, in our own epoch have not been those of warriors, whether just or unjust, but of civilians, the non-combatant sacrifices of total war. Noncombatants are molded from the same civic stuff as war fighters. And it is this shaping to and for a way of life that needs to be tended to if we are to assess the power civic identification retains to construct individual and collective identities.

In the recent past, we learned how "Baghdad Schoolchildren Are Made Ready for War," the correspondent for the *New York Times* noting that children were readied for "sacrifice" through "weekly outdoor military drill," during which they chanted, ranted, and play-acted their loyalty to their 'father-leader,' President Saddam Hussein, and hurled insults at President Bush."[16] We have learned of protests that have resulted in upper-class martyrs as members of the upper class immolate themselves to counter what they perceive to be a stark injustice. "Dramatic self-sacrifice," *Time* magazine calls it, and quotes the father of a young man who burns himself alive, "My son has done the right thing. Some good will flow out of his sacrifice."[17] President Fidel Castro's political troubles are noted given his need to appeal, incessantly, "for sacrifice at precisely the moment when his moral right to rule Cuba is more widely questioned than ever before."[18] One of the slogans of the Mothers of the Disappeared in Argentina read: "Those Who Die for Life Cannot Be Called Dead," as these women sought to make sense of the unwilling sacrifice of their sons and daughters to a repressive regime. And a Russian philosopher, Alexei Losev, whose work has been rediscovered as state communism crumbles, told a tale of his own self-sacrificing love for Russia in late 1941, at the height of the war, after a German air raid bombed out his home near Moscow's Arbat Square, killing his family. What is remarkable is not so much the totality of identification and sacrifice he proclaims and extols but the fact that young Glasnost-era Soviet writers should foreground Losev's essay, "Motherland," as an alternative to the depredations of Communist rule, speaking, as it does, to wholehearted involvement with community of a sort that need not be coerced. A sample of Losev's chilling yet powerful words:

> The common life is our Motherland. She brings us into this world, and, then receives us after our death. . . . Outside a community there is not an individual. . . . There is nothing in a human being that is above his community. He is an embodiment of his community . . . but what does one call this personal life, this life of an individual, when a person is born or he dies, when he grows up or withers away, when he is healthy or ill, and all this taking place within the sphere of communal life, a correct, normal, and natural state of the world, in which everything separate, isolated, specific, personal, and unique manifests itself only in the context of an integral whole, in the context of communal life, in the

context of things necessary, legitimate, normal, harsh, and inevitable,
but nevertheless, one's own, dear and precious, in the context of one's
Motherland.
    Such a life is called a sacrifice. Motherland calls for sacrifice. The
life of the Motherland is in itself an eternal sacrifice.[19]

Being part of a way of life is no simple process of inculcation into a
society's rules and practices; rather, it is a matter of creating and sustaining
the identities of persons and collectivities. John Donne pined that "no man is
an island"; current critics, both left and right, insist each of us exists in a
dense web of social relations. Images of being 'at home,' of a homeland, of
being homeward bound are visions of safety, enclosure, special and particular
ties. "Homelessness," whether that of individuals or whole peoples, is most
often constructed as a personal tragedy, a social problem, or a volatile
geopolitical dilemma. Individuals carry images of home within them and
project those images out into and upon their worlds. Nations are conceived as
large and either warring or friendly families. Studies of children indicate that
the human young occupy a densely textured *political* world at whose core lies
the notion of 'homeland'. Robert Coles, in his work, *The Political Life of
Children*, finds that attachment to homeland is personalized by children as
motherland or fatherland. "Nationalism works it way into just about every
corner of the mind's life," Coles writes, adding that if an observer is attuned
to the symbolism and imagery deployed by children, he or she will find "a
nation's continuing life . . . enmeshed in the personal lives of its children."[20]
    Children seize upon symbols and have ready access to a nation's "name,
its flag, its music, its currency, its slogans, its history, its political life."
Coles notes that the entrenched notion of a homeland is double-edged, at once
inward-looking—a place where one "gets one's bearings," a domicile, a
source of spiritual and social nourishment—and outward-projecting—
protecting us from "them," from foreigners who, all too easily, become
enemies. Both aspects of homeland imagery turn up in "the developing
conscience of young people" everywhere, concludes Coles after studying the
politics of children on five continents.[21]
    The upshot of Coles's story is modern nationalism, *sic et non*.
Inevitable, yes, in some form or another, for we must all locate ourselves in
a particular place. Good or bad? Both. The nationalism in personal identity
may, on the one hand, encourage social commitment to and for one's
homeland and its people; on the other hand, it may energize fear and hatred of
the homelands of others. One way or another we are all marked, deeply and
permanently, by the way political life gets embodied in images of motherland
and fatherland—so much so that the human body itself is politicized, taking
on the markings of one civic realm as compared to another.
    In the post–World War II era, new nationalisms have deployed war—or,
perhaps better put, colonial wars have created new nationalisms. Between
1945 and 1968, sixty-six countries became independent. Benedict Anderson

notes that *every* successful revolution since 1945 has been defined in national terms and that the end of nationalism is "not remotely in sight." Nationalism is the most "universally legitimate form" and "universally legitimate value in the political life of our time."[22] This nation is an "imagined political community—and imagined as both inherently limited and sovereign."[23] Imagined because each member of such a community lives in some image of communion with each other. As well, communities can be distinguished by the style in and through which they are imagined.

Sovereignty enters the picture for obvious reasons. It is a concept constitutive of as well as derivative from nation-state formation and identity: a Western historic form that has been, and continues to be, universalized. Sovereignty incorporates both a drive toward freedom from the domination of another as well as a particular understanding of power. Historically, much of the power of the concept of sovereignty lay precisely in its encoding of the absolute, perpetual, indivisible power of a masculinized deity, a deity whose power was absolute and from everlasting to everlasting, as a penultimate political form. State power, the power of the legitimate ruler and promulgator of laws, tamed and ordered domestic politics even as it set the boundary for autonomous self-sovereignty. The earthly sovereign shared many of the attributes of his divine counterpart. For Bodin, for example, sovereignty is the power of an absolute *dominus* over a vast domestic space.

If there is any force to my musings concerning the metaphysical traces embedded in the full-blown theory of sovereignty, the genealogy of the concept is nested in the powerful and pervasive construction of God's sovereign dominion, force, and will over what would have remained a formless void had He not exercised His omnipotent volition. Sovereignty over time shifts from king to state, and this state cannot alienate its sovereignty. As God's will is singular. so must the sovereign's be—at least once it is formulated as a "general will," and most certainly this singularity must pertain in "foreign affairs."

The constructions of sovereignty allow us to make more sense of the will-to-sacrifice as it shifts from personal liege loyalty to a feudal lord to an abstract, juridical, imagined tie that nevertheless calls forth sacrifice in its/his (the sovereign's) name. But another dimension must be added to this already rich mulch. I noted above that most modern nation-states are construed in feminine terms. The Sovereign may bear a masculinized face but the nation itself is feminized, a mother, a sweetheart, a lover. One can rightly speak, as Anderson does, of "political love," a love that retains the fraternal dimensions of medieval *caritas* but incorporates as well a maternalized loyalty symbolized domestically: the nation is home and home is mother. No more than one chooses one's parents does one choose one's country, and this adds even greater force to the nature of political love. We fall in love early through language, "encountered at mother's knees and parted with only at the grave," and through this language "pasts are restored, fellowships are imagined, and futures dreamed."[24] Demanding but well-nigh irresistible—a *force majeure*. The child's will-to-sacrifice flows from embodied ties to both parents that project outward into a more generalized relationship to a feminized motherland, a masculinized sovereign state. No wonder most of us most of the time 'obey.'

One of the most poignant and horrible instances of sacrifice and obedience in our time is the terrible blood sacrifice demanded by the sovereign gods of the fascist state who construed their nation not so much in language as in blood. And loyalty reverted to a personal bond, an oath to a godlike leader. We all know of the Final Solution, but few know of the Final Sacrifice—the term is Gerhard Rempel's from his book, *Hitler's Children: The Hitler Youth and the SS*. Starving, bewildered Hitler Youth were thrown into the final months of the war when Hitler and "determined SS officers conspired to generate a children's crusade to shore up crumbling defenses and offer thousands of teenagers as a final sacrifice to the god of war."[25] The schemes were brutal; the results horrifying. Thousands of children between the ages of 8 and 17 perished in suicidal sabotage attempts and last-ditch stands. Five thousand young people, male and female, were thrown into the "twilight of the gods" in the last spasm of the agony of Berlin; 500 survived. What was most astonishing to observers was the determination of these children to "do their duty until they were literally ready to drop. They had been fed on legends of heroism for as long as they could remember. For them the call to 'ultimate sacrifice' was no empty phrase."[26] The grotesquery of all this signifies, in admittedly extreme form, the macabre dimension of the will-to-sacrifice as it has been constituted in the politics of an unusually virulent form of sovereignty.

The nation-state is a phenomenon that cannot be imagined or legislated out of existence. Needing others to define ourselves, we will remain inside a state/nation-centered discourse of war and politics, for better and for worse, so long as states remain the best way we have devised for protecting and sustaining a way of life in common. But we can try to tame and limit the demands of sovereignty; we can, perhaps, move toward what I am tempted to call a postsovereign politics. I have in mind a politics that shifts the focus of political loyalty and identity from sacrifice (actual or *in situ*) to responsibility. My target is both images of the sovereign self as an unproblematic, unified, sharply boundaried phenomenon as well as the sovereign state in its full-blown, untrammeled instantiation.

A politics *sans* sovereignty: is it possible? What would it look like? How would it forge civic identities in such a way that blood sacrifice, that of the self or enemy others (whether internal or external) is not so pervasive a demand and possibility? I cannot develop a vision of such a politics here in any full-blown sense, but I can indicate where we should turn for help: to the rich body of thought penned by Central Europeans over the past several decades. I have in mind Adam Michnik and Vaclav Havel as the two central figures in creating a theory of civil society, a politics, in opposition to authoritarian, sovereign state apparatuses. Havel writes of politics as "practical morality . . . humanly measured care for our fellow human beings."[27] He never uses the word sovereignty in any of his writings; nor has he, to my knowledge, launched into sovereign discourse since his election as president of Czechoslovakia. But he does write of identity and responsibility; of accountability and deed doing. What is most astonishing about his letters from prison is the fact that they are utterly devoid of maudlin, self-sacrificial constructions. They *are* filled, however, with a sense of identity as an ongoing, lifelong process of becoming—no notion of a completed sovereign self here—and of responsibility as that which cannot be cut to the measure of a man's hubris. And sovereign discourse historically has been nothing if not hubristic.

Havel writes of a post-totalitarian system and antipolitical parties, in his struggle to get away from the rigidities and excesses of the discourse of war and sovereignty. He urges us into a postsovereign political discourse, a move from sacrifice to responsibility: "I feel that this arrogant anthropocentrism of modern man, who is convinced he can know everything and bring everything under his control, is somewhere in the background of the present crisis. It seems to me that if the world is to change for the better it must start with a change in human consciousness, in the very humanness of modern man."[28]

An ethic of responsibility means one is answerable, accountable to another, for something; one is liable to be called to account. One is also a being, capable of fulfilling an obligation or trust; reliable; trustworthy. This presumes, indeed requires, a particular construction of what Charles Taylor calls "the modern identity," one constituted in and through the notion of self-responsible freedom. Softening the demands of the iron grip, sovereignty=sacrifice, does *not* mean so loosening the bonds of reason that the self flies off in all directions and can find no good reason to prefer *this* to *that* and can hear in such notions as "responsibility" only a dour and crabby moralism. A few final thoughts as intimations of an alternative, then:

Hélène Carère d'Encausse recently argued that attachment to a nation is "an accomplishment of civilized man, not a regression. The nation-state is not a tribal construction. Elements of familialism and tribalism may reverberate and are certain features of any genealogical construction of the modern identity, but they do not dominate." Identification with a national "imagined community" is a complex, many-sided construction. It taps particularism and universalism. Indeed, one might argue it *requires* such, being composed of normatively vital aspects of both ethnicity and universal values, organic integration and voluntarism. Human beings require concrete reference groups in order to attain individuality and identity, but too complete immersion in such groups limits the boundaries of identity and of identification to fixed familial, tribal, or territorial lines. John A. Armstrong, in a recent piece on "Contemporary Ethnicity," worries that extreme voluntarist individualism leads to the loss of a coherent identity.[29] Statist demands that extract the 'last full measure of devotion' that most of us would willingly offer to family and dear friends, is a corrective device to our current deracination. That is, modernity denatures nonvoluntarist obligations and commitments, then reconstitutes and abstracts them as mandated blood sacrifice in the name of the collective, a sacrifice of "radical severity," in political theorist George Kateb's words.

Kateb muses interestingly on the question of sacrifice as a mandated obligation. According to Kateb, no one has a moral obligation to die; hence, conscription is illegitimate. One *may* sacrifice oneself for a "child or a defenseless loved one," but to construe this possibility in contractual terms is "to cheapen it." Kateb detects a perhaps unavoidable conundrum in modern universalistically cast constitutional republics: on the one hand, and in light of individualist construals, the social group is not idolized; the collective is not sacralized. This makes possible, or should, the free flow of "self-sacrificing love" toward particular individuals or groups. On the other hand, a "mandated obligation to die" emerges with greatest force "only in an individualist moral universe" in which persons have been stripped of ties of great robustness and insistency to particular others. Kateb's argument leaves us suspended in a political and moral universe in which sacrifice is legally mandated, yes, but in which the legitimacy of such demands is ongoingly challenged. The demand and the challenge are both reactions to a strongly individualist social order.

Feminist moral theorizing, now poised between the poles of the so-called justice v. care perspectives, offers no promise of a resolution in this matter. Critics of the justice perspective—critical because it posits an autonomous moral agent capable of applying fundamental rules through the use of abstract reason and in the service of universal values—offer, as an alternative, care—the caring, connected self. But the sacrificial political identity I have traced is very much a relational, embedded, interdependent self. Care—*caritas*—sacrifice: these are ancient themes, not new ones; primal constructions, not modern discoveries. What we require is a complex moral universe, a world of justice *and* mercy, autonomy *and* caring, particular ties *and* universal aspirations. In such a universe, one adumbrated in the work of a Michnik or a Havel, freedom and responsibility are living possibilities; the self is very much a modern identity, at once committed yet aware of the irony and limits to all commitments; prepared to sacrifice, but wary of all calls to sacrifice. This identity is, in the main, antiheroic. The heroic emerges, when it does, as a modern form of "*Hier ich stande. Ich kann nicht anders.*" The stress is on the "*Ich*," and the presumption is that none should be commanded to do the supererogatory; none should be *required* to give the last full measure of devotion. But to live in a universe in which no *one* was prepared, in which no such "*Ich*" was any longer constructed and nothing was worth sacrificing for, would be to live in a moral universe impoverished beyond our poor powers of imagination.

The final words shall be Havel's:

> The problem of human identity remains at the center of my thinking about human affairs . . . as you must have noticed from my letters, the importance of the notion of human responsibility has grown in my meditations. It has begun to appear with increasing clarity, as that fundamental point from which all identity grows and by which it stands or falls; it is the foundation, the root, the center of gravity, the constructional principle or axis of identity, something like the "idea" that determines its degree and type. It is the mortar binding it together, and when the moral dries out, identity too begins irreversibly to crumble and fall apart. (That is why I wrote you that the secret of man is the secret of his responsibility.)

This, remember, from a man who insists one must never lose one's sense of absurdity.[30]

Notes

1. All citations are drawn from Elshtain, *Women and War.*
2. Jean-Jacques Rousseau, *The Government of Poland* (Indianapolis: Bobbs-Merrill, 1972), 87.
3. Jean-Jacques Rousseau, *Emile*, trans. Allan Bloom (New York: Basic Books, 1979), 37–38.
4. I recognize, of course, that Hegel's *Kriegstaat* is also a *Richtstaat*. This underscores my point that wars in a state system are not random flailings but are extraordinarily complex, rule-governed human activities.
5. See the complete discussion in Elshtain, *Women and War*, 73–75.
6. From *The Western Way of War* (New York: Alfred A. Knopf, 1989), 107.
7. Ernst H. Kantorowicz, *The King's Two Bodies: A Study in Medieval Political Theology* (Princeton, NJ: Princeton University Press, 1957), 237.
8. Kantorowicz, *The King's Two Bodies*, 237.
9. Kantorowicz, *The King's Two Bodies*, 241, citing a letter by Pope Urban II.
10. Kantorowicz, *The King's Two Bodies*, 242.
11. Kantorowicz, *The King's Two Bodies*, 244.
12. J. Glenn Gray, *The Warriors* (New York: Harper Colophon, 1970), 47.
13. All citations from *Women and War*, 211–212.
14. Kantorowicz, *The King's Two Bodies*, 245.
15. *From Max Weber: Essays in Sociology*, ed. H. H. Gerth and C. Wright Mills (New York: Oxford University Press, 1946), 335.
16. Elaine Sciolino, "Baghdad Schoolchildren Are Made Ready for War," *New York Times*, 8 January 1991, A7.
17. Edward W. Desmond, "Fatal Fires of Protest," *Time*, 15 October 1990, 63.
18. Charles Lane, "Low Fidelity," *The New Republic*, 7 and 14 January 1991, 25–30, 28.

19. Alexei Losev, "Motherland," *The Literary Gazette Int.*, May 1990, 14–15.

20. Robert Coles, *The Political Life of Children* (Boston, MA: Atlantic Monthly Press, 1986), 60.

21. Coles, *The Political Life of Children*, 63.

22. Anderson, *Imagined Communities*, 13.

23. Anderson, *Imagined Communities*, 15.

24. Anderson, *Imagined Communities*, 140.

25. Gerhard Rempel, *Hitler's Children: The Hitler Youth and the SS* (Chapel Hill: University of North Carolina Press, 1989), 233. See also Jay W. Baird, *To Die for Germany* (Bloomington: Indiana University Press, 1990).

26. Rempel, *Hitler's Children*, 241.

27. Vaclav Havel, *Living in Truth* (London: Faber and Faber, 1986), 155.

28. Vaclav Havel, *Disturbing the Peace* (New York: Alfred A. Knopf, 1990), 11. A tall order, intimations of the long haul, if not the long march.

29. See Hélène Carère d'Encausse, "Springtime of Nations," *The New Republic*, 21 January 1991, 17–22; and John A. Armstrong, "Contemporary Ethnicity: The Moral Dimension in Comparative Perspective," *The Review of Politics* 52 (Spring 199): 163-168, p. 166.

30. Vaclav Havel, *Letters to Olga* (New York: Henry Holt, 1989), p. 145.

7

Feminists and Realists View Autonomy and Obligation in International Relations
Christine Sylvester

> ... and the gravest problems arise from theories of the world founded
> upon a conception of man that is concealed and for this reason never
> examined.   —Kenneth W. Thompson[1]

This chapter explores concealments of autonomous and minimally obligated man—and gender more generally—in realist international relations theory and practice. It also reveals activities by women in international relations that subvert realist autonomies and rewrite obligations in more feminist ways.

The seemingly generic term "realist" has been posed as a way of "examining reality as it really is—without subscribing to Realist assumptions."[2] In practice, however, realism can smokescreen Realist strivings for autonomy from men's and women's "real" experiences of relationships and unchosen obligations, thereby reinforcing, in unexpected ways, the view proffered by Hedley Bull and Carsten Holbraad that "international relations is not one of those subjects in which it can be assumed that new studies represent an advance on old ones."[3]

The Realist-realist gender concealments may have to do with shared groundings in liberalism.[4] The feminist writings of Nancy Hirschmann, Carole Pateman, and Cynthia Enloe help us see how that connection works and how certain forms of liberalism can erase women from spheres of significance. Hirschmann addresses the unacknowledged gendering of freedom, recognition, and obligation in Western liberal theory, and traces this concealment to defensiveness experienced by males in the process of becoming properly gendered as men;[5] one sees within her treatise the origins of defensively positionalist realist states.[6] Pateman writes about a conquest-based sexual contract predating the hypothetical liberal social contract that brought Leviathans into existence;[7] both contracts are alive today within the gendered operations of many neorealist and neoliberal institutionalist regimes. Enloe offers glimpses of women engaged in liberal exchanges and reciprocities that should figure into realist theories of international relations, but do not; she argues in effect that viewing these activities from women's standpoints reveals the false gender blindness of the realist imperium and makes it more difficult for the rule of emperors to continue.[8]

There are other clues to disguised gender in Realist-realist overlaps and skepticisms that complicate and enrich, order and disorder everyone's theories and arguments, and there are concrete actions that women engage in within international relations that reveal the limitations of our usual understandings of the field. After exploring the meanings of autonomy and obligation presented by Hirschmann, Pateman, Enloe, and others, compared to meanings encrusted in international relations theory, the paper veers off "strangely" onto highly contextualized terrains where women operate in, around, and against realist forms of autonomy and obligation in everyday international relations. This portion of the discussion provides gender "takes" on James Keeley's point that "disorder and resistance can persist in the face of realist ordering or be created by it,"[9] and suggests ways that seemingly insignificant disorderings begin to recast a field.

Feminist Issues of Autonomy and Obligation

Nancy Hirschmann addresses the tendency of consent theorists to make "obligation" an inferior second term to "freedom" and probes the related and gendered meanings of "autonomy" that give rise to this practice. She implicitly agrees with arguments casting social contract liberalism as a politics of negativity. In Benjamin Barber's terms, this politics has "enthroned not simply the individual but the individual defined by his perimeters, his parapets, and his entrenched solitude."[10] To Hirschmann the negativity has to do with equations in liberal theory of "individuals" with men—a connection Barber's statement reveals. She argues that masculine identity is embedded in notions of inherently and naturally free individuals, and, correlatively, in the idea that "the only legitimate limitations are those imposed by the self."[11]

As is the wont of many feminist standpointers—that is, feminists who believe women's experiences of subordination give them opportunities to view reality in different and more accurate ways than the ways of those who subordinate women[12]—Hirschmann finds the origins of masculine self-preserving theory in gendering experiences that make it difficult for adult males to valorize connectedness as the main principle of sociality. Her feminist psychoanalytic account begins with a young infant supposing its mother's body is part of itself, and then discovering that self is not "subsumed in the one who supplies [its] needs, who is most generally across cultures, female."[13]

For boys, that discovery begins a struggle to suppress original psychic femaleness. This path is not foreordained in "nature," but rather conforms to cultural notions that gender is an exclusive category of identity that must be learned. Becoming male entails an exaggerated emphasis on separation: "a boy defines himself against the mother, as "not-mother."[14] She becomes an object of difference, an "other," as he develops "a conception of agency that abstracts "individual will (the ability to make choices and act on them) out of the context of the social relationships within which it develops and within which it is exercised, because those relationships are threatening by definition."[15]

The properly gendered man then denies the heteronomous roots of his gender identity and embraces a reactive form of autonomy, that is, "a separateness and independence that is a reaction against others."[16] In public society, the reactively autonomous mental stance creates "discrete and controlled points of contact, only through rule-governed and role-defined structures."[17] It reconnects separated and wary individuals through formal "rights" and creates obligations as chosen restraints on what Nancy Rosenblum describes as "a masterless person, free of deference and ascriptive attachments and privileges, though not without norms and attachments altogether."[18] Nonvoluntary consent becomes oxymoronic when, in fact, the basis for a model of voluntary consent is a set of gender rules that men learn involuntarily.

In liberal political theory, the cast of masculine reactive autonomy appears in stories of abstract social contracts entered into, seemingly, by "orphans who have reared themselves, whose desires are situated within and reflect nothing but independently generated movement."[19] Realist international relations theory follows in this mold, even as it focuses on those anarchic spaces that elude social contract; for it depicts states as primitive "individuals" separated from history and others by loner rights of sovereignty—backed up, for good measure, by military hardware—and involved in international conventions and institutions only on a voluntary basis.[20]

The world looks different to girls, because they are mothered by physically similar beings and face no social messages to be unlike mother in order to attain proper status as women. A girl thereby develops a sense of empathetic connection to the world: "self and other will constitute a continuum for her."[21] This does not mean she is free of struggles to differentiate from mother; those tend to occur in adolescence, when issues of psychosexual individuality come to the fore. It does mean that experiences associated with being mothered by a physical similar, in combination with social reinforcements of mother-daughter sameness, contribute to a sense of relational autonomy, whereby girls and then women find their identity within the context of relationships rather than in opposition to them.

If this is so, then many of the relationally grounded obligations women assume also fail to fit the liberal model of chosen restraints one can disavow if it is in one's interest to do so. Feminine differentiation is "a particular way of being connected to others,"[22] and often that connection takes the form of child care or of responsibility for children abandoned or disavowed by their fathers. In a piece for the *Village Voice*, Enloe argues that such responsibilities are the basis of media comminglings of "womenandchildren" into the symbols, victims, and dependents states exist to protect in an international crisis. This caricature reinforces the sense that women's connections entail unchosen obligations; but it also denigrates the content of those obligations by presenting women as "family members rather than independent actors, presumed to be almost childlike in their innocence about the realpolitik of international affairs."[23]

How do adult men come to dominate women and to denigrate their obligations after "escaping" psychic femaleness? Feminist psychoanalytic thinking implies that patriarchal right derives from women's position as mothers: as long as primary caretaking falls to women, identity differentiation occurs first against her and then against others. Carole Pateman, however, argues that "the meaning and value accorded to motherhood in civil society is . . . a consequence of the patriarchal construction of sexual difference as political difference."[24] This construction has origins in a symbolic sexual contract that subordinated women before the social contract came into effect. The social contract divided sociality into public and private realms—state and civil society—and the pre-existing sexual contract contributed the idea that "the private sphere is part of civil society but is separated from the 'civil' sphere."[25]

Pateman reconstructs the sexual contract to show the basis of women's later subordination in society:

> Hobbes states in Leviathan that in the war of all against all "there is no man who can hope by his own strength, or will, to defend himself from destruction, without the help of confederates." But how can such a protective confederation be formed in the natural condition when there is an acute problem of keeping agreements [owing to the isolation and mutual wariness of all]? The answer is that confederations are formed by conquest, and, once formed, are called "families." . . . In Leviathan . . . a family "consists of a man, and his children; or of a man, and his children, and servants together; wherein the father or master is the sovereign." . . . If one male individual manages to conquer another in the state of nature the conqueror will have obtained a servant . . . [If] a male individual manages to conquer a female individual [t]o protect her life she will enter into a contract of subjection—and so she too becomes the servant of a master."[26]

Thus, in a condition free of systemic domination-subordination relations, the conquest of women does indeed occur with motherhood. But in this case, mother is equal to men, though she must defend her infant and herself in the state of nature. Defending two people, one of whom is helpless, disadvantages women vis-à-vis unfettered or confederation-strengthened men, and we are conquered. Conquered peoples become politically subordinate, and therefore we might say that subsequent gendering processes root out that subordinate psychic femininity in boys.[27]

This story explains why men are dominant forces inside those families that are ostensibly outside the important realms of civil society, and why men exclude women from participation in the original social contract and thereafter from public spaces of "significance." It reinforces Hirschmann's sense that "voluntarist theories of obligation can be read, at least in part, as theories of power, with power conceived as domination."[28]

A different approach to knowledge and power emerges when we start from women's more relationally oriented world and add the consideration that choiceless relations also characterize men's initiation into sociality. For girls, the process of attaining identity involves less defensiveness, and the Rubicons dividing self from others—and creating sovereigns and servants—can seem imaginary. This may be the reason Hobbes's "family" women later "consent" to enter marriage contracts in civil society: the conqueror is not an alien so much as he is a potential community member. Properly gendered boys, meanwhile, fail to see that the autonomous self is already connected rather than also connected.[29] In this sense, relational autonomy incorporates the experiences of both sexes and is a reasonable starting point for liberal theory. Obligation must then be reformulated to account for "the very human experience of choicelessness, and for the fact—so adamantly denied by consent and social contract theory—that choices exist in contexts" of relationship.[30]

Cynthia Enloe's *Bananas, Bases, and Beaches: Making Feminist Sense of International Relations* is different in scope and approach from the political theories elaborated by Hirschmann and Pateman, and yet parallels them nicely. Enloe offers an extended look at women's contributions to international relations and argues that realist practice depends on, but is presented as autonomous from, activities of and oligations to women. "Our" field is normally silent about the theoretical implications of women's embeddedness in international relations—as representatives of imperialism, as workers in global factories, as marketing logos affixed to export products, and so forth. To Enloe this means:

> Women's roles in creating and sustaining international politics have been treated as if they were "natural" and thus not worthy of investigation. Consequently, how the conduct of international politics has *depended* on men's control of women has been left unexamined. This has meant that those wielding influence over foreign policy have escaped responsibility for how women have been affected by international relations.[31]

In keeping gender off the agenda and isolated from the realm of significance, realism reveals "how much power it takes to maintain the international political system in its present form," and how much this power "hides the workings of both femininity and masculinity."[32] For example, governments rely on masculinized and feminized sacrifice to sustain a readiness for war in order to preserve state sovereignty. Masculinized sacrifice wins honor through battle, while feminized sacrifice at home is considered second order (except by Jean-Jacques Rousseau)—references to patriotic mothers and the odd tribute to women combatants notwithstanding.[33]

Although Enloe does not say it directly, the bedrock issue for her, as for Hirschmann, seems to be obligation and the falsely unitary concept of reactive autonomy that denies or buries international *relationships* in the language of liberal exchange-oriented contracts. The alternatives may lie on the unexplored cusp of reactive and relational autonomy, where for Enloe the international is personal and for Hirschmann "the point is to call attention to the fact that men already are consensually obligated in many ways and that these obligations are appropriate to human relations but our public ideology will not allow us to recognize this fact."[34]

Autonomy and Obligation in International Relations Theory

The texts of classical Realism establish reactive autonomy as a norm of international relations while keeping autonomous and minimally obligated liberal man in the shadows. Since Realism has been hegemonic, some claim, for three hundred years,[35] its stance on this matter fills many spaces between Realism and "realism."

In the work of Hans J. Morgenthau, autonomy figures directly into the sixth principle of political realism:

> Intellectually, the political realist maintains the autonomy of the political sphere, as the economist, the lawyer, the moralist maintains theirs . . . the political realist is not unaware of the existence and relevance of standards of thought other than political ones [but] as a political realist, he cannot but subordinate those other standards to those of politics.[36]

Initially the domain of the "individual" political realist, his reactive autonomy is transposed onto the state. That state is "free to manage its internal and external affairs according to its discretion, in so far as it is not limited by treaty or what we have earlier called common or necessary international law."[37] Obligations are approved warily: "No nation has the right, in the absence of treaty obligations to the contrary, to tell any other nation what laws it should enact and enforce, let alone enact and enforce them on the latter's territory."[38] While both of these postures prevent social fusion, a condition of subverted relationship, they also enable one heroic egoist to destabilize those few obligations to others that arise in realist international relations: "without my consent your decision does not bind me [and] without my consent there is no decision."[39] Each state is thus a heroic exhibitionist using its sovereign privatization as a public act to stand aloof from or to thwart other would-be conquering heroes.[40] That sovereignty is a romantic fiction or breached principle—often violated, in fact, by *realpolitik* decisionmakers—seems to have little impact on the abstract theoretical point.

Realists often look askance at interdependence because it connotes to them "some degree of vulnerability by one party to another."[41] What is to be avoided is a situation that gives a state power over another, for then conflict is likely to result rather than cooperation. Hence, in relationships among states,

> just as in households or community conflicts, one way to establish peace is to eliminate or minimize contact among opponents or potential adversaries. Separation from other units, if that were possible, would mean less contact and thus less conflict.[42]

Indeed, it is in the household, say feminist revealers, that the realist has honed his separation skills.

Richard Ashley argues that Morgenthau does leave room for statesmen and theorists to reinterpret the community tradition of realism in ways that reflect "the internal history of the community and its internalized context."[43] Conceptions of man are part of that internalized context, but they are 'concealed and for this reason never examined' because realism is autonomous from communities with different identities and interpretations of international relations. Again to quote Morgenthau, "the great mass of the population is to a much greater extent the object of power than it is its wielder."[44] This view resonates with Antonio Gramsci's view that a state achieving that delicate combination of consent and coercion of liberal hegemony becomes the outer ditch of civil society, wherein the [state] bureaucracy is "the crystallization of the leading personnel—which exercises coercive power, and at a certain point becomes a [realist] caste."[45]

In the realist story, man is metaphorically fused to his state to form a reactive self who is celebratory of freedom. That self-state is obligated by social contract to ensure the survival of nationals amid unrul(y) forces of anarchy. Yet he-it draws considerable identity not from multiple relational ties with the society under contract but from similar (id)entities floating unattached in the international "out there." The potential for relational forms of autonomy, given in the fact that the self-state is in relationship with its protector-protected, from whom it draws obligations, thus squares off against the "freedom" of anarchy and loses.

Schools of thought representing differences within Realism keep the field disconnected from noncaste populations and free from gender-aware interpretations. They do, however, connect the state to other states in interesting, but nonetheless reactively autonomous ways.

The hegemonic stability story, for example, suggests that international order is best ensured when one of the most heavily resourced states—truly the heroic individualist—assumes leadership and provides collective goods for otherwise conflictual sovereign states. Here the hegemonic mother of a boy's earliest memories and fears is seemingly transposed into the good state acting obligingly to rid a world to which it is connected of harmful vulnerabilities. Yet the hegemon conducts its relations "at discrete and controlled points of contact through rule-governed and role-defined structures"—regimes—within a competitive political framework where would-be defectors defer to the high costs of cheating.[46] Moreover, "many of the gains from hegemony have been less in the line of collective goods than private ones, accruing primarily to the hegemon and thus helping maintain its hegemony."[47] Regime contracts thus tip the benefits toward already strong parties in a neurotic and inappropriate parody of mothering.

Tellingly confused autonomies and obligations can also be found in *Man, the State, and War*, Kenneth Waltz's nearly neorealist celebration of an anarchic state system.[48] Here, state policies are interdependent along lines described in Rousseau's metaphor of the stag hunt. That is, there is no automatic mechanism to adjust clashing interests, and so balances form in which the freedom of choice of any one state is limited by the actions of all others. Waltz simultaneously maintains that "pursuing a balance-of-power is still a matter of choice," and that "the alternatives are those of probable suicide on the one hand and the active playing of the power-politics game on the other."[49] He also says, in a statement resonating somewhat with feminist psychoanalytic understandings of men's choiceless relations, that:

> the balance of power is not so much imposed by statesmen on events as it is imposed by events on statesmen. It is not to be eliminated by declamation but, if it is to be eliminated at all, by altering the circumstances that produce it. The circumstances are simply the existence of a number of independent states that wish to remain independent. Freedom is implied in the word "independence" but so is the necessity of self-reliance.[50]

In that statement Waltz throws authorship of the balance "problem" onto abstract "events" man is simply forced to confront—as when a boy baby confronts the otherness of mother. To alter the situation entails altering the circumstances of false independence. So far so feminist. But one cannot alter the circumstances by continuing to assume either that independent states exist *a priori* or that, through wish-based actions, they manage to be independent despite international interdependencies and ties to nation. Such assumptions leave states backed up against a domestic space, in which women's experiences could cast shadows on notions of reactive and minimally obligated relationships but are not allowed to do so. Furthermore, the independence assumed here leaves states forever facing "the residual zone of historical determinacy still to be brought under control in the name of reasoning man."[51] Since there is little likelihood that realists can themselves alter the circumstances of state (fantasies of) independence, owing to their community concealments of man and their domestication of women, everyone is stuck.

In Waltz's *Theory of International Politics*, the anarchic dynamics of the system triumph and have a certain choiceless leveling effect on states, rendering those (id)entities functionally similar and somewhat predictable. Foundational sameness, we learn from feminist psychoanalytic writings, can enhance empathetic relationships. Indeed, to some, Waltz's neorealist states "determine their interests and strategies on the basis of calculations about their own positions in the system"[52] of relations, and sometimes find mutual interest in formal associations or regimes. Neorealist associations, however, are arenas of defensive vigilance that tilt states in the direction of reactive autonomy. Waltz writes: "In a self-help system each of the units spends a portion of its efforts, not in forwarding its own good, but in providing the means of protecting itself against others."[53] The result is that "interdependence is always a marginal affair."[54] Waltz's structure tames relational autonomy.

Robert Keohane accurately argues, I submit, that neorealism fails to take into account institutional characteristics of the system and therefore provides no way for the system to change except when the capabilities of states change. To understand world politics, we must explore the ways institutions emerge and "affect incentives facing states."[55]

In Keohane's account, regime formation is a process of cooperation "that involves the use of discord to stimulate mutual adjustment."[56] Through planning and negotiation, using a variety of resources, and calling upon preexisting conventions—without which communication would be difficult—"decisions involving international regimes [become] in some meaningful sense voluntary."[57] Once regimes form, often "in the utilitarian social contract tradition,"[58] they can connect self-helpers by offering high quality information to policymakers and by developing norms of honesty and straightforwardness that participants can internalize to counter realist values.

State obligations initially chosen on the basis of specific reciprocities can metamorphose into "regime-supporting behavior[s deemed] . . . beneficial to us even though we have no convincing evidence to that effect."[59] The attainment of this diffuse reciprocity enables states to "contribute one's share, or behave well toward others . . . in the interests of continuing satisfactory overall results for the group of which one is a part, as a whole."[60] Although Keohane wisely notes that "diffuse reciprocity in the absence of strong norms of obligation exposes its practitioners to the threat of exploitation,"[61] his neoliberal institutionalist framework offers promising relational innovations.

But there is a dilemma built into it as well. Among a priori sovereign identities, each entity may be leery of decisions that could alter the structure of the system and undermine reactive autonomy (the British concern about a united Europe). Functionalists of old had an answer to such identity crises: put the matter in the hands of Lilliputian technocrats who will enmesh Gulliver in unobtrusive relational ties. Under neoliberal institutionalism, sneaked interdependencies come alive and are quickly restrained: only after states reach a threshold of satisfaction with chosen obligations to one another (specific reciprocities) can they be tempted into diffuse reciprocity. Thus the neoliberal difference from realism is hidebound to realist vigilances. Unchosen obligation is tamed.

Other schools of thought in international relations base their prospects on similar unleashings and tamings. World Order analysts, for instance, admonish us to break with state-centric understandings of power and interest, but some among them would replace that "reality" with an international society of "man."[62] Then there are deconstructors who reveal many concealed power moves in international relations but have yet to undertake systematic deconstructions of gender in realist literatures;[63] man thereby retains "his privileged place as the sole author and principal character in their stories."[64]

Although post–international relations theories are also promising, they are likewise not yet awake to the issue of gender in international relations. In one case the tropes of autonomy are trotted out to indicate how foreign activities undertaken by social groups in industrialized societies now pose "autonomy and interdependence [as] constituent aspects of the position held by social groups or their directing elites respectively in relation to the national-political actors."[65] One looks in vain for women and men in these autonomous social groups and for notions of obligation that are less tied to calculated outcomes. One wonders whether this is another case of masculinity concealed in international (post–international, transnational) relations.[66]

In perusing vast realist literatures, even in this cursory way, feminist standpointers notice the recurrences of reactive autonomy and minimal obligations in ostensibly gender-free international relations. This is the quality that binds realism, neorealism, and neoliberal institutionalism to one another. What strategies can disorder and destabilize the entrenched concealments?

Women in the Interstices of Realist Autonomy and Obligation

At the intersections of theory and day-to-day realities of realist practice we can locate sites of women's struggles with, through, and against the reactively stuck state and the community of realism that theory both constructs and reflects. The sites and the struggles are empirically visible— Enloe has sighted them. And yet they are hidden from view when one engages in theoretical flights of freedom from obligations to the supporting actors of the drama. To reveal women's concrete struggles is to challenge the realist story of reactive autonomy and its corollary that gender is insignificant to international relations. It is to take up Sarah Brown's suggestion that "the proper object and purpose of the study of international relations is the identification and explanation of social stratification and of inequality as structured at the level of global relations."[67] It is to join realism's experience-based castings of a field—its partialities orchestrated into the grand production—with other experiences and productions.

The first site features activities complicit with realism that actually subvert the reign of reactive autonomy and disorder realist expectations. Fawn Hall is at this site, where she helps a realist engineer of foreign policy to pursue his voluntary association with the Contras, and protects him from government agencies acting to reconnect him to the sphere of legal obligation. Her shreddings feed his fantasy of mastering history, something that eluded him during the Vietnam War, when "we were winning but the press was portraying our victories as defeats."[68] Her testimonies before Congress uphold a heroic script of old realism enlivened by a patriotic man. That she carves out an identity through her relationship with North is revealed in her private choice of a Contra lover; here she commingles the personal with the international in ways that are not supposed to figure into the world of realism.

Hall's actions are ostensibly on the side of realist triumphs. But her relational autonomies within realism alienate her twice from the field she serves: first, from the realist state that seeks to tame her boss; and second, from the liberal realm of privacy that is supposedly the location of romantic secrets. At the same time she is twice obligated to realism—through her identification with North's division of sociality into us/them and insiders/outsiders, and through the Contra lover as heroic state in formation.[69] Her actions do not change history, but they do reveal that the realist community is not without its internal subversions at the hands of loyal women. This is a crucial revealing if one is to recast realism as a partial view of the world.

At this site we can also identify diplomats' wives, who daily serve realist politics and who have done so until recently in the absence of recognition. These unpaid servants of national interest create conditions of cozy relational autonomy for men inclined to reactivity in the diplomatic arena. They make the conduct of affairs of state sociable, and they do so not because they are recruited by the state but because the marriage contract carries the private obligations of servants into the public arena of conquerors.

Once upon a recent time, the realist state was obligated only to the diplomat. As a result of lobbying by the Association of American Foreign Service Wives, the US State Department in 1972 declared the foreign service wife a private person. This "new" status conflated her previous duties with a kind of ceremonial independence from them. Choiceless obligations in her wifely tasks did not end, because the sexual contract was still in force; but the end of liberal rights was served. This outcome underscores feminist cautions about the coop(t)erative potential of liberalism even as it reveals its realist-thumping potential.[70]

The next site of women in international relations emerges into view when we examine realist statesmen in their workplaces, and provides its own set of vantage points for rewriting theory. "Nearly ninety per cent of the secretaries and clerical personnel at the World Bank are women, but women occupy less than 3 per cent of its 'senior level' positions."[71] In 1984 the female staff at the United Nations "made up more than half of the Secretary General's staff, but held only 22.3 per cent of the professional international civil-service posts, as compared with 83 per cent of its clerical and secretarial jobs."[72] How can women be so nonrecognizable within organizations that exist to tame uncooperative aspects of the realist world?

We might begin by following Pateman's lead, and suggesting that the sexual contract underlying liberal theory simply makes its way into international contracts negotiated by realist states, as do other dominance-subordination relations; for example, the formerly contracted terms of colonialism are the basis of today's North-South statuses. It is also possible, from a feminist psychoanalytic view, that relationally trained women accept lower positions in the hope that their contributions will advance the interests of the group (the organization) as a whole and will be reciprocated in due time. A diffusely cooperative sense of obligation does not work, however, in contexts where a field of study and its community of practitioners recognize no particular obligations to women and to their characteristic ways of relating. The regimists are "free" to operate inside international organizations under the self-interested norms of their realist masters. Diffuse reciprocators, who behave in more generously obligated ways, are exploited.

Keohane argues that "repayment of political and economic debts in a strictly bilateral context may increase confidence, enabling actors to take a broader view of their common interests."[73] Payment of debts to women regime workers would, by this logic, nurture a sense of common obligation.

Notwithstanding a Coordinator for the Improvement of the Status of Women in the Secretariat of the United Nations, and the attention paid to women during the United Nations Decade for Women, the debts remain largely unpaid. When gender is considered, neoliberal institutionalist theory is only partially helpful in understanding regimes. To bring women in, however, could transform rather than modify that theory.[74]

At a third site in international relations, women give up on liberal struggles against the liberal-realist oppressor and embrace post-hegemonic processes aimed specifically at promoting transformed rather than reciprocated obligations. Their actions feature what Hirschmann refers to as "working out the content of obligations within the context of connection . . . [rather than attempting] to predefine feminist obligation . . . in the standard fashion of analytic philosophy."[75] The connections are with women, and that move acknowledges the importance of bringing voices of absent presences into theory and practice, not simply in the sense of "allowing voices to express themselves [as women advocacy groups in international regimes do] but helping them realize their expression, and attempting to see and understand the world from these other perspectives."[76]

Enloe briefly mentions one such case in relationships forming between women soldiers and military wives that cross boundaries heretofore unchallenged in realist military practice. The basis of this defiance of convention is, ironically, the realist state's unconventional invitation to women soldiers to be more than the absent or protected ones of lore, while, however, designating them as less than military men in the tasks they can perform. Military women emerge "in between," assuming supportive roles by taking on highly technological tasks in a military suffering the effects of too few good men. As they respond to these liberal "opportunities," some women recruits bump against the misogynist attitudes of the military and find more in common with wives than with insider career peers. There is a certain choicelessness woven into their context, and in that choicelessness is an opportunity to rescript the type of autonomy that has long prevented military people from crossing lines of status.

Women's peace encampments have also occupied this site, taking a hand in revealing realist security as permeable and oppressive. Their efforts took shape in response to contracts forged between the United States and its European allies to bring new US nuclear weapons to already missile-clogged countries. Some women, who supposedly have no agency of their own in international relations, protested these contracts in ways that demonstrated the weaknesses of nuclear defenses: they public(ized) the private movements of US "secret" convoys carrying cruise missiles to points of deployment throughout the United Kingdom; they mixed the metaphors of war and peace by painting peace signs on convoy trucks and putting implements of domesticity (potatoes) up truck exhaust pipes; and they climbed into convoy vehicles and rode along with autonomous military men.[77]

In the process of formulating such strategies, encampers developed nonhierarchical, nonlinear, and nonreciprocal methods of decisionmaking to anticipate or prefigure "a simple, peaceful, postnuclear society."[78] Their methods were not bereft of discord nor were their strategies totally new; but neither were they beholden to received conventions:

> At the peace camp each woman does what she thinks is necessary, so there are no rosters or lists of who has to do what. . . . This is very unfamiliar to some people, who exclaim in frustration, "why don't they organize something?" To their credit, women at the camp have not given in to this demand but have created a space that allows many women to ask instead, "What do I want to do?" Some feel alienated and do not return, but others become much more autonomous and effective than they would if they merely followed other people's directives.[79]

In a more realist context, a situation of every woman doing what she thinks is necessary would suggest that each was a victim of anarchic structure and had to rely on self-help strategies until conventions and then contractual agreements could bring stable relations. Indeed, some recount how in the absence of rule-governed behaviors at the Seneca Women's Peace Camp, a free-rider problem emerged such that "suckers" ended up doing more work, experiencing burnout and resentment.[80] Yet the logic of the exercise was to recast politics instead of rehearsing old rules of organization. This produced some burnout but also some innovative decision-making procedures:

> The meeting started out with hard-line opposing views and consensus seemed unlikely. But acting on the suggestion of a participant to break into smaller circles of like opinion, including a middle-ground group, and create a circle within a circle, each group taking its turn, the discussion proceeded. Without fear of judgement now, because speaking with those with whom we felt most at ease—while the others listened in. And so speaking more deeply than before. When we formed one large circle again, the talk was no longer strained. . . . And consensus, to the astonishment of all, I think, was reached easily.[81]

A meeting such as this, recorded in such "strange" incoherent language, differs both from the realist bargaining environment, with its "free-riders" and "suckers," and from what Hirschmann describes as "liberal dialogue":

> "Liberal dialogue" of political theory is an interaction of two totally separate individuals who have particular points of view and try to "win" by convincing the other person: it again replicates the struggle for recognition, to have your views recognized without recognizing the other.[82]

The Seneca meeting as a model features, instead, a conversation that proceeds from the assumption that "people will really listen to what others say, will attempt to incorporate those views into themselves, and indeed become somewhat transformed by that incorporation."[83]

Such techniques provide spaces for political action that are in between reactive and relational autonomies, in between chosen and unchosen obligations. They do not banish all problems of sociality, such as "free-riding," because women who come to adulthood following relational scripts may rebel against them as restrictive; or, suffering the ill effects of systematic denigrations of relationship, women may take care not to caretake. The camps were real arenas of sociality rather than restricted places of coercive contracts (entailing the punishment of defectors) or of impossible goody-goodyism.

When women peace campers stepped out of roles scripted for them—often taking their children with them—the outer ditch was threatened with having neither defenders nor defense against such insubordinating tactics. The lingering message from the encampments, therefore, is that women should form more "strange" conversations at the fence of realist defense, including in those conversations diplomats' wives, women serving in national militaries, and women caught in regimes. A messy and surely unrul(y) alliance such as this would demonstrate generalized commitment to a different "group" than realist theory recognizes, acknowledge women's relationships as politically significant, and help develop obligations across differences based on listening to what the "others" to realism say about international relations. Theory written from various points within this alliance would undoubtedly rattle realism's cage.

Another Recasting

The exercise of revealing concealed sites of women's struggles in, with, and against liberal-realist international relations shows not only that men and women are already connected to the field, but that realism is simultaneously ordered and disordered by women's activities in relation to the activities of masculine theorists, states, and organizations. Reinscribers of realist international relations must take note of simultaneous power directions and read each backwards and forwards.[84] Consider what happens to one neorealist analysis when its gender concealments are so read.

Zeev Maoz argues that when a strong state enhances its power by acquiring extra resources, it may end up losing control over outcomes. This happened to Turkey during the Balkan wars of 1912–1913 and to Israel after its invasion of Lebanon in 1982.[85] Added resources enabled such states to do things they could not have done previously, and this altered their preference structure and the stakes for other self-helping states. The resource inferiors then ganged up against the superior states in order to limit further power-aggrandizing activities.

Women are nonrecognized resources for realist states, occupying positions ranking with oil, geography, industrial capacity, and military preparedness as contributions to power. When an already strong state seeks more power by appropriating more women to its cause—as the United States might be perceived to have done by sending mothers to the Persian War front, what are the consequences? What are the results when the United States continuously taps into the voluntarism of women living around its overseas military bases in order to comfort its troops? What types of women-aggrandizing actions reorder strong state preferences, and when, if ever, do such power moves become worthy of disordering confrontations by "inferior" states?

Some precedents exist in international relations for gang-ups against people-aggrandizing state behaviors. When the Soviet state tried appropriating Jewish citizens to itself (or preventing others from doing so), strong and less strong states (Israel) ganged up against it. The concern of those ganging up against the Soviet state may be explained by the fact that many people prevented from leaving the Soviet Union were the best-educated scientists and people of letters in the country.[86] What about contexts in which the ganging-up states have little hope of or little to gain by appropriating the victims for themselves? Do they still "see" the resource appropriation and calculate it as potentially productive of new and dangerous priorities? Do they still gang up?

When the South African state repeatedly appropriated rural black women as a social security service for migrant laborers, this aggrandizement was not interpreted by antiapartheid states as a state effort to free up funds for other power moves. When black men were detained without trial, or after trials of dubious validity, however, a moderate ganging-up cry could be heard in the capitals of Europe and North America. The freeing of Nelson Mandela was the cause célèbre, not the freeing of women from servitude to the white state, even though few ganging-up states would seek to appropriate Mandela for their own power.

On the one hand, none of this is unexpected. It took a female member of the European parliament to see that the multilaterally negotiated Multi-Fibre Agreement (MFA) would "allow multinational companies to exploit women."[87] Why would unilateral power moves against women come to anyone's notice? Indeed, "systematic violence against women is treated as 'customary' or as a 'private matter,' and thus immune to international condemnation."[88] Women are seemingly not resources of the state when they are not named as such by realists.

On the other hand, revealing women as resources shows that Maoz's thesis is partial and perhaps inaccurate unless he can explain why this resource does not fit predictions based on other types of resources. He needs to specify the types of resource appropriations that can lead a strong state to lose control over outcomes.

But let us not stop with this point. Rather let us play out Maoz's logic on feminist rather than realist terms. On our terms, the "inferior" actors are feminist organizations and theorists. The "strong" actors are realist theorists and states. Maoz claims that strong actors can lose control over outcomes by failing "to attribute to opponents the ability to adjust their strategies to an environment in which they become increasingly inferior."[89] From the foregoing analysis, it is clear that realist efforts to appropriate wives for the foreign service resulted in a movement by equality-minded women to gang up on several offending strong states, primarily the United States and Great Britain. Similarly, instead of acting as proper "base women"—offering succor to US troops in the United Kingdom—Greenham Common women dashed the convention of realist womanhood. That Enloe then revealed both cases and others for all to read, shows that women-appropriating actions by states may be disordered by ganging-up activities at the cusp of that infamous domestic/international dichotomy. The Maoz article is redeemed.

Feminists and women strugglers might not win theory in the decisive ways realists find significant; after all, Greenham Common women did not prevail on their own against theater nuclear weapons in Great Britain. If one stands at the nexus of the win/lose dichotomy, however, one can lose the effort to command international relations and win new self-confidence and political skills for future challenges. To think in terms of absolute success or failure, of theory takeovers versus realist retrenchments, is to be governed by the reactively autonomous habit of establishing identity against and in opposition to others. It is also to reinforce realist international relations as a totality to be supplanted completely, rather than as a partial reality filtered through the standpoints of some men.

A Chorus of Concluding Objections

The "theories we use to understand and explain the world of international politics [are] not divorced from who does the theorizing"[90] and the practice. Until now, an assortment of realisms have dominated the theoretical and practical aspects of international relations, projecting a certain sense of autonomy onto larger playing fields and all the while denying that gender suits up at all. The feminist standpoint approach usefully reveals hidden conceptions of man in realism, alerts us to a community in reactive autonomy from women, and helps us locate theory-subverting activities that are not supposed to have significance.

A standpoint feminist, however, can anticipate a bevy of complaints about this exercise. First, there is the cry that we wildly confound levels of analysis by moving from individuals to states, from infant gendering to social theory, from Chiquita Banana to GATT. Gendering lessons in infancy and youth must be separated from phenomena associated with the abstract level of the international system.

This particular complaint seems to illustrate reactive autonomy in the practices of science. Concern to separate phenomena into discrete and independent categories of analysis leads to artificial islands of sociality reattached through statistical bridging mechanisms. Research that questions the accuracy of separability assumptions may reveal that the warning cry of ecological fallacy—Confound Not the Levels of Analysis—hides interconnected power relations. Hirschmann, Pateman, and Enloe implicitly unravel the conventional prohibition against juxtaposing levels of analysis to reveal its power text and carve out some space for more accurate social theory.

Second, there is the argument that the feminist standpoint approach jumps the tracks of mainstream theory and takes off in an opposite direction, even though the gendered self it hangs on to has an authorial signature so overdetermined by early experiences that it could be a tyrannical menace. The concept "women" may not be available as a foundation for a new direction, given that its meanings are subject to historical change and therefore are indeterminate.[91] Relational autonomy may not exist either, except as a political creation of societies bound and determined to find reasons why women are not equipped for public affairs. Reactive autonomy may be a parody of class, race, and locational myopias; or it may be something women need more of in response to strangulating relationships that prime them for more responsibilities (obligations) than men carry, or that lead to neurotic manifestations of caring.[92]

Indeed, we do not want to catch ourselves in the trap that has gripped realism for so long: ethnocentricity as truth. In proceeding with feminist international relations it behooves us to investigate a wide range of locally understood autonomies and obligations and to use them to recast "our" world, "refus[ing] to see all right and good on one side only."[93] Our project calls for skepticism toward bandwagoning standpoints that would smite that realist (or misguided postmodernist) with the certainty of an emperor. It calls for foregrounding contextualized autonomies and obligations by focusing on sited struggles not easily reduced to stereotypes about what is relational and what is reactive.

We need not shatter the realist window in the course of this exercise, because it does offer us a partial view. From studies of constructs like "reciprocity" we learn about conditions that may inspire some groups to exit our proposed relationships, reject our caring rescriptings, and manipulate agreements. We do need to explain to those who want us to replace realism with something else, however, that we are not talking about talking about feminist international relations; we are adding our (I would argue partial) views to the picture. Our revelations, though "strange," are realist-disordering and space-opening—for women, theory, and alternative practice.

Notes

I am grateful to the participants of the Wellesley Conference on Gender and the State in International Relations, and to members of the School of International Relations at the University of Southern California, for offering stimulating thoughts on this chapter. I revised the original paper while I was a senior visiting scholar at the Center for International Studies, University of Southern California.

1. Kenneth W. Thompson, *Political Realism and the Crisis of World Politics: An American Approach to Foreign Policy* (New York: Kennikat, 1960), 12.

2. Robert Keohane, *International Institutions and State Power: Essays in International Relations Theory* (Boulder, CO: Westview, 1989), 68, note 17.

3. Hedley Bull and Carsten Holbraad, eds., in Martin Wight, *Power Politics* (New York: Holmes and Meier, 1978), 20.

4. Arthur Stein, *Why Nations Cooperate: Circumstances and Choices in International Relations* (Ithaca: Cornell University Press, 1991), chapter 1. This is not an uncontroversial claim. James Dougherty and Robert Pfaltzgraff describe realism as "basically conservative, empirical, prudent, suspicious of idealistic principles, and respectful of the lessons of history," in *Contending Theories of International Relations: A Comprehensive Survey*, 3d ed., (New York: Harper and Row, 1990), 7. Postmodernist critics tend to emphasize that there is no one direction of thought in any theory; rather the directions are created through community readings. See R. B. J. Walker, "Realism, Change, and International Political Theory," *International Studies Quarterly*, 31 (1987): 65–86.

5. Nancy Hirschmann, "Freedom, Recognition, and Obligation: A Feminist Approach to Political Theory," *American Political Science Review*, 83 (1989): 1227–1244.

6. Joseph Grieco defines a defensive positionalist as a state that wants "to know what the impact will be of virtually any relationship on [its] relative defensive capabilities." *Cooperation Among Nations: Europe, America, and Non-Tariff Barriers to Trade* (Ithaca: Cornell University Press, 1990), 10.

7. Pateman, *The Sexual Contract*.

8. Enloe, *Bananas, Bases, and Beaches*.

9. James Keeley, "Toward A Foucauldian Analysis of International Regimes," *International Organization* 44 (1990): 93.

10. Benjamin Barber, "Liberal Democracy and the Costs of Consent," in *Liberalism and the Moral Life*, ed. Nancy Rosenblum (Cambridge, MA: Harvard University Press, 1989), 59.

11. Hirschmann, "Freedom," 1227.

12. See the discussion of feminist standpoint in Harding, *The Science Question in Feminism*. For an application to international relations, see Christine Sylvester, "The Emperors' Theories and Transformations: Looking at the Field Through Feminist Lenses," in *Transformations in the Global Political Economy*, ed. Dennis Pirages and Christine Sylvester (London: Macmillan, 1990), 230–254.

13. Hirschmann, "Freedom," 1230.

14. Hirschmann, "Freedom," 1230.

15. Hirschmann, "Freedom," 1231. Terry Eagleton uses a similar argument to describe Immanuel Kant's aesthetic representation of the sublime in *The Ideology of the Aesthetic* (London: Basil Blackwell, 1990), noting that:

> to attain full moral stature we must be wrenched from the maternal pleasures of Nature and experience in the majesty of the sublime the sense of an infinite totality to which our feeble imaginations will never be equal. . . . In the sublime, morality and feeling for once come together but in negative style: What we feel is how immeasurably Reason transcends the senses, and thus how radically 'unaesthetic' our true freedom, dignity, and autonomy are. (p. 91)

16. Hirschmann, "Freedom," 1230–1231.

17. Hirschmann, "Freedom," 1238.

18. Nancy Rosenblum, *Another Liberalism: Romanticism and the Reconstruction of Liberal Thought* (Cambridge, MA: Harvard University Press, 1987), 29.

Michel Foucault would find the projection of men's lived experiences on the world symptomatic less of lessons from childhood than of general modernist tendencies to construct regimes of knowledge-power establishing authority for certain practices. See *The Order of Things: An Archaeology of the Human Sciences* (New York: Random House, 1973). See also Richard Ashley's discussion of Foucault's ideas, as relevant to international relations, in "Living on Border Lines."

19. Di Stefano, "Masculinity as Ideology," 639.

20. The depiction of states as primitive individuals is from Alexander Wendt and Raymond Duvall, "Institutions and International Order," in *Global Changes and Theoretical Challenges: Approaches to World Politics of the 1990s*, ed. Ernst-Otto Czempiel and James N. Rosenau (Lexington, MA: Lexington Books, 1989), 55.

21. Hirschmann, "Freedom," 1230.

22. Chodorow, *The Reproduction of Mothering*, 107.

23. Cynthia Enloe, "Womenandchildren: Making Feminist Sense of the Persian Gulf Crisis," *Village Voice*, 25 September 1990, p. 29.

24. Pateman, *The Sexual Contract*, 34.

25. Pateman, *The Sexual Contract*, 11.

26. Pateman, *The Sexual Contract*, 47–48.

27. Women are the ones fettered by infants in the war of all against all because Hobbes initially grants them (family-less) mother rights: "every woman that bears children, becomes both a mother and a lord [over the child]." See Thomas Hobbes, *Philosophical Rudiments Concerning Government and Society*, in *The English Works of Thomas Hobbes of Malmesbury*, vol. 2 (Germany: Scientia Verkag Aalen, 1966), 116, quoted in Pateman, *The Sexual Contract*, 44. In return for her nurturing, the child "agrees" that "being grown to full age he become not her enemy" (Hobbes in Pateman, *The Sexual Contract*, 44). Thus the mother-child relationship is a contract that eventually wins for the mother an ally in the war of all against all. Presumably, having an ally reduces the likelihood that she will be conquered; yet, given the logic of the argument, she never makes it to that point without falling under a master, because the child is a free rider for many years. Men conquered by other men also become servants in Hobbes's scheme of things. That they are later released and women are not implicates the marriage contract as the vehicle of servitude for civic women.

28. Hirschmann, "Freedom," 1240.

29. Christine Di Stefano, "Rethinking Autonomy," paper presented at the annual meeting of the American Political Science Association, San Francisco, 1990, 36.

30. Hirschmann, "Freedom," 1241.

31. Enloe, *Bananas, Beaches, Bases*, 4.

32. Enloe, *Bananas, Beaches, Bases*, 3 and 11.

33. See Elshtain, *Women and War*.

34. Hirschmann, "Freedom," 1242.

35. K. J. Holsti, *The Dividing Discipline: Hegemony and Diversity in International Theory* (Boston: Unwin Hyman, 1985), vii. See also Robert Gilpin, *War and Change in World Politics* (Cambridge: Cambridge University Press, 1981), 7.

36. Hans J. Morgenthau, *Politics among Nations: The Struggle for Power and Peace*, 3d ed. (New York: Alfred Knopf, 1965), 11–12.

37. Morgenthau, *Politics Among Nations*, 315.

38. Morgenthau, *Politics Among Nations*, 315–316.

39. Morgenthau, *Politics Among Nations*, 316.

40. See discussion of heroic individualism in Rosenblum, *Another Liberalism*, chapter 5.

41. Paul R. Viotti and Mark V. Kauppi, *International Relations Theory: Realism, Pluralism, Globalism* (New York: Macmillan, 1987), 56.

42. Viotti and Kauppi, *International Relations Theory*, 57, quoting Steven Spiegel and Kenneth Waltz, eds., *Conflict in World Politics* (Cambridge, MA: Winthrop, 1971), 454–74.

43. Richard Ashley, "Political Realism and Human Interests," *International Studies Quarterly* 25 (1981): 214.

44. Morgenthau, *Politics Among Nations*, 103. This means that realism features "a kind of dialogue that is echoed in many a male-dominant marriage . . . [wherein] the dependent female . . . is asked to maintain and adjust the intersubjective understandings, values, and ethics of the whole family in accord with the demands and opportunities emerging from the 'man's world'" (Ashley, "Political Realism," 225). Yet this gender imbalance in power casts doubt on Ashley's claim that the hermeneutic dialogue has been bounded by the addition of technical realism's stylized form and concerns; rather, parts of a potential dialogue are bounded by realism's internal gender concealments.

45. Antonio Gramsci, *Selections from Prison Notebooks*, ed. and trans. Quinton Hoare and Geoffrey Newell Smith (London: Lawrence and Wishart, 1971), 246. Robert Keohane points out that "many Marxian interpretations of hegemony turn out to bear an uncanny resemblance to Realist ideas, using different language to make similar points." See *After Hegemony: Cooperation and Discord in the World Political Economy* (Princeton, NJ: Princeton University Press, 1984), 32.

46. See Charles Kindleberger, *The World in Depression, 1929–1939*, (Berkeley: University of California Press, 1973); also Gilpin, *War and Change in World Politics*.

47. Bruce Russett, "The Mysterious Case of Vanishing Hegemony: Or, Is Mark Twain Really Dead?" *International Organization* 39 (1985): 208. Stephen Krasner makes a similar point about the hegemon's ability to shape the trade system to its own ends, as does Gilpin with repect to multinational corporations. See Krasner's "State Power and the Structure of International Trade," *World Politics* 18 (April 1976); and Gilpin's *U.S. Power and the Multinational Corporation* (New York: Basic Books, 1975).

48. Kenneth Waltz, *Man, the State, and War* (New York: Columbia University Press, 1959). Viotti and Kauppi define neorealism as:

> a label applied to those realists who are interested in explaining state behavior under conditions of anarchy and who emphasize the importance of the structure of the international system and how this influences and constrains state behavior. The term may also have negative connotations in the eyes of some critics who claim that the neorealists have neglected the importance of values and norms as stressed by earlier realists such as Hans Morgenthau (Viotti and Kauppi, *International Relations Theory*, 599).

49. Waltz, *Man, State, and War*, 205.

50. Waltz, *Man, State, and War*, 209.

51. Ashley, "Living on Border Lines," 286.

52. Keohane, *International Institutions and State Power*, 41.

53. Kenneth Waltz, *Theory of International Politics* (Reading, MA: Addison-Wesley, 1979), 105.

54. Kenneth Waltz, "The Myth of National Interdependence," in *The International Corporation*, ed. Charles Kindleberger (Cambridge, MA: MIT Press, 1970), 206.

55. Keohane, *International Institutions and State Power*, 11.

56. Keohane, *After Hegemony*, 46. This may not be his final statement on the issue, since in "International Relations Theory: Contributions of a Feminist Standpoint," *Millennium* 18 (1989): 245–253, he raises questions about reciprocity that hint at cooperation through empathy.

57. Keohane, *International Institutions*, 104.

58. Keohane, *International Institutions*, 101.

59. Keohane, *International Institutions*, 114.

60. Keohane, *International Institutions*, 146.

61. Keohane, *International Institutions*, 149.

62. This is Holsti's encapsulation of work in the World Order Models Project genre. See *The Dividing Discipline*, 47. WOMP literature evokes voices of the oppressed, including women, but has tended to espouse a humanist future, a term feminists find historically justifying of men-centered cultures. See discussion in Christine Sylvester, "Some Dangers in Merging Feminist and Peace Projects," *Alternatives* 8 (1987): 493–510.

In *One World, Many Worlds: Struggles for a Just World Peace* (Boulder, CO: Lynne Rienner, 1988, xii), however, R. B. J. Walker argues that "groups like WOMP, journals like *Alternatives*, as well as the work of peace researchers and alternative development groups, provided some of the few spaces in which fundamental questions about the interconnected and global character of contemporary human life could be raised in a critical manner at all." That global civilization relies in part on women's struggles is a theme more evident in *One World, Many Worlds* than in most previous world order writings.

63. One notices an earnest, but nonetheless passing, nod at feminist concerns in the special issue of *International Studies Quarterly* on "Speaking the Language of Exile: Dissidence in International Studies" (34, 3, 1990). There, women are mentioned as suffering exile from professionalized international relations, but our dilemmas are not considered important enough to warrant article-length treatment by a feminist.

64. Jane Flax, *Thinking Fragments: Psychoanalysis, Feminism, and Postmodernism in the Contemporary West* (Berkeley: University of California Press, 1989), 226.

65. Werner Link, "Reflections on Paradigmatic Complementarity in the Study of International Relations," in *Global Changes and Theoretical Challenges*, ed. Czempiel and Rosenau, 104.

66. There is considerable room in James Rosenau's framework of post–international relations to insert feminist standpoints on relational autonomy, because he seeks to move "beyond the interaction of states and . . . into the wellsprings of national and local politics as well as into the ways in which individual orientations and actions are translated into collective outcomes." See his *Turbulence in World Politics: A Theory of Change and Continuity* (Princeton, NJ: Princeton University Press, 1990), xiv.

67. Sarah Brown, "Feminism, International Theory, and International Relations of Gender Inequality," *Millennium* 17 (1988): 461.

68. Robin Morgan, *The Demon Lover: On the Sexuality of Terrorism* (London: Methuen Press, 1989), 174, quoting from Donald Moore in George

Hackett with Richard Sandza, "With Ollie North in the 'Eye of the Hurricane,'" *Newsweek*, 13 July 1987, 17.

69. Adapted from Michael Walzer's discussion in *Obligations* (Cambridge, MA: Harvard University Press, 1970), 221, and Morgan's discussion of "The Deadly Hero" in *The Demon Lover*, chapter 2.

70. On liberalism's co-optive potential see Brown, "Feminism, International Theory," 461–464. On liberalism's radical future in the hands of feminists, see Eisenstein, *The Radical Future of Liberal Feminism*.

71. Enloe, *Bananas, Beaches, and Bases*, 120.

72. Enloe, *Bananas, Beaches, and Bases*, 121.

73. Keohane, *International Institutions and State Power*, 150.

74. In order for the theory truly to distinquish itself from realism, it would have to break from a convention of cooperative autonomy in realist international relations to which it also subscribes. This convention rehearses "anarchy" as a necessary prerequisite for rational action in international relations. If the crutch of cooperative autonomy were kicked away, diffuse reciprocity would be revealed as the acceptance of similarities between elite men as the basis of the "group," for the good of which regimes form. Recast the "group" and the implications for regimes and their chroniclers could be profound. See discussion in my "Reginas and Regimes: Feminist Musings on Cooperative Autonomy in International Relations," paper presented at the 1991 International Studies Association meetings, Vancouver, and the discussion forthcoming in Christine Sylvester, *Feminist Theory and International Relations in a Postmodern Era*, Cambridge: Cambridge University Press.

75. Nancy Hirschmann, *Rethinking Obligation* (Ithaca: Cornell University Press, forthcoming), chapter 6, 2–3, typescript.

76. Hirschmann, *Rethinking Obligation*, chapter 6, 6, typescript.

77. Gwyn Kirk, "Our Greenham Common: Feminism and Nonviolence," in *Rocking the Ship of State*, ed. Harris and King, 117.

78. Kirk, "Our Greenham Common: Feminism and Nonviolence," 117.

79. Gwyn Kirk, "Our Greenham Common: Not Just a Place But A Movement," in *Rocking the Ship of State*, ed. Harris and King, 264.

80. Peregrine Schwartz-Shea and Debra D. Burrington, "Free Riding, Alternative Organization, and Cultural Feminism: The Case of Seneca Women's Peace Camp," *Women and Politics* 10 (1990): 1–37.

81. Rhoda Linton, "Seneca Women's Peace Camp: Shapes of Things to Come," in *Rocking the Ship of State*, ed. Harris and King, 243.

82. Hirschmann, *Rethinking Obligation*, chapter 6, 7, typescript.

83. Hirschmann, *Rethinking Obligation*, chapter 6, 8, typescript.

84. Enloe, *Bananas, Beaches, and Bases*, 196.

85. Zeev Maoz, "Power, Capabilities, and Paradoxical Conflict Outcomes," *World Politics* 41 (1989): 239–266.

86. I am grateful to Eileen Crumm for pointing this out to me.

87. Quoted in Georgina Ashworth, "An Elf Among the Gnomes: A Feminist in North-South Relations," *Millennium* 17 (1988): 499.

88. V. Spike Peterson, "Whose Rights?" *Alternatives* 15 (1990): 305.

89. Maoz, "Power, Capabilities," 246.

90. Holsti, *The Dividing Discipline*, viii.

91. Denise Riley, *"Am I That Name"? Feminism and the Category of "Women"* (Minneapolis: University of Minnesota Press, 1988), chapter 1.

92. See Sylvester, "Some Dangers in Merging Feminist and Peace Projects."

93. Elshtain, *Women and War*, 257.

8

Gender and Critique in the Theory of International Relations

R. B. J. Walker

What is to be made of recent signs of critical ferment in the Anglo-American analysis of international relations? Few, if any, clear directions seem to be emerging. Despite persistent attempts to discipline some of the more provocative recent avenues of inquiry by invoking presumed standards of scientific objectivity or policy relevance, the theoretical pluralism and metatheoretical explorations that began to attract attention about a decade ago continue to challenge established orthodoxies. They especially challenge the ground on which claims about science, objectivity, policy, and relevance have been sustained as standards of political and scholarly judgment.[1]

Some critics privilege demands for historical perspective, and thus explore philosophies of history and the dilemmas of historicism. Some privilege the need for a properly global political economy, and thus question accounts of interstate behavior abstracted from the demands and transformations of contemporary capitalism. Some seek to revive epistemologies of interpretation against positivist and utilitarian accounts of empirical science. Some seek to grapple with the ontological and political challenges launched by all those currents of philosophical critique that have expressed, since at least the early decades of this century, a profound skepticism toward the most basic presuppositions of modern life and thought. Most recently, many of these forms of critique have been given new vitality and direction within specifically feminist accounts of both contemporary world politics and Anglo-American theories of international relations as distinctively gendered practices. Drawing upon some of the most forceful but also difficult insights of contemporary social and political theory, as well as on an increasing self-awareness of the politics of "women's place" and "women's time," feminist voices have begun to make themselves heard in what has been one of the most gender-blind, indeed crudely patriarchal, of all the institutionalized forms of contemporary social and political analysis.[2]

In this chapter, I take a seemingly oblique cut into the complex problems that are posed by attempts to generate critical perspectives on international relations theory in general and attempts to juxtapose claims about feminism and international relations theory in particular. I suggest that what links many of the most interesting forms of critique in the recent literature on international relations, and what is of crucial significance in recent attempts to understand world politics as a gendered practice, is an insistence on the highly problematic character of political identity in the modern world. What is at stake, I believe, is not just the possibility of adding certain excluded voices to the discipline of international relations as it is presently conceived. It is, rather, the possibility of challenging the grounds on which the theory of international relations has been constructed as a constitutive margin that simultaneously limits and affirms an historically specific account of political identity within a spatially bounded community.[3] The attempt to develop feminist perspectives on world politics cannot be restricted to the critique of theories of international relations alone. It is not by accident that feminist critiques have only established a minimal presence in this specific discipline. The extent to which this specific discipline has remained impervious to almost any form of philosophical or political critique gives some indication of its role in generating and legitimating what is taken to be crucial and incontrovertible about political life within the sovereign state.

The central constitutive principle of modern political life is generally acknowledged to be state sovereignty. Indeed, it is so central that it is usually relegated to the (hegemonic) status of a simple and reified given, or reduced to the dry technicalities of law and constitutionalism. It is also no accident, therefore, that recent critical ferment in the theory of international relations has been accompanied by the revival of interest in state sovereignty as an especially dense political practice. It is through the principle of state sovereignty, in particular, that questions about political identity have been answered by an appeal to specifically modern ontologies.[4] If it is the case that recent feminist critiques do draw our attention to the problematic status of modern political identities, then these critiques also must be drawn to interrogate state sovereignty as a constitutive political practice. Once state sovereignty is interrogated seriously in this way, it can no longer be treated as the great foundational myth of origin—and destination. Critical theories of international relations, then, including those articulated under the specific rubric of feminism, must necessarily engage not only the parochialisms and closure of one modern academic discipline but also the limits of a specific account of political life—an account of which that discipline is but a pale, but immensely important reflection: a confirming reflection, that is, of the identity of that which is reflected. The fact that it is possible to use in this context such a problematic term as "reflection," with all its ocular resonances of grand Cartesian and Augustinian dichotomies, is perhaps enough to indicate the scale of the disruptions that may—but only may—arise from the juxtaposition of feminism and theories of international relations.

*   *   *

Consider, to begin with, the acutely provocative term "world politics": a term that simultaneously signifies both the readily familiar and the utterly mysterious. It is a term used to refer to forms of human endeavor (international, or, more accurately, interstate relations) that are known, in some accounts, through apparent historical repetitions of the natural and tragic order of things. It also suggests, however, a groping for something that, by these very same accounts, simply cannot be. "World politics" is at once a banality and yet a contradiction in terms; references to it are nevertheless quickly absorbed into popular discourses and scholarly procedures.

Take the mystery first, a mystery compounded of diversity and denial. Rather a lot seems to be going on in "the world" that can be construed as "political." The difficulty, most would admit, is to know quite what to make of the terms "world" and "politics" in this context. The thawing of ethnic conflicts in Eastern Europe; plans by the US Army to burn stockpiles of nerve gas on a lonely Pacific atoll; the vagaries and surprises of arms reductions talks between the United States and Soviet Union; the relative advantage of Japanese over US industries in technologies deemed "critical" for national defense; selective application of IMF conditionality; the repudiation of a Brezhnev Doctrine here and the reassertion of a Monroe Doctrine there; the development of a tourist trade centered on prostitution in, say, Manila, or the nearest convention center: any such listing of "events" generates puzzlement as to how they might all be understood as part of a broader pattern of processes and structures, of determinations, contingencies, and unintended consequences. Despite all the controversy arising from claims about the status of laws, explanations, and models in scientific analysis, a very large proportion of the literature on international relations remains absorbed by the difficulties of classification: by the ontological choices that are affirmed by particular categories of inclusion and exclusion; by inherited denotations of the political, the economic, the social, the cultural; by judgments about the significant and the insignificant, the real and the imaginary.

The difficulty of knowing how to treat the multiplicity of events that might be construed as world politics is overcome in a variety of ways by different theoretical perspectives. Some now speak of a world society, or a global political economy, and seek to delineate the contours of a totalizing narrative to end all totalizing narratives. World politics then promises to become a synonym for a planetary polity populated by "humanity." Others

are more impressed by the enduring resilience of one specific strategy of
classification, a strategy confident that some things are indeed important and
others trivial. The term "world politics" is then merely a rather awkward
synonym for "interstate relations"—awkward because, strictly speaking,
relations between states are not supposed to have the same political character
as life within states. This is the crucial implication of injunctions against the
"domestic analogy" as well as of the discursive rituals in which "realism" is
opposed to "utopianism" in this context. It is the one theme that links all
those writers who have been woven into various accounts of a tradition of
international relations theory. For, according to the dominant traditions of
explicitly political thought, politics is something that can only occur within
a coherent political community, in a *polis*, or its more complex successors.
Within the community, it is possible to aspire to Justice, Reason,
Enlightenment, and History. Between communities we have to make do with
mere relations: with order perhaps, or a crude power politics, but not a
political community in which procedures of democratic accountability or,
perhaps, articulations of a collective identity might become a plausible
aspiration.[5]

Thus the utterly mysterious turns into the readily familiar.
The kaleidoscope of the front page is deciphered and codified into the
significant and the marginal, the high politics and the low economics, the
necessary and the contingent, the tragic and the naive. It is not that the
familiar categories attract unanimous approval. On the contrary, most
analysts seem to concede that whatever is going on in "the world" is
rather more complex and puzzling than the available categories of
explanation. Hence the constant attempts to explain patterns of
interdependence, regimes, institutions, cosmopolitan cultural forms, and so
on. Some even go so far as to suggest that, for the first time, "humanity" is
now caught up in shared and increasingly integrated systems, in a "world
order," "planetary society," or "global civilization." Yet even if one is
impressed by the increasingly global articulation of economic structures,
technological capacities, modes of communication, and the circulation of
capital, the meaning of "world politics" remains deeply obscure, caught
between remembrances of continuity and intimations of irreducible
complexity and novelty.

*   *   *

Similar problems arise in relation to attempts to articulate specifically
feminist perspectives on world politics and international relations. Again it is
necessary to confront a mystery of diversity and denial, a proliferation of
events, experiences, and processes that is nevertheless erased by the claim
that women's place and women's time already have their only effective
political expression in the sovereign state.

Perhaps only one useful generalization about the vast discourse that has emerged around contemporary feminism is possible: there is no single feminist perspective. Most entries into this discourse are guarded by more or less discriminating systems of classification: socialist, liberal, or radical; essentialist or historicist; empiricist, standpoint, poststructuralist. Such classifications may well be necessary guides to a complex terrain, but they are also evidence of the profusion of possibilities, as well as of the discursive rituals through which critique is tamed and co-opted.[6] Moreover, few of these systems of classification fail to evoke a vague sense of guilt about the ethnocentricism of philosophical and political traditions that have made these classifications possible. In the context of "world politics" and "international relations" especially, aspirations for a greater sensitivity to feminist concerns ought to lead to a greater sensitivity to the diversity of situations in which women act in different parts of "the world."[7]

The difficulty of coming to terms with the diverse experiences of women's place and women's time is in fact an aspect of the difficulty of specifying any clear meaning to the term "world politics." For example, it may seem that many events that we understand as part of world politics bear no relationship to gender. Yet it is not difficult to see how, in principle, arms control negotiations, advanced technologies, or the burning of toxins in far-off places might all be subjected to feminist enquiry quite as appropriately as might tourist prostitution. While it may be true that feminism easily conjures up the names of brave intellectual explorers—a de Beauvoir, for example, or a Kristeva—it equally conjures up a diversity of brave activists struggling in difficult and dangerous circumstances. Moreover, while both feminist theory and practice have, for most, become indelibly associated with explicitly Western situations, the encounter of feminism and world politics can hardly afford to ignore women's experiences of other cultural traditions or their struggles for survival in situations of extreme poverty and structural violence in all parts of the world.

Still, in the categories of modern political analysis, the diversity of women's experiences is captured and simplified in the same way as the diversity of all those events that might be interpreted as an aspect of world politics. To state the matter bluntly, while vague and inchoate accounts of world politics may allow us to distinguish women's experiences and struggles as a crucial part of contemporary political life, the categories of contemporary theories of international relations systematically render these experiences and struggles invisible. This point has been made with great cogency in the recent literature on feminism and international relations, but it is also a point that is, at a certain level, quite obvious. It is certainly no less obvious, for example, than the point that the categories of international relations theory have rendered class conflicts invisible or the point that these categories reify the ethnocentric hubris of particular cultures. In this sense, at least, accounts of the absence of women's experiences from the representations of international relations theory are not entirely without precedent.

A full account of the conditions under which this invisibility has become possible is well beyond the scope of the present analysis, but five avenues of enquiry may be sketched briefly. Together, these five avenues of enquiry indicate how and why contemporary feminist critiques of the theory of international relations are inevitably drawn into struggles around that detonative site designated by the sign of modernity/postmodernity.

First, there is the manner in which theories of statist political community have resolved a specific account of gender relations into a specific resolution of the relation between temporality and spatiality. Here Machiavelli offers a useful point of departure, though neither a clear point of origin nor of inspiration. Second, there is the articulation of theories of statist political community within a binary account of available political identities: in Andrew Linklater's telling terminology, through a choice between men and citizens. Third, there is the manner in which these resolutions of space, time, and identity have been articulated and reified within the principle of state sovereignty, a principle nearly sufficient, I believe, to generate all the characteristic categories, debates, and forms of critique in contemporary theories of international relations. Fourth, there is the parallel elaboration of these resolutions of space, time, and identity within three other problematics generated by early modern accounts of political community: specifically in relation to the legitimation of private property, to the freedoms and obligations of autonomous individuals, and to the relationship between autonomous reason within and the absence of autonomous reason beyond the centered political community of the sovereign state. Finally, there are the political strategies through which the conditions and assumptions that fostered these specific resolutions have been treated as the natural presuppositions of contemporary political life. By drawing attention to each of these themes in turn, however briefly, I hope to suggest just how far beyond the existing disciplinary categories feminist critiques of contemporary international relations theory must go.

*   *   *

It is rather odd that Machiavelli is caricatured most often as the spokesman for an account of political life that is distinctly uninteresting. Advice about the need for violence, duplicity, and intrigue is not difficult to come by, even in the texts of the most edifying moral traditions. His specific advice only becomes interesting and memorable when placed in the context of the specific questions he was trying to answer and the intellectual resources that were available for answering them.[8] In this sense, Machiavelli is remembered less as the author of specific maxims than as someone who developed an account of political life in which maxims were elevated to the pinnacle of political wisdom. For maxims are not laws. They do not reflect the eternal authority of heaven. They respond only to possibilities and probabilities—to chance, temporality, and *fortuna*.

It is also odd that Machiavelli is so often given an honorary place as a carrier, even initiator, of the supposed tradition of political realism in international relations, while the political erotics of *virtù* and *fortuna* find scarcely a mention. It is even more puzzling that Machiavelli's maxims should have been enshrined in an account of an enduring tradition, given his repeated insistence on the impermanence and contingency of life on earth and on the sheer difficulty of establishing a lasting legacy, one fit to be remembered past one's own inevitable mortality. As befits a politicized erotics, the encounter between *fortuna* and *virtù* is always uncertain. And if, by taking advantage of the knowledge that timing is everything, the man of *virtù* succeeds in seducing the bitch goddess, he also knows that what timing might bring, time will surely take away. Machiavelli's political erotics are distinctively chauvinistic, but it is a chauvinism that cuts more than one way.

It is useful to reflect on this particular moment in the emergence of modern political thought, for it is really the only well-known point at which questions about gender are raised explicitly in relation to questions about the location and character of political community as such. To the extent that gender has since been treated as problematic within the received traditions of political thought, this early modern account of political community has been treated as a given—except that the degree of ambivalence and uncertainty expressed by Machiavelli has given way to the more forthright assertions of Thomas Hobbes: no more *fortuna*; and not much temporality. The skill and uncertainties of tennis play give way to the demands of Reason, law, and the great Leviathan. Where, in Machiavelli, it is possible to locate women's place precisely in women's time, at least abstractly, in Hobbes, time is simply fixed in a particular place, the great Euclidean space of the territorial state.[9]

*   *   *

References to Hobbes in feminist scholarship usually arise in connection with two well-established and important fields of investigation. Some examine the relation between gender politics and the development of the mechanistic ontologies crystallized by Galileo and his contemporaries. In this case, the familiar themes of disenchantment, the collapse of the Great Chain of Being, and the shift from feudalism to capitalism are augmented by accounts of a move from a woman-centered universe—portrayed, for example, in Renaissance cosmologies—to a male-centered universe expressed by the founding fathers of modern science and philosophy.[10] Others have a more explicit focus on the way the early modern contract theorists managed to reconstruct legitimations of patriarchal authority despite the radical and equalitarian character of their critiques of feudal hierarchies.[11] In the context of theories of international relations, however, an additional, though complementary, line of analysis also seems important, one that to some extent has been taken up in recent feminist critiques of war and militarism.[12] Here the focus is less on the relative valence of "male" and "female" in different cultures or historical periods than on the fusion of gender distinctions into a unitary political identity, an identity that nevertheless retains its own characteristic ambivalence.

It is worth reminding ourselves why Hobbes fits so uneasily into accounts of a realist tradition of international relations. Hobbes's state of nature is a condition arising from structural relations between individuals in a finite space who are both autonomous and equal. He clearly understood that states are not like individuals: they are less vulnerable to violence than are individuals and they are unequal to each other.[13] Consequently, what Hobbes calls a state of war is not difficult to reconcile with accounts of the modern system of states as a relatively coherent "society," one characterized less by incessant conflict than by regularized and even institutionalized forms of cooperative accommodation.[14] Given the clarity with which Hobbes refuses to make a sharp distinction between political community within states and anarchy between them, it is necessary to ask why he has nevertheless become so closely associated with precisely this distinction. It may be, for example, that theorists of international relations have simply not read him. Or, perhaps they have come to confuse the *de jure* sovereign equality expressed in international law with the *de facto* inequality of superpowers and microstates. Or that the atomistic individualism that is expressed so radically by Hobbes has become so deeply ingrained in modern consciousness that it is simply applied to everything—a possibility made especially plausible by the overwhelming hegemony of liberal utilitarian microeconomics in late twentieth-century social and political thought.

Hobbes was certainly radical in certain key respects. His simple assertion that the human condition can be understood as a consequence of the autonomy and equality of individuals challenged the prevailing assumptions of continuity and hierarchy. This assertion, of course, grew out of a long and complex struggle to shape a new understanding of human identity. Hobbes, like Descartes, or Luther, may be understood as a rather late participant in a profound cultural transformation in which autonomous subjectivities came to be defined against God, Nature, or Humanity.[15] Having crystallized a moment of autonomy, the early modern thinkers were driven to find ways whereby the autonomous individual, the knowing subject, and the inner conscience might be reconciled with the world from which they had been, ambiguously, alienated or freed.

Hobbes's response to this problem is crucial, and its significance for contemporary theorists of international relations goes beyond either his cooptation into accounts of a tradition or the fecundity of analogies with his structural rendition of a state of nature. It is crucial because it formalizes a specific resolution of the relationship between autonomous individuals and universalizing accounts of Nature, God, and Humanity through the claims of particular states. It is the particular state, ordered according to the principles of universal geometric reason (and thus, possibly, according to the word of God), that affords a home for the individual, a source of protection, a condition of liberty under the law, a reconciliation of freedom and necessity, of separation and participation.

The difficulty, of course, concerns the precise status of the universality that is expressed by the sovereign state. The force of the necessity that drives individuals into contractual relations with each other may derive from some "higher" duty to preserve God's handiwork, or it may derive from merely pragmatic and utilitarian, and thus purely temporal and contingent, considerations. Hence the long-standing controversies about the status of Hobbes's account of political obligation. (Hence also the grand irony of all attempts to use modernist accounts of autonomous reason in order to castigate critics of that historically specific account of reason, and autonomy, for their nihilism, relativism, and political irresponsibility.) More significantly, despite the appeal to principles of universal reason, the reconciliation of the autonomous individual and other autonomous individuals in a particular society does not lead to a reconciliation with humanity as such. On the contrary, the reconciliation of particular and collective on the terrain of the universalizing appeal yet particularistic authority of the sovereign state affirms the irresolvable conflict between the claims of citizenship and the claims of humanity.

Many of the political thinkers of the early modern period were absorbed by the seriousness of this problem. Andrew Linklater rightly characterizes the development of thinking about international relations not as a debate between congealed traditions but as a continuing struggle to come to terms with the moral tensions—identified by a wide range of early modern theorists—between the claims of obligation to fellow citizens of a political association and claims of obligation to the remainder of humanity.[16] The statist resolutions identified by Hobbes—resolutions that have since become paradigmatic for our understanding of the content and locus of authentically political life—simply affirm the priority of claims arising from citizenship within a particular community.

Thus, insofar as we might look to Hobbes for insight into the dilemmas of contemporary world politics and the theory of international relations, we are drawn to engage first and foremost with a particular construction of the political, and of the conditions under which international relations theory is then constructed by negation—by negation, that is, of a unitary political identity. Hobbes participates in the articulation and legitimation of a new account of political identity in early modern Europe. This new, unitary identity absorbs and overwhelms all other identities. Hobbes's defense of the principle of equality remains very striking. It affirms the relative absence of familiar social differentiations in his analysis. Considerable interpretive tenacity is required, for example, to locate asymmetries of class, culture—or gender.[17] When they are located, they are found in the familiar form of particulars masquerading as universals. Two possibilities are extended: the free individual and the member of humanity. And both possibilities are affirmed yet denied by the claims of the sovereign state. Gone is the sense of politics as a struggle between gendered energies. Gone too are the old privileging strategies of hierarchical order. Instead, the *virtù* of the prince has become the enduring Reason of state. *Fortuna* and time have been tamed. The world has become populated by individuals who know themselves politically only as abstract subjects; free yet constrained by law; citizens, but humans only to the extent that they can realize their humanity through the twin sovereignties of state and subjectivity—the abstract autonomies whose conditions of production and reproduction have simply vanished from sight.

*   *   *

Wedged somewhere between the symbolic and contested names of Machiavelli and Hobbes lie the apparently simple claims of state sovereignty. Recognized to be the key constitutive moment of modern political life, the principle of state sovereignty is simultaneously the most enduring silence in modern political discourse. Always mentioned, but then taken for granted, it guards the distinction between the supposedly authentic politics within and the mere relations between states. Consequently, it also guides our understanding of the alternative forms of political practice that might be available now.

The disjunction between the clear codifications of state sovereignty and the messy articulation of states and borders has been noted often enough. In this sense, the claim to sovereignty can be understood as one of the most important practices of states as well as a formalization of their identity. Moreover, in some of the recent literature, attempts have been made to understand state sovereignty as a political practice in relation to the ontological assumptions, axiological consequences, and discursive rituals that are both expressed in and generated by the explicitly modernist claims of state sovereignty. In Richard Ashley's work, for example, we find an incisive analysis of how a metaphysics of presence and absence—the metaphysics assumed in the Hobbesian privileging of an internal reconciliation of individual and humanity within the state—continues to govern contemporary accounts of community and anarchy.[18] It is this metaphysics, not the familiar dogmatic assertions about the way things are, nor the more recent injunctions about the validity of empiricist epistemologies, that provides the crucial legitimation of dominant conceptual categories and research strategies.

The so-called "levels-of-analysis" schema, for example, is little more than a simple reification of the spatial demarcation of political community codified by the principle of state sovereignty but turned on a vertical axis. Transformed into the dominant strategy of classification and pedagogy, into a merely analytical device for sorting what goes where, it turns ontological densities into methodological shallows. Naturalizing options that arose and were affirmed in the early modern era, it denies the possibility of any historical transformation of these accounts of autonomy, equality, space, time, and identity.[19]

At least three groups of ontological resolutions must be unpacked from the simple claim to a monopoly of power and/or authority by the sovereign state. This claim resolves, in brief, the relationship between unity and diversity, between self and other, and between space and time. It does so by drawing on the philosophical and cultural practices of an historically specific civilization (whether read through Weber as modernity, through Marx as capitalism, or through others as Western, patriarchal, and so on) driven by the need to realize and yet control those moments of autonomy—primarily individual, private property, and state—that emerged from the dissolution of hierarchies in early modern Europe. To put this slightly differently, state sovereignty articulates an exceptionally elegant answer to questions about political identity—about who the "we" is that engages in political life— given the collapse of previous answers articulated on the basis of hierarchical continuities.

As a response to questions about whether "we" are citizens, humans, or somehow both, the principle of state sovereignty affirms that we have our primary and often overriding political identity as participants in a particular community, but asserts that we retain a connection with "humanity" through our participation in a broader global—international—system. As citizens, we may aspire to universal values, but only on the tacit assumption that the world "out there," that supposedly global or states system, is in fact a world of particular states—of dangers, or of other communities, each aspiring to some notion of goodness, truth, and beauty. The central difficulty here concerns whether these notions are different (in which case we get international conflict and, at best, pragmatic rules of accommodation) or the same (in which case we may be, like Kant, mildly optimistic about a universal peace between autonomous republican—or liberal, or democratic— states). Moreover, as citizens within states, it becomes possible to envisage a home, a space, for politics in which temporal order might unfold —though not in the manner of *fortuna*—toward progress, development, and fulfillment. In the space between states, however, we are left with mere contingencies and recurrences. All hopes of temporal progress are dismissed as aberrant utopian dreams.

Contemporary accounts of state sovereignty have centered on whether it remains adequate to contemporary conditions. Yet these accounts, whether concluding in favor of obstinacy or of obsolescence, tend to reproduce a metaphysics of presence and absence that is intrinsic to the principle of state sovereignty itself. It is in this context, for example, that it is possible to understand many of the characteristic difficulties of important literatures on "world order," "interdependence," and so on.[20] It is in this context, also, that it is possible to understand some of the specific conditions under which the resolutions of state sovereignty have remained plausible. Some of these conditions are addressed by forms of international political economy that make a serious attempt to read the state in relation to class hegemonies established in the context of the global dynamics of capitalism. Other conditions are examined by analyses that draw on poststructuralist readings of the discourses of modernity; that is, on the manner in which legitimations of the principle of state sovereignty rest ultimately on an account of a sovereign subject as the founding identity of modern political life. Accounts of defense policy that stress the function of claims about security as a disciplining of common identity at home have often begun from a similar insight.[21]

Whatever else they may do or seek to achieve, attempts to develop a specifically feminist critique of theories of international relations must also engage with these historically specific conditions of possibility. For the problem is not that questions about gender have been excluded from theories of international relations. Accounts of gender identity—and of all other identities, not least those that might be articulated in relation to concepts of class and culture—are *already* incorporated into the most fundamental assumptions that permit an account of international relations to be constructed at all. Just as disciplinary conventions encourage the treatment of "ethics" or "culture" as something that must be brought to international relations,[22] as an intersection between distinctive and possibly irreconcilable phenomena, so also do these conventions encourage a similar account of gender. In fact, theories of international relations, even or perhaps especially those that are most single-mindedly realist or positivist, already express axiological and cultural positions. They also express an account of gender identity, an identity more familiarly known as the universalizing abstraction of "rational man."

*   *   *

As a practice, the principle of state sovereignty appears to be abstract. As an apparent abstraction, it is an immensely dense and effective political practice. As a politics of presence and absence, it is ever present as the condition of the possibility of modern political discourse, an empty principle that may be left to the technical quibbles of lawyers and the banal squabbles of realists/idealists and thus rendered ever absent as the condition of possibility that can be taken for granted, the point of origin and eternal return, the ground from which all may be surveyed, identified, and located.

It is easy enough to see why contemporary feminist critiques of international relations theory might be especially interested in unpacking or deconstructing claims about state sovereignty. It is, after all, a crucial reification of human identity as a particular rendition of rational man. Contemporary feminist thought has been profoundly concerned with the problematic character of political identities that—while often discussed separately from the specific principle of state sovereignty—can be understood as part of the modern, or Western, or bourgeois, attempt to resolve all claims to unity and diversity, and thus all possibilities in space and time, in a moment of autonomy.

The proliferation of descriptive terms, however—modern, bourgeois, Western, and, now, perhaps, patriarchal—is more than a little troubling. Explanations of the substantive content of claims to state sovereignty have emerged from all directions. Fixed under the sign of modernity, it can be understood in relation to transitions from hierarchies to discontinuities, from the integrations of Aristotle/Aquinas to the chasms of Augustine/Descartes, from the collective and organic to the individualistic and the mechanistic. In this context, especially, we might expect to find references to the travails of scholasticism and secularism, or the traumatic march of instrumental reason. Fixed under the sign of the bourgeoisie, state sovereignty can be understood in relation to the modalities of possessive individualism, the specificities of the capitalist state, and the antinomies of bourgeois thought. In this context, especially, we might expect to see analyses of the resonance between state sovereignty and the concept of private property, that other paradigmatic expression of spatial separations between included and excluded, part and whole, rational and lazy. Fixed under the sign of the West, state sovereignty appears as an expression of cultural peculiarities, of some essential quality of a civilization that is somehow afraid of nature, or dialectics, or tradition. Whether cast in the terms of Marx or Weber, understood as ethnocentricism or ideology, the apparent silence of a legal principle soon swells to encompass a large part of the literature on the modern human condition.

Reification and commodification, rationalization and disenchantment, objectification and representation, class determination and the relative autonomy of the state: encounters between claims to state sovereignty and the critical enquiries of modern social and political theory are not difficult to construct. Nor is it difficult to see a continuity among these critical enquiries and many of the concerns emerging from contemporary feminist theory. Yet it is worth examining this continuity more closely. State, class, race, age, and gender: the hyphenated "isms" of contemporary social and political analysis express a refusal of unicausalities and linear histories, a proliferation of cross-disciplinary perspectives, and a deep suspicion of any relapse into the

understood in this way have come to be treated as a cause for considerable celebration. For Weber, however, celebration was accompanied by a sense of despair at the costs of disenchantment, at the sweeping of all meaning to the margins of modern existence, at the iron cage of an efficient but meaningless world.

What Weber presents as the tragic ambivalence of modernity, contemporary theories of international relations present as a simple bifurcation: classical realism and neorealism; historicism and structuralism; historical/interpretive/normative speculation and social science. In this bifurcating understanding, moreover, classical realism is severed from its informing problematic, and is presented as a simple-minded account not only of the way things are, but, through an even more simple-minded appeal to a tradition, of the way things have always been. Neorealism, on the other hand, clings resolutely to the technical ground of epistemology and method, conveniently forgetting that modern epistemology and method depend on ontological constructions of knower and known, subject and object, categories and world, that are themselves constitutive of the modernity that is being explained.

It is with Weber, in short, that we can find a crucial reformulation of the modernist resolution of philosophical options expressed in the principle of state sovereignty. But this reformulation does not retain the optimistic reading of universal reason shared by, say, Hobbes and Kant. On the contrary, the resolution of universality and particularity in the sovereign state leads to the celebration of national will in a world of irreconcilable national wills. It is not surprising, therefore, that Weber's negative reading of modernity has come to seem rather embarrassing, in need of repudiation through a forthrightly positive attitude to Enlightenment, modernity, and instrumental reason.

Several contemporary trends can be read in this context:

- A new celebration of Kantian republicanism as the condition of possibility of peace.
- A rereading of traditional accounts of the possibility of interstate cooperation in terms of assumptions about the instrumental rationality of autonomous actors (essentially a reworking of the move from passions to interests that was articulated in relation to individuals sometime between Hobbes and Adam Smith).
- A strong antipathy to relapsing into any of the forms of historicism and thus, supposedly, into relativism—which, in view of the historical fate of Weberian power politics, is certainly understandable.
- An insistence, nonetheless, that appeals to Enlightenment or utilitarian efficiency remain deeply problematic. From Nietzsche, to Weber, to the early Frankfurt School, to recent skirmishes around

attempts to articulate a postmodernist attitude, modernist resolutions of philosophical options—the resolutions enshrined in the principle of state sovereignty and recast in a powerfully pessimistic way by Weber—have been treated as deeply implicated in the violence of the present rather than as a way out.

$$*\quad*\quad*$$

We live in what is widely seen as a reflective moment in contemporary social and political thought. The postwar celebration of modernist conceptions of progress, and the accompanying revival of positivistic conceptions of scientific enquiry, have been faltering for the past quarter-century. It is true that the revival of late nineteenth-century neo-Kantianism expressed in T. S. Kuhn's account of knowledge-constitutive categories was quickly absorbed into the church of empirical social science, though it was neo-Kantianism, it might be noted, against which the dogmas of logical positivism had been asserted in the first place. Even in the 1960s, however, it was difficult to engage with the literature on the philosophy of social science without realizing just how deeply aspirations for objective empiricism had been corroded, not only by obscure European philosophers of language and interpretation but even by the more skeptical (Humean and neo-Kantian) currents within empiricism itself.

As a reflective moment, though, this is also a moment of paradox. Sociologically, the orthodoxies of positivist social science remain hegemonic. Standards of professional training and research funding are still informed by the myth of the white coat. Philosophically, however, these orthodoxies are dissolving. Defenders of empirical method have been forced to become much more modest in their claims and much more sophisticated in their treatment of the logic of explanation, the requirements of model building, or the relation between hypothesis formation and data construction. Methodological orthodoxies have given way to a sometimes disconcerting proliferation of research strategies, many of them informed by the once despised professions of literature, philosophy, history, and political theory.

The theory of international relations offers a rather extreme example of this paradox. As a specifically US social science, one that became institutionalized at the height of postwar modernism and positivism, it remains deeply informed by the epistemological prejudices of that particular place and time. Though the field holds some memory of other possibilities, historicism, philosophy, political theory, and "values" are associated with traditions that are viewed as either dangerous or silly.

This explains, at least in part, the distinctly minor role played by any kind of critical theory of international relations. It also explains the extent to which debate about the possibilities of such a critique remain so caught up in questions about epistemology. The attempt to identify the sources and substance of a critical theory still seems to require a lengthy preface reminding us that we are indeed living in a postpositivist era, and that once epistemological obsessions are relaxed, some rather difficult and important ontological and axiological questions still need to be addressed. It is in this context that I would like to recapitulate and underline some of the central implications of the argument developed above.

First, it will be noted that I have explicitly refrained from attempting to apply insights from contemporary feminist theory directly to the theory of international relations. There are many reasons for this, notwithstanding my own judgment that contemporary feminist theory is one of the most crucial sites of both critical and creative political exploration. Most simply, perhaps, feminist theory is not a collection of insights that may be applied. As a fractured and heavily contested discourse, it remains a site of active political struggle. Most importantly, though, for my purposes here, it is essential to understand how questions of gender are already resolved—unsatisfactorily—in the constitutive categories of the discipline.

Most particularly, I have tried to suggest that it is essential to understand how questions of gender, along with all other questions about political identity, are resolved in an historically specific way by the principle of state sovereignty. They are also resolved, in a derivative way, by all those discourses that build on the primary resolutions of state sovereignty. The theory of international relations, I have suggested, is simply one of those derivative discourses. It continues to reproduce the articulation of universality and diversity, self and other, and space and time that was fixed, within a distinctively modern metaphysics, in early modern Europe. Notoriously, attempts to articulate alternative accounts of political identity—especially in terms of culture, class, and local community—have been captured within the resolutions of state sovereignty: the nation-state, socialism in one country, and the erosion of participatory community. Attempts to develop a critique of international relations theory in terms of identities of gender must necessarily come to terms with the extent to which the resolutions of state sovereignty remain persuasive. Not least, we have the basis here for yet another way of categorizing (and thus controlling) various kinds of feminist theory: those that find these resolutions to be plausible, and that therefore continue to work with received accounts of political community, and those that do not.

Second, to approach the problem in this manner is to highlight the priority of ontological and axiological questions. Many classifications of the feminist literature simply presume an epistemological interest. The popular trinity of empiricist, standpoint, and poststructuralist, for example, can be understood in this way. That is, we can focus on questions of identity either in relation to the abstract densities of state sovereignty or to the constructions of economy, individual subjectivity, or cultural otherness that have been framed within a parallel logic. Either way, we engage with ontological and axiological accounts of autonomy that gave rise to modern epistemology in the first place. Even to speak of objectivity or subjectivity is already to assume a world of subjects and objects which have to be reconciled through a process of knowing.

Third, these subjects and objects did not appear out of thin air. Modern conceptions of autonomous subject and objective world are usually understood as products of complex social processes, primarily those codified under terms like "the transition from feudalism to capitalism" or "from tradition to modernity." These processes can be analyzed with some degree of specificity, albeit through highly contested theoretical traditions (which have themselves been constituted through the processes that are being explained). Questions about ontology and axiology, therefore, lead directly to questions about the historical construction of political practice.

To put the matter this way seems, fourth, to affirm the continuing vitality of social and political theory rather than to strengthen the currently privileged status of an empirically conceived social science. This affirmation, however, also seems to challenge the familiar distinction between politics within states and mere relations between them, the distinction that has been the silent condition permitting the construction of received understandings of social and political theory. The affirmation ironically seems to challenge not only the myth of a tradition of international relations theory but also, and more crucially, the myth of a tradition of political theory as the story of life, liberty, and the pursuit of happiness/property in the bounded polis/state. Thus it might be said that the aspiration for a feminist theory of international relations is fundamentally misguided. Such an aspiration retains the assumption that political life can be divided into two distinct realms—an assumption codified in the principle of state sovereignty, which already expresses an account of political identity in which gender is systematically suppressed and silenced. A feminist theory of world politics, however, might be understood as a different matter. Here the difficulty is merely that of identifying possibilities for political community other than the bounded community of state, and of knowing what differences critical feminist practices might make to their achievement.

Fifth, in stressing the extent to which accounts of gender are already written into the resolutions of state sovereignty, I have emphasized a fairly abstract pattern of presence and absence in which women are silenced in a manner that affirms the sovereign voice of man. The lineage of this pattern presumably might be traced back to earlier and especially religious sources. Much of modern thought can be understood as a secularized reworking of the play of dualisms crystallized by Augustine. The pattern of presence and absence, however, can also be understood in relation to the manner in which women have been located—the household, domesticity, the labor of reproduction, the voice of peace—and thus been treated as apolitical in general and irrelevant to international relations in particular. It may be true that even the most radical of democracies stops at the door marked "national security," but those recesses of civil society in which women have their place cannot even claim rights to enter the estate. The silencing and depoliticization of women can be understood in terms of the marginalization of women's place and women's time, but so in turn can the authoritative voice of sovereignty be understood in terms of valorizations of the merely domestic, the merely reproductive, the merely nurturing, the explicitly passive voice of women.

A sixth group of implications may be simply hinted at in a metaphor, a metaphor of domesticity that nonetheless suggests a possible reading of at least some aspects of contemporary world politics. A woman's place is in the kitchen. In the kitchen are three modern conveniences. In one corner—call it, say, Central Europe—the freezer has been unplugged. Offensive odors have been sensed. Elsewhere—but nowhere in particular—the microwave is on full power, its invisible energies accelerating and transforming not only the rotting remains but seemingly everything within range. Over there—in the red-light district, perhaps, or in zones of exclusion not far from here—the garbage pail, clean on the outside, perhaps, but one would not want one's children playing in or living near it.

Like all metaphors, no doubt, this one has serious limits. But then so do those other textualizations of international relations—the conquest of *fortuna* by the virile hero or the rational sovereign; the ostinato affirmation of Man, the state, and international system as "levels," choices, and possibilities; or the story of life before international relations followed by the eternal debates, the tragic necessities, the deferred expectations. Women do have different stories to tell. Many would not begin with the benign appearance of state sovereignty. As a principle this is only an (immensely elegant and historically persuasive) answer to questions theorists of international relations no longer take seriously. The question to which it is an answer— who are we, given the palpable fragility of historically constituted certainties?—remains with us, whoever we are. Feminist critiques of international relations theory can certainly help to articulate this question a little more clearly. But to insist on the importance of this question is to call for more than just a more active intersection between feminism and international relations.

Notes

1. I treat "international relations" as an *object* of enquiry, as one constitutive aspect of contemporary world politics. It is of interest primarily as an expression of the spatial and temporal limits of specifically modern forms of political life rather than as a more or less persuasive account of contemporary world politics. For an extended critique of "international relations" in these terms, a critique that informs the argument developed here, see my *Inside/Outside:*

International Relations as Political Theory (Cambridge: Cambridge University Press, 1992).

For a comprehensive discussion of the wide range of interpretations that have been burdened with the label "critical theory of international relations," see Jim George and David Campbell, "Patterns of Dissent and the Celebration of Difference: Critical Social Theory and International Relations," in "Speaking the Language of Exile: Dissidence in International Studies," Special Issue of *International Studies Quarterly*, 34: 3, September 1990, edited by Richard K. Ashley and R. B. J. Walker, 269–294.

References to the term "critical" are fraught with difficulty. At the very least, it is necessary to distinguish between forms of critique that retain a commitment to modified forms of empiricism (postpositivism), those that take up various currents of interpretive or hermeneutic analysis, those that seek to extend Marxian political economies, those that are attracted to a Habermasian faith in Enlightenment conceptions of universal reason, and those that are informed by post-Nietzschean skepticism about philosophies of identity. Use of terms like "critical" or "reflectivist" to designate a single mode of analysis or group of scholars who work outside the presumed mainstream inevitably turns into a transparent rhetorical ploy that both legitimizes the presumed mainstream and trivializes the serious philosophical and political differences that ought to be apparent among contemporary "patterns of dissent."

My own use of the term "critical" derives most generally from various attempts to extend Kant's explorations of the conditions of possibility of knowledge in the context of post-Kantian skepticisms about the spatiotemporal guarantees that informed Kant's own account of universal rationality. It is in this specific sense that it is possible to trace the highly problematic status of social and political critique throughout the twentieth century, a status that has merely become more obvious in the wake of contemporary reflections on language, subjectivity, and so on. It is in this sense, also, that currently influential attempts to distinguish between modernity and postmodernity are so misleading.

Many of the characteristic gestures of the supposedly postmodern have been treated as part of the modern world since the early nineteenth century. Indeed, one of the key issues raised by most recent forms of critical theory, whatever their differences, is not some primordial divide between the modern and the postmodern—and thus between the objectivist and the relativist, the responsible and the irresponsible—but the erasure of critical scholarship in the name of an epistemologically legitimated social science that continues to treat ontological difficulties much as King Canute treated the incoming tide. While many interesting, and in my judgment very important, openings have been made under the sign of the postmodern, it is important to recognize continuities with earlier moments of critique, not least, given their significance for established forms of international relations theory, in the writings of Hobbes and Hume or in the characteristic disputes of European social theory between 1890 and 1920. In fact, much of the current literature on the critical theory of international relations, including the present essay, can be understood in part as an attempt to reopen earlier moments of critique that have been closed off both by the pretensions of a positivistic/utilitarian social science and by superficial claims about political realism. Similarly, I take it that attempts to articulate feminist social and political theory must engage a legacy of failed and co-opted critiques, must work within and against established accounts of what it means to be human, political, progressive, and so on, rather than simply to renounce all that has come before as fatally and irretrievably tainted. It will not do to invent some new paradigm, theory, or technique informed by the presumption of some more authentic essence, or to announce some new agent of history that might finally take the place of Newton's eternal categories or Hegel's universalizing *Geist*. As I try to show in this essay, there is rather more at stake in attempts to take a critical, reflective, or feminist stance toward theories of international relations than either the provision of better theories and explanations—as these are often conceived by claimants to an empiricist, rationalist, utilitarian, or realist mainstream—or the assertion of an already established identity from which international relations might be better surveyed.

2. For example: Grant and Newland, eds., *Gender and International Relations*; Tickner, *Gender in International Relations*; Sylvester, *Feminist Theory and International Relations in a Postmodern Era*; Peterson, "Clarification and Contestation: A Conference Report on Women, the State and War—What Difference Does Gender Make?" (Los Angeles: University of Southern California Center for International Studies, 1989); Runyan and Peterson, "The Radical Future of Realism"; Elshtain, *Women and War*; Elshtain and Tobias, *Women, Militarism, and War*; Enloe, *Does Khaki Become You?*; Enloe, *Bananas, Beaches and Bases*; and Cohn, "Sex and Death."

3. In this respect, "international relations" has much in common with the institutionalization of anthropology as a scholarly discipline, except that the fixing of center and margin in anthropology (modern and primitive, advanced and developing) has occurred as a reification of temporal trajectories, whereas international relations has depended on the reification of spatial exclusions. It is instructive, however, that although international relations has borrowed rather promiscuously from disciplines that have been able to take established forms of social and political order more or less for granted—especially sociology and economics—neither the theoretical traditions nor theoretical controversies of anthropology have been of much interest to students of international relations. In both cases, however, problems arising from the reification of otherness and the presumption of universal standards of rationality are much in evidence.

4. For a more extended discussion, see Walker, *Inside/Outside*; and Walker, "Sovereignty, Identity, Community." The attempt to unsettle the specifically modern account of political identity that informs the principle of state sovereignty is central to Ashley, "Untying the Sovereign State," Ashley, "Living on Borderlines"; Richard K. Ashley and R. B. J. Walker, "Reading Dissidence/Writing the Discipline: Crisis and the Question of Sovereignty in International Studies," in Ashley and Walker, "Speaking the Language of Exile," 367–416; and Michael Shapiro, "Sovereignty and Exchange in the Orders of Modernity," *Alternatives* 16 (Fall 1991): 447–478. Important attempts to insist that sovereignty is a concrete historical practice rather than a permanent and abstract legal code include Janice Thompson, "Sovereignty in Historical Perspective: The Evolution of State Control over Extraterritorial Violence," in *The Elusive State: International and Comparative Perspectives*, ed. James Caporoso (Newbury Park, CA.: Sage, 1989), 227–254; and Cynthia Weber, "Writing the State: Political Intervention and the Historical Constitution of State Sovereignty," Ph.D. diss., Arizona State University, May 1991.

5. On the significance of the "domestic analogy" in the theory of international relations, see Hidemi Suganami, *The Domestic Analogy and World Order Proposals* (Cambridge: Cambridge University Press, 1989).

6. It should be fairly obvious that my own sense of the proliferation of controversies about the significance of contemporary feminism is especially influenced by the ongoing encounter between feminist and poststructuralist forms of social and political theory, not least because this encounter has so effectively

highlighted the problematic character of historically constituted claims about nature, culture, and gender identity. Helpful introductions to recent debates include Nicholson, ed., *Feminism/Postmodernism*; Marianne Hirsch and Evelyn Fox Keller, eds., *Conflicts in Feminism* (New York: Routledge, 1990); Irene Diamond and Lee Quimby, eds., *Feminism and Foucault: Reflections on Resistance* (Boston, MA: Northeastern University Press, 1988); Jennifer Allen and Iris Marion Young, eds., *The Thinking Muse: Feminism and Modern French Philosophy* (Bloomington and Indianapolis: Indiana University Press, 1989); Jardine, *Gynesis*; Toril Moi, *Sexual/Textual Politics: Feminist Literary Theory* (London: Methuen, 1985); Judith Butler, *Gender Trouble: Feminism and the Subversion of Identity* (New York: Routledge, 1990); Joan Cocks, *The Oppositional Imagination: Feminism, Critique, and Political Theory* (New York: Routledge, 1989); and Chris Weedon, *Feminist Practice and Poststructuralist Theory* (Oxford: Basil Blackwell, 1987).

7. Among a vast literature, see, for example, Mies, *Patriarchy and Accumulation*; Bernard, *The Female World from a Global Perspective*; and Jayawardena, *Feminism and Nationalism in the Third World*. Unfortunately, it must be said that neither feminist nor critical social and political theory in general has been especially sensitive to the dilemmas of ethnocentricism, although helpful meditations are not difficult to find: recent examples include Gayatri Chakravorty Spivak, *The Post-Colonial Critic: Interviews, Strategies, Dialogues* (New York: Routledge, 1990); and Rey Chow, *Woman and Chinese Modernity: The Politics of Reading Between East and West* (Minneapolis: University of Minnesota Press, 1991).

8. I draw here on a large and vigorously contested literature on Machiavelli as well as on my own attempt to treat Machiavelli's questions—but not the historically specific metaphysics of space and time that informed either his answers or his way of asking the questions—as a way of destabilizing claims about a tradition of political realism in the theory of international relations; see *Inside/Outside*, chapter 2, an earlier version of which appeared as "'The Prince' and 'The Pauper': Tradition, Modernity, and Practice in the Theory of International Relations," in *International/Intertextual Relations*, ed. Der Derian and Shapiro, 25–48.

9. An impressive literature has now accumulated detailing the silences of Western political discourse on questions of gender. See, especially, Elshtain, *Public Man, Private Woman*; Okin, *Women in Western Political Thought*; Pateman, *The Sexual Contract*; Mary Lyndon Shanley and Carole Pateman, eds., *Feminist Interpretations of Political Theory* (Cambridge: Polity Press, 1991). and Brown, *Manhood and Politics*. Despite the devastating critique of established categories effected by such literature, it can also be read as evidence of the extent to which assumptions about the character and location of political community that inform the received traditions of political theory remain deeply entrenched. The addition of women's experiences to existing traditions of modern political thought does not automatically show how prevailing accounts of political community could have been, or might now become, otherwise. For a reading of this problem within contemporary struggles for socialism, see Warren Magnusson and R. B. J. Walker, "Decentring the State: Political Theory and Canadian Political Economy," *Studies in Political Economy* 26 (Summer 1988):37–71; and Magnusson, "The Reification of Political Community," in *Contending Sovereignties: Rethinking Political Community*, ed. R. B. J. Walker and Saul H. Mendlovitz (Boulder, CO: Lynne Rienner, 1990), 45–60.

10. For example, see Merchant, *The Death of Nature*. Unfortunately, renditions of the origins of modernity in terms of a crude mechanist/organicist

division still overwhelms many forms of critical enquiry—most notably those concerned with either gender or environment—that ought to have become especially sensitive to the reification of both dichotomies and histories.

11. Pateman, *The Sexual Contract*.

12. Elshtain, *Women and War*.

13. Thomas Hobbes, *Leviathan*, ed. C. B. MacPherson (London: Penguin, 1977), chapter 13.

14. Hedley Bull, *The Anarchical Society* (London: Macmillan, 1977).

15. See especially the classic discussion in Ernst Cassirer, *Individual and Cosmos in Renaissance Philosophy* (1927), trans. M. Domandi (New York: Harper and Row, 1963).

16. Andrew Linklater, *Men and Citizens in the Theory of International Relations* (London: Macmillan, 1982).

17. Witness, for example, the controversial character of C. B. Macpherson's interpretation in *The Political Theory of Possessive Individualism: Hobbes to Locke* (Oxford: Clarendon, 1962). An important exception to the prevailing silence on Hobbes and gender is Carole Pateman, "'God Hath Ordained to Man a Helper': Hobbes, Patriarchy and Conjugal Right," in Shanley and Pateman, eds., *Feminist Interpretation*, 53–73.

18. Ashley, "Untying the Sovereign State."

19. Walker, *Inside/Outside*, chapter 6.

20. Walker, "World Order and the Reconstitution of Political Life," in *The Constitutional Foundations of World Order*, ed. Richard Falk, Robert Johansen, and Samuel Kim (Albany: State University of New York Press, 1992).

21. James Der Derian, *On Diplomacy: A Genealogy of Western Estrangement* (Oxford: Basil Blackwell, 1987); David Campbell, "Global Inscription: How Foreign Policy Constitutes the United States," *Alternatives* 15 (Summer 1990): 263–286; Bradley Klein, "How the West Was One: Representational Practices of NATO," in "Speaking the Language of Exile," ed. Ashley and Walker, 311–325.

22. Walker, *Inside/Outside*, chapter 3; Walker, "The Concept of Culture in the Theory of International Relations," in *Culture and International Relations*, ed. John Chay (New York: Praeger, 1990), 3–17.

23. Raymond Aron, "Max Weber and Power Politics," in Otto Stammer, ed., *Max Weber and Sociology Today*, trans. K. Morris (Oxford: Basil Blackwell, 1979), 83–100 and Hans J. Morgenthau, *Scientific Man vs. Power Politics* (Chicago: University of Chicago Press, 1946).

24. Stephen Turner and Regis Factor, *Max Weber and the Dispute over Reason and Value* (London: Routledge and Kegan Paul, 1984) offer an especially helpful discussion of Morgenthau's political realism in this context.

Selected Bibliography

Abrams, Philip. 1988. Notes on the Difficulty of Studying the State (1977). *Journal of Historical Sociology* 1 (March): 58–89.

Ackelsberg, Martha, and Irene Diamond. 1987. Gender and Political Life: New Directions in Political Science. In *Analyzing Gender*, edited by Beth B. Hess and Myra M. Ferree. Newbury Park, CA: Sage.

Afshar, Haleh, ed. 1987. *Women, State, and Ideology: Studies from Africa and Asia.* Albany: State University of New York Press.

Anderson, Benedict. 1983. *Imagined Communities.* London: Verso.

Anderson, Perry. 1974. *Lineages of the Absolutist State.* London: New Left Books.

Anderson, Perry. 1974. *Passages from Antiquity to Feudalism.* London: Verso NLB.

Arthur, Marilyn B. 1977. "Liberated" Women: The Classical Era. In *Becoming Visible: Women in European History*, edited by Renate Bridenthal and Claudia Koonz, 62–89. Boston, MA: Houghton Mifflin.

Arthur, Marilyn B. 1984. Early Greece: The Origin of the Western Attitude Toward Women. In *Women in the Ancient World*, edited by J. Peradotto and J. P. Sullivan. Albany, NY: SUNY Press.

Ashley, Richard. 1988. Untying the Sovereign State: A Double Reading of the Anarchy Problematique. *Millennium* 7, 2 (Summer): 227–72.

Ashley, Richard. 1989. Living on Borderlines: Man, Poststructuralism, and War. In *International/Intertextual Relations*, edited by James Der Derian and Michael J. Shapiro, 259–322. Lexington, MA: Lexington Books.

Atkinson, Jane Monnig. 1982. Review Essay: Anthropology. *Signs* 8, 2: 236–58.

Balbo, Laura. 1982. The Servicing Work of Women and the Capitalist State. In *Political Power and Social Theory*, vol. 3, edited by Maurice Zeitlin. Greenwich, CT: JAI Press.

Balbo, Laura. 1987. Crazy Quilts: Rethinking the Welfare State Debate from a Woman's Point of View. In *Women and the State: The Shifting Boundaries of Public and Private*, edited by Anne Showstack Sassoon. London: Hutchinson.

Baron, Ava. 1987. Feminist Legal Strategies. In *Analyzing Gender*, edited by Beth B. Hess and Myra M. Ferree. Newbury Park, CA: Sage.

Benhabib, Seyla. 1987. The Generalized and the Concrete Other. In *Feminism as Critique*, edited by Seyla Benhabib and Drucilla Cornell. Minneapolis: University of Minnesota Press.

Benn, S. I. and G. F. Gaus, eds. 1983. *Public and Private in Social Life.* London: Croom Helm.

Bennett, Jane. 1987. *Unthinking Faith and Enlightenment: Nature and the State in a Post-Hegelian Era.* New York and London: New York University Press.

Berman, Ruth. 1989. From Aristotle's Dualism to Materialist Dialectics: Feminist Transformation of Science and Society. In *Gender/Body/Knowledge,* edited by Alison Jaggar and Susan Bordo, 224–255, New Brunswick, NJ & London: Rutgers University Press.

Bernard, Jessie. 1981. *The Female World.* New York: Free Press.

Bernard, Jessie. 1987. *The Female World from a Global Perspective.* Bloomington: Indiana University Press.

Bleier, Ruth. 1984. *Science and Gender: A Critique of Biology and Its Theories on Women.* Oxford: Pergamon.

Boals, Kay. 1975. Political Science: Review Essay. *Signs* 1, 1 (Autumn): 161–174.

Bordo, Susan. 1988. Feminist Skepticism and the Maleness of Philosophy. *The Journal of Philosophy* 85, 11: 619–626.

Bordo, Susan. 1990. Feminism, Postmodernism, and Gender-Scepticism. In *Feminism/Postmodernism,* edited by Linda Nicholson. New York and London: Routledge.

Boris, Eileen, and Peter Bardaglio. 1983. The Transformation of Patriarchy: The Historic Role of the State. In *Families, Politics, and Public Policy,* edited by Irene Diamond. New York and London: Longman.

Bourdieu, Pierre. 1977. *Outline of a Theory of Practice.* Cambridge: Cambridge University Press.

Brocke-Utne, Birgit. 1985. *Educating for Peace.* Oxford: Pergamon.

Brown, Carol. 1981. Mothers, Fathers, and Children: From Private to Public Patriarchy. In *Women and Revolution,* edited by Lydia Sargent. Boston, MA: South End Press.

Brown, Sarah. 1988. Feminism, International Theory, and International Relations of Gender Inequality. *Millennium* 17: 461–76.

Brown, Wendy. 1988. *Manhood and Politics: A Feminist Reading in Political Theory.* Totowa, NJ: Rowman and Littlefield.

Burstyn, Varda. 1983. Economy, Sexuality, Politics: Engels and the Sexual Division of Labour. *Socialist Studies/Etudes Socialiste: A Canadian Annual 1983.* University of Manitoba.

Burstyn, Varda. 1983. Masculine Dominance and the State. In *The Socialist Register,* edited by R. Miliband and J. Saville. London: Merlin Press.

Butler, Judith. 1990. Gender Trouble, Feminist Theory, and Psychoanalytic Discourse. In *Feminism/Postmodernism,* edited by Linda Nicholson. New York and Routledge: Routledge.

Cameron, Barbara. 1983. The Sexual Division of Labour and Class Struggle. *Society for Socialist Studies.* Manitoba: University of Manitoba.

Cantarella, Eva. 1987. *Pandora's Daughters: The Role and Status of Women in Greek and Roman Antiquity.* Baltimore, MD: Johns Hopkins Press.

Caporaso, James A., ed. 1989. *The Elusive State.* Newbury Park, CA: Sage.

Carneiro, Robert. 1970. A Theory of the Origin of the State. *Science* 169: 733–38.

Carnoy, Martin. 1984. *The State and Political Theory.* Princeton, NJ: Princeton University Press.

Charlton, Sue Ellen, Jane Everett, and Kathleen Staudt, eds. 1989. *Women, the State, and Development.* Albany: State University of New York Press.

Chase-Dunn, Christopher. 1990. World-State Formation: Historical Processes and Emergent Necessity. *Political Geography Quarterly* 9, 2 (April): 108–130.

Chase-Dunn, Christopher, and Thomas D. Hall, eds. 1991. *Core/Periphery Relations in Precapitalist Worlds.* Boulder, CO: Westview.

Chatterjee, Partha. 1989. Colonialism, Nationalism, and Colonised Women: The Contest in India. *American Ethnologist* 16, 4: 622–633.

Chevillard, Nicole, and Sebastien Leconte. 1986. Slavery. In *Women's Work, Men's Property*, edited by Stephanie Coontz and Peta Henderson. London: Verso.

Chodorow, Nancy. 1978. *The Reproduction of Mothering.* Berkeley: University of California Press.

Cixous, Helene. 1976. The Laugh of the Medusa. *Signs* 1 (Summer): 875–893.

Claessen, Henri J. M., and Peter Skalnik, eds. 1978. *The Early State.* The Hague: Morton Publishers.

Clark, Lorenne M. G. 1976. The Rights of Women: The Theory and Practice of Male Supremacy. In *Contemporary Issues in Political Philosophy*, edited by J. King-Farlow and W. Shea. New York: Neal Watson Academic Publications.

Cohen, Ronald. 1978. Introduction. In *Origins of the State*, edited by Ronald Cohen and Elman R. Service. Philadelphia, PA: Institute for the Study of Human Issues.

Cohen, Ronald, and Elman R. Service, eds. 1978. *Origins of the State: The Anthropology of Political Evolution.* Philadelphia, PA: Institute for the Study of Human Issues.

Cohn, Bernard S., and Nicholas B. Dirks. 1988. Issues and Agendas: Beyond the Fringe: The Nation State, Colonialism, and the Technologies of Power. *Journal of Historical Sociology* 1, 2: 224–229.

Cohn, Carol. 1987. Sex and Death in the Rational World of Defense Intellectuals. *Signs* 12 (Summer): 687–718.

Connell, R. W. 1990. The State, Gender, and Sexual Politics: Theory and Appraisal. *Theory and Society* 19: 507–544.

Coontz, Stephanie, and Peta Henderson, eds. 1986. *Women's Work, Men's Property.* London: Verso.

Corrigan, Philip, ed. 1980. *Capitalism, State Formation, and Marxist Theory.* London: Quartet Books.

Corrigan, Philip, and Derek Sayer. 1985. *The Great Arch: English State Formation as Cultural Revolution.* Oxford and New York: Basil Blackwell.

Cox, Robert W. 1983. Gramsci, Hegemony, and International Relations: An Essay in Method. *Millenium* 12, 2: 162–75.

Cox, Robert W. 1986. Social Forces, States, and World Orders: Beyond International Theory. In *Neorealism and Its Critics*, edited by Robert O. Keohane. New York: Columbia University Press.

Dahlerup, Drude. 1987. Confusing Concepts—Confusing Reality: A Theoretical Discussion of the Patriarchal State. In *Women and the State: The Shifting Boundaries of Public and Private*, edited by Anne Showstack Sassoon. London: Hutchinson.

Dalby, Simon. 1992. Security, Modernity, Ecology: The Dilemma of Post–Cold War Security Discourse, *Alternatives* 17:95–133.

Derrida, Jacques. 1976. *Of Grammatology.* Translated by G. C. Spivak. Baltimore, MD: Johns Hopkins.

Diamond, Irene, and Gloria Feman Orenstein, eds. 1990. *Reweaving the World: The Emergence of Ecofeminism.* San Francisco, CA: Sierra Club Books.

Di Stefano, Christine. 1983. Masculinity as Ideology in Political Thought: Hobbesian Man Considered. *Women's Studies International Forum* 6: 633–44.

Di Stefano, Christine. 1990. Dilemmas of Difference: Feminism, Modernity, and Postmodernism. In *Feminism/Postmodernism*, edited by Linda Nicholson. New York and London: Routledge.

Di Stefano, Christine. 1991. *Configurations of Masculinity: A Feminist Perspective on Modern Political Theory*. Ithaca, NY & London: Cornell University Press.

Dobash, R. Emerson, and Russel Dobash. 1979. *Violence Against Wives: A Case Against the Patriarchy*. New York: The Free Press.

Easton, David. 1981. The Political System Besieged by the State. *Political Theory* 9, 3: 303–325.

Eisenstein, Zillah R. 1981. *The Radical Future of Liberal Feminism*. New York: Longman.

Eisenstein, Zillah R. 1983. The State, the Patriarchal Family, and Working Mothers. In *Families, Politics, and Public Policy*, edited by Irene Diamond. New York and London: Longman.

Eisenstein, Zillah R. 1984. *Feminism and Sexual Equality: Crisis in Liberal America*. New York: Monthly Review Press.

Eisler, Riane. 1987. Human Rights: Toward an Integrated Theory for Action. *Feminist Issues* 7, 1: 25–46.

Elshtain, Jean Bethke. 1981. *Public Man, Private Woman: Women in Social and Political Thought*. Princeton, NJ: Princeton University Press.

Elshtain, Jean Bethke. 1982. Political Theory Rediscovers the Family. In *The Family in Political Thought*, edited by Jean B. Elshtain. Amherst: University of Massachusetts Press.

Elshtain, Jean Bethke. 1987. *Women and War*. New York: Basic Books.

Elshtain, Jean Bethke, and Sheila Tobias, eds. 1990. *Women, Militarism, and War*. Savage, MD: Rowman and Littlefield.

Enloe, Cynthia. 1983. *Does Khaki Become You?* Boston, MA: South End Press.

Enloe, Cynthia. 1987. Feminists Thinking About War, Militarism, and Peace. In *Analyzing Gender*, edited by Beth B. Hess and Myra M. Ferree. Newbury, CA: Sage.

Enloe, Cynthia. 1990. *Bananas, Beaches, and Bases: Making Feminist Sense of International Politics*. Berkeley: University of California Press.

Evans, Peter B., Dietrich Rueschemeyer, and Theda Skoçpol. 1985. On the Road Toward a More Adequate Understanding of the State. In *Bringing the State Back In*, edited by Peter B. Evans, Dietrich Rueschmeyer, and Theda Skoçpol. New York: Cambridge University Press.

Fausto-Sterling, Anne. 1986. *Myths of Gender: Biological Theories About Women and Men*. New York: Basic Books.

Farganis, Sondra. 1989. Feminism and the Reconstruction of Social Science. In *Gender/Body/Knowledge*, edited by Alison Jaggar and Susan R. Bordo. New Brunswick and London: Rutgers University Press.

Fee, Elizabeth. 1981. Is Feminism a Threat to Scientific Objectivity? *International Journal of Women's Studies* 4: 378–392.

Ferguson, Kathy E. 1987. Male-Ordered Politics: Feminism and Political Science. In *Idioms of Inquiry: Critique and Renewal in Political Science*, edited by Terence Ball. Albany: State University of New York.

Ferguson, Kathy E. 1983. Toward a New Anarchism. *Contemporary Crises* 7 (January): 39–57.

Ferguson, Yale H., and Richard W. Mansbach. 1988. *The Elusive Quest: Theory and International Politics*. Columbia, SC: University of South Carolina Press.

Ferguson, Yale H., and Richard W. Mansbach. 1989. *The State, Conceptual Chaos, and the Future of International Relations Theory*. Boulder, CO and London: Lynne Rienner.

Ferree, Myra M., and Beth B. Hess. 1987. Introduction. In *Analyzing Gender*, edited by Beth B. Hess and Myra M. Ferree. Newbury Park, CA: Sage.

Flax, Jane. 1987. Postmodernism and Gender Relations in Feminist Theory. *Signs* 12: 621–643.

Foley, Helene P. 1981. The Conception of Women in Athenian Drama. In *Reflections on Women in Antiquity*, edited by H. P. Foley. New York: Gordon and Breach.

Foucault, Michel. 1980. *The History of Sexuality*. Vol 1. Translated by R. Hurley. New York: Vintage.

Foucault, Michel. 1980. *Power/Knowledge*. Edited by C. Gordon. New York: Pantheon.

Franzway, Suzanne, Dianne Court, and R. W. Connell. 1989. *Staking a Claim: Feminism, Bureaucracy, and the State*. Oxford: Polity Press.

Fraser, Nancy, and Linda J. Nicholson. 1990. Social Criticism Without Philosophy: An Encounter Between Feminism and Postmodernism. In *Feminism/Postmodernism*, edited by Linda J. Nicholson. New York and London: Routledge.

Gailey, Christine Ward. 1984. Women and Warfare: Shifting Status in Precapitalist State Formation. *Culture* 4: 61–70.

Gailey, Christine Ward. 1985. The State of the State in Anthropology. *Dialectical Anthropology* 9: 65–89.

Gailey, Christine Ward. 1987. *Kinship to Kingship: Gender Hierarchy and State Formation in the Tongan Islands*. Austin: University of Texas Press.

Gailey, Christine Ward. 1987. Evolutionary Perspectives on Gender Hierarchy. In *Analyzing Gender*, edited by Beth B. Hess and Myra M. Ferree. Newbury Park, CA: Sage.

Gellner, Ernest. 1983. *Nations and Nationalism*. Ithaca, NY: Cornell University Press.

Giddens, Anthony. 1987. *The Nation-State and Violence*. Vol. 2 of *A Contemporary Critique of Historical Materialism*. Berkeley and LA: University of California Press.

Gilligan, Carol. 1982. *In a Different Voice*. Cambridge, MA: Harvard University Press.

Gimbutas, Marija. 1982. *Goddesses and Gods of Old Europe, 7000–3500 B.C.* Berkeley: University of California Press.

Glennon, Lynda. 1979. *Women and Dualism: A Sociology of Knowledge Analysis*. New York: Longman Press.

Gordon, Linda. 1990. *Women, the State, and Welfare*. Madison: University of Wisconsin.

Gramsci, Antonio. 1971. *Selections from the Prison Notebooks of Antonio Gramsci*. Translated by Q. Hoare and G. N. Smith. New York: International Publishers.

Grant, Rebecca. 1989. Feminist Criteria in International Relations Theory. Paper presented at the International Studies Association Meeting, London.

Grant, Rebecca, and Kathleen Newland, eds. 1991. *Gender and International Relations*. Bloomington and Indianapolis: Indiana University Press.

Gross, Elizabeth. 1986. Conclusion. In *Feminist Challenges: Social and Political*

Theory, edited by Carole Pateman and Elizabeth Gross. Boston, MA: Northeastern University Press.

Grossholtz, Jean. 1983. Battered Women's Shelters and the Political Economy of Sexual Violence. In *Families, Politics, and Public Policy*, edited by Irene Diamond. New York and London: Longman.

Haas, Jonathan. 1982. *The Evolution of the Prehistoric State*. New York: Columbia University Press.

Hall, John, ed. 1986. *States in History*. New York: Basil Blackwell.

Halliday, Fred. 1987. State and Society in International Relations: A Second Agenda. *Millennium* 16: 215–230.

Halliday, Fred. 1988. Hidden from International Relations: Women and the International Arena. *Millennium* 17: 419–428.

Hanmer, Jalna. 1978. Violence and the Social Control of Women. In *Power and the State*, edited by Gary Littlejohn, Barry Smart, John Wakeford, and Nira Yuval-Davis. New York: St. Martin's Press.

Haraway, Donna. 1988. Situated Knowledges: The Science Question in Feminism and the Privilege of Partial Perspective. *Feminist Studies* 14: 575–599.

Haraway, Donna. 1989. *Primate Visions: Gender, Race, and Nature in the World of Modern Science*. New York: Routledge.

Haraway, Donna. 1991. *Simians, Cyborgs, and Women: The Reinvention of Nature*. New York: Routledge.

Harding, Sandra. 1982. Is Gender a Variable in Conceptions of Rationality? A Survey of the Issues. *Dialectica* 36: 225–242.

Harding, Sandra. 1986. *The Science Question in Feminism*. Ithaca, NY: Cornell University Press.

Harding, Sandra, ed. 1987. *Feminism and Methodology*. Bloomington: Indiana University Press.

Harding, Sandra. 1991. *Whose Science? Whose Knowledge?* Ithaca, NY: Cornell University Press.

Harding, Sandra, and Merrill Hintikka, eds. 1983. *Discovering Reality: Feminist Perspectives on Epistemology, Metaphysics, Methodology, and the Philosophy of Science*. Dordrecht, Netherlands: D. Reidel Publishing Co.

Harrington, Mona. 1988. Feminism and Foreign Policy. Paper presented to the annual meeting of the American Political Science Association, Washington, DC.

Harris, Adrienne, and Ynestra King, eds. 1989. *Rocking the Ship of State: Toward a Feminist Peace Politics*. Boulder, CO: Westview.

Hartsock, Nancy. 1983. *Money, Sex, and Power*. New York: Longman.

Hawkesworth, Mary E. 1989. Knowers, Knowing, Known. *Signs* 14, 3 (Spring): 533–557.

Heise, Lori. 1989. Crimes of Gender. *Worldwatch* (March-April): 12–21.

Hekman, Susan. 1987. The Feminization of Epistemology. *Women & Politics* 7: 65–83.

Hess, Beth B., and Myra Marx Ferree, eds. 1987. *Analyzing Gender: A Handbook of Social Science*. Newbury Park, CA: Sage.

Hevener, Natalie Kaufman. 1983. *International Law and the Status of Women*. Boulder, CO: Westview.

Hodge, John L., Donald K. Struckmann, and Lynn Dorland Trost. 1975. *Cultural Bases of Racism and Group Oppression*. Berkeley, CA: Time Readers Press.

Hooks, Bell. 1984. *Feminist Theory: From Margin to Center*. Boston, MA: South End Press.

Ikenberry, G. John. 1986. The State and Strategies of International Adjustment. *World Politics* 39 (October): 53–77.

Irigaray, Luce. 1985. *This Sex Which Is Not One.* Ithaca, NY: Cornell University Press.

Jaggar, Alison. 1983. *Feminist Politics and Human Nature.* Totowa, NJ: Rowman and Allanheld.

Janssen-Jurreit, Marielouise. 1982. *Sexism: The Male Monopoly on History and Thought.* Translated by V. Moberg. New York: Farrar, Straus, & Giroux.

Jardine, Alice A. 1985. *Gynesis: Configurations of Woman and Modernity.* Ithaca, NY & London: Cornell University Press.

Jayawardena, Kumari. 1986. *Feminism and Nationalism in the Third World.* London: Zed Books.

Jones, Kathleen. 1990. Citizenship in a Woman-Friendly Polity. *Signs* 15: 781– 812.

Jones, Kathleen, and Anna Jonasdottir, eds. 1988. *The Political Interests of Gender.* London: Sage.

Keuls, Eva C. 1985. *The Reign of the Phallus: Sexual Politics in Ancient Athens.* New York: Harper and Row.

Keller, Evelyn Fox. 1985. *Reflections on Gender and Science.* New Haven, CT: Yale University Press.

Keohane, Robert O. 1988. International Institutions: Two Approaches. *International Studies Quarterly* 32, 4: 379–96.

Kerber, Linda K. 1988. Separate Spheres, Female Worlds, Women's Place: The Rhetoric of Women's History. *The Journal of American History* 75, 1 (June): 9–39.

Kirby, Andrew. 1989. State, Local State, Context, and Spatiality: A Reappraisal of State Theory. In *The Elusive State,* edited by James A. Caporaso. Newbury, CA: Sage.

Klein, Bradley S. 1988. After Strategy: The Search for a Post-Modern Politics of Peace. *Alternatives* 13 (July): 293–318.

Krasner, Stephen D. 1984. Review Article: Approaches to the State. *Comparative Politics* 16, 2: 223–246.

Kratochwil, Friedrich. 1986. Of Systems, Boundaries, and Territory: An Inquiry into the Formation of the State System. *World Politics* 39: 27–52.

Kratochwil, Friedrich, and John Gerard Ruggie. 1986. International Organization: A State of the Art on an Art of the State. *International Organization* 4 (Autumn): 753–75.

Kristeva, Julia. 1977. *About Chinese Women.* New York: Urizen.

Krouse, Richard W. 1982. Patriarchal Liberalism and Beyond. In *The Family in Political Thought,* edited by Jean B. Elshtain. Amherst: University of Massachusetts Press.

Lamphere, Louise. 1977. Review Essay: Anthropology. *Signs* 2, 3: 613–27.

Laurin-Frenette, Nicole. 1980. The Women's Movement and the State. *Our Generation* 15, 2 (Summer): 27–39.

Lawrence, Philip K. 1987. Strategy, the State, and the Weberian Legacy. *Review of International Studies* 13: 295–310.

Leacock, Eleanor. 1981. *Myths of Male Dominance.* New York: Monthly Review Press.

Lerner, Gerda. 1986. *The Creation of Patriarchy.* New York: Oxford University Press.

Levi, Margaret. 1981. The Predatory Theory of Rule. *Politics and Society* 10, 4: 431–465.

Lloyd, Genevieve. 1984. *The Man of Reason: "Male" and "Female" in Western Philosophy.* Minneapolis: University of Minnesota Press.

Lovenduski, Joni, and Jill Hills, eds. 1981. *The Politics of the Second Electorate.* London: Routledge and Kegan Paul.

MacDonald, Sharon. 1987. Drawing the Lines—Gender, Peace, and War: An Introduction. In *Images of Women in Peace and War*, edited by Sharon MacDonald, Pat Holden, and Shirley Ardener. London: Macmillan.

MacKinnon, Catharine E. 1983. Feminism, Marxism, Method, and the State: Toward Feminist Jurisprudence. *Signs* 8: 635–58.

MacKinnon, Catharine E. 1989. *Toward a Feminist Theory of the State.* Cambridge, MA: Harvard University Press.

Malson, Micheline R., Jean F. O'Barr, Sarah Westphal-Wihl, and Mary Wyer, eds. 1989. *Feminist Theory in Practice and Process.* Chicago and London: University of Chicago Press.

Mann, Michael. 1984. The Autonomous Power of the State. *Archives Européènes Sociologiques* 25: 185–213.

Mann, Michael. 1986. *The Sources of Social Power.* Vol. 1. Cambridge: Cambridge University Press.

Mann, Michael. 1988. *States, War, and Capitalism.* New York: Basil Blackwell.

Merchant, Carolyn. 1980. *The Death of Nature: Women, Ecology, and the Scientific Revolution.* New York: Harper and Row.

Mies, Maria. 1986. *Patriarchy and Accumulation on a World Scale: Women and the International Division of Labour.* London: Zed Books.

Mies, Maria. 1988. Introduction. In *Women: The Last Colony*, edited by Maria Mies, Veronika Bennholdt-Thomsen, and Claudia von Werlhof. London and New Jersey: Zed Books.

Mies, Maria, Veronika Bennholdt-Thomsen, and Claudia von Werlhof. 1988. *Women: The Last Colony.* London and New Jersey: Zed Books.

Migdal, Joel S. 1990. The State in Society: Struggles and Accommodations in Multiple Areas. *States and Social Structures Newsletter* 13: 1–5.

Minh-ha, Trinh T. 1989. *Woman, Native, Other: Writing Postcoloniality and Feminism.* Bloomington and Indianapolis: Indiana University Press.

Mohanty, Chandra Talpade. 1984. Under Western Eyes: Feminist Scholarship and Colonial Discourses. *Boundary 2*, 12, 3: 333–58.

Mosse, George L. 1985. *Nationalism and Sexuality: Respectability and Abnormal Sexuality in Modern Europe.* New York: Howard Fertiz.

Nash, June, and Maria Fernandez-Kelly, eds. 1983. *Women, Men, and the International Division of Labor.* Albany: State University of New York Press.

Nelson, Barbara J. 1989. Women and Knowledge in Political Science. *Women & Politics* 9, 2: 1–25.

Neufeld, Mark. 1990. The Reflexive Turn and IR Theory. Paper presented to the annual meeting of the Canadian Political Science Association, Victoria, May.

Neufeld, Mark. 1991. Interpretation and the "Science" of International Relations. Paper presented to the International Studies Association Meeting. Vancouver, March.

Nicholson, Linda, ed. 1990. *Feminism/Postmodernism.* New York and London: Routledge.

Nicholson, Linda. 1986. *Gender and History.* New York: Columbia University Press.

Norton, Theodore Mills. 1982. Contemporary Critical Theory and the Family: Private World and Public Crisis. In *The Family in Political Thought*, edited by Jean B. Elshtain. Amherst: University of Massachusetts Press.

O'Brien, Mary. 1981. *The Politics of Reproduction*. London and Boston: Routledge and Kegan Paul.

Okin, Susan Moller. 1979. *Women in Western Political Thought*. Princeton, NJ: Princeton University Press.

Paggi, Leonardo, and Piero Pinzauti. 1985. Peace and Security. *Telos*, no. 63: 3–40.

Parpart, Jane L., and Kathleen A. Staudt, eds. 1988. *Women and the State in Africa*. Boulder, CO: Lynne Rienner.

Pateman, Carole. 1983. Feminist Critiques of the Public/Private Dichotomy. In *Public and Private in Social Life*, edited by S. Benn and G. Gaus. New York: St. Martin's Press.

Pateman, Carole. 1985. *The Problem of Political Obligation*. Berkeley: University of California Press.

Pateman, Carole. 1986. Introduction. In *Feminist Challenges*, edited by Carole Pateman and Elizabeth Gross. Boston, MA: Northeastern University Press.

Pateman, Carole. 1988. *The Sexual Contract*. Stanford, CA: Stanford University Press.

Peterson, V. Spike. 1988. An Archeology of Domination: Historicizing Gender and Class in Early Western State Formation. Ph.D. diss., The American University, Washington, DC.

Peterson, V. Spike. 1990. Whose Rights? A Critique of the "Givens" in Human Rights Discourse. *Alternatives* 15: 303–344.

Peterson, V. Spike. 1991. Gendered States and States of Gender. Unpublished ms.

Peterson, V. Spike. 1991. Transgressing Boundaries: IR Theory, Feminism, and States. Unpublished ms.

Pitkin, Hanna Fenichel. 1984. *Fortune Is a Woman: Gender and Politics in the Thought of Niccolò Machiavelli*. Berkeley, CA: University of California Press.

Poggi, Gianfranco. 1978. *The Development of the Modern State*. Stanford, CA: Stanford University Press.

Pomeroy, Sarah B. 1975. *Goddesses, Whores, Wives, and Slaves: Women in Classical Antiquity*. New York: Schocken Books.

Randall, Vicky. 1987. *Women and Politics: An International Perspective*. 2d ed. Chicago, IL: University of Chicago Press.

Rapp, Rayna. 1979. Review Essay: Anthropology. *Signs* 4, 3: 497–513.

Reardon, Betty. 1985. *Sexism and the War System*. New York: Columbia University Teachers College.

Robbins, Kittye Delle. 1983. Tiamat and Her Children: An Inquiry Into the Persistence of Mythic Archetypes of Woman as Monster/Villainess/Victim. In *Face to Face*, edited by Meg McGavran Murray. Westport, CT: Greenwood Press.

Rorty, Richard. 1979. *Philosophy and the Mirror of Nature*. Princeton, NJ: Princeton University Press.

Rorty, Richard. 1985. Solidarity or Objectivity? In *Post-Analytic Philosophy*, edited by J. Rajchman and C. West. New York: Columbia University Press.

Rosenau, James N. 1989. The State in an Era of Cascading Politics. In *The Elusive State*, edited by J. Caporaso. Newbury Park, CA: Sage.

Ruddick, Sara. 1989. *Maternal Thinking*. Boston, MA: Beacon Press.

Ruggie, John Gerard. 1983. Continuity and Transformation in the World Polity. *World Politics* 35: 261–285.

Runyan, Anne Sisson. 1988. Feminism, Peace, and International Politics: An

Examination of Women Organizing Internationally for Peace and Security. Ph. D. diss., American University, Washington, DC.

Runyan, Anne Sisson. 1990. Gender Relations and the Politics of Protection. *Peace Review* (Fall).

Runyan, Anne Sisson, and V. Spike Peterson. 1991. The Radical Future of Realism: Feminist Subversions of IR Theory. *Alternatives* 16: 67–106.

Runyan, Anne Sisson, and V. Spike Peterson. Forthcoming. *Global Gender Issues*. Boulder, CO: Westview.

Ryan, Michael. 1982. *Marxism and Deconstruction*. Baltimore, MD: Johns Hopkins University Press.

Sacks, Karen. 1982. *Sisters and Wives: The Past and Future of Sexual Equality*. Urbana: University of Illinois Press.

Sassoon, Anne S., ed. 1987. *Women and the State*. London: Hutchinson.

Schiebinger, Londa. 1989. *The Mind Has No Sex: Women in the Origins of Modern Science*. Cambridge, MA: Harvard University Press.

Scott, Joan. 1986. Gender: A Useful Category of Historical Analysis. *American Historical Review* 91: 1053–75.

Seager, Joni, and Ann Olson. 1986. *Women in the World: An International Atlas*. New York: Simon and Schuster.

Sederberg, Peter C. 1984. *The Politics of Meaning: Power and Explanation in the Construction of Social Reality*. Tucson: University of Arizona Press.

Segal, Lynne. 1987. *Is the Future Female? Troubled Thoughts on Contemporary Feminism*. New York: Peter Bedwick Books.

Sen, Gita, and Caren Grown, eds. 1987. *Development, Crises, and Alternative Visions: Third World Women's Perspectives*. New York: Monthly Review Press.

Shiva, Vandana. 1988. *Staying Alive: Women, Ecology and Development*. India: Kali for Women and London: Zed Books.

Silverblatt, Irene. 1988. Women in States. *Annual Review of Anthropology*: 427–60.

Skoçpol, Theda. 1985. Bringing the State Back In: Strategies of Analysis in Current Research. In *Bringing the State Back In*, edited by Peter B. Evans, Dietrich Rueschmeyer, and Theda Skoçpol. New York: Cambridge University Press.

Spender, Dale. 1981. Introduction. In *Men's Studies Modified*, edited by Dale Spender. Oxford and New York: Pergamon Press.

Spender, Dale, ed. 1981. *Men's Studies Modified: The Impact of Feminism on the Academic Disciplines*. Oxford and New York: Pergamon Press.

Stiehm, Judith. 1983. The Protected, the Protector, the Defender. In *Women and Men's Wars*, edited by Judith Stiehm. Oxford: Pergamon Press.

Stiehm, Judith, ed. 1983. *Women and Men's Wars*. Oxford: Pergamon Press.

Stimpson, Catharine R. Women as Knowers. 1984. In *Feminist Visions*, edited by Diane Fowlkes and Charlotte McClure. University, AL: University of Alabama Press.

Stone, Merlin. 1976. *When God Was a Woman*. New York: Harcourt Brace Jonanovich.

Sylvester, Christine. 1989. Feminist Postmodernism, Nuclear Strategy, and International Violence. Paper presented at the International Studies Association Meeting, London, March.

Sylvester, Christine. Forthcoming. *Feminist Theory and International Relations in a Postmodern Era*. Cambridge: Cambridge University Press.

Thomas, George M., and John Meyer. The Expansion of the State. *Annual Review of Sociology* 10: 461–82.

Tickner, J. Ann. 1989. Redefining Security: A Feminist Perspective. Unpublished ms.

Tickner, J. Ann. 1992. *Gender in International Relations: Feminist Perspectives on Achieving Global Security*. New York: Columbia University Press.

Tilly, Charles, ed. 1975. *The Formation of National States in Western Europe*. Princeton, NJ: Princeton University Press.

Tilly, Charles. 1985. War Making and State Making as Organized Crime. In *Bringing the State Back In*, edited by Peter B. Evans, Dietrich Rueschemeyer, and Theda Skoçpol. New York: Cambridge University Press.

Tilly, Charles. 1990. *Coercion, Capital, and European States, AD 990–1990*. Cambridge, MA: Basil Blackwell.

Tilly, Louise A., and Joan W. Scott. 1978. *Women, Work, and Family*. New York: Holt, Rinehart, and Winston.

Tinker, Irene, ed. 1990. *Persistent Inequalities*. New York and Oxford: Oxford University Press.

Tong, Rosemarie. 1989. *Feminist Thought: A Comprehensive Introduction*. Boulder, CO: Westview.

Trebilcot, Joyce, ed. 1983. *Mothering: Essays in Feminist Theory*. Totowa, NJ: Rowman and Allanheld.

Tronto, Joan. 1987. Beyond Gender Difference to a Theory of Care. *Signs* 12, 4: 644–63.

United Nations. 1991. *The World's Women: 1970–1990 Trends and Statistics*. New York: United Nations.

Vickers, Jill McCalla. 1990. At His Mother's Knee: Sex/Gender and the Construction of National Identities. In *Women and Men: Interdisciplinary Readings on Gender*, edited by Greta Hoffmann Nemiroff. Toronto: Fitzhenry & Whiteside.

Von Werlhof, Claudia. 1988. On the Concept of Nature and Society in Capitalism. In *Women: The Last Colony*, edited by Maria Mies, Veronika Bennholdt-Thomsen, and Claudia von Werlhof. London and New Jersey: Zed Books.

Waerness, Kari. 1987. On the Rationality of Caring. In *Women and the State: The Shifting Boundaries of Public and Private*, edited by Anne Showstack Sassoon. London: Hutchinson.

Walker, R. B. J. 1988. State Sovereignty, Global Civilization, and the Rearticulation of Political Space. World Order Studies Program. Occasional Paper No. 18. Center for International Studies. Princeton, NJ: Princeton University.

Walker, R. B. J. 1990. Sovereignty, Identity, Community: Reflections on the Horizons of Contemporary Political Practice. In *Contending Sovereignties: Rethinking Political Community*, edited by R. B. J. Walker and Saul H. Mendlovitz. Boulder, CO: Lynne Rienner.

Walker, R. B. J. 1990. Sovereignty, Security, and the Challenge of World Politics. *Alternatives* 15, 1: 3–28.

Whitworth, Sandra. 1989. Gender and International Relations: Beyond the Inter-Paradigm Debate. *Millennium* 18, 2: 265–272.

Wilson, Elizabeth. 1977. *Women and the Welfare State*. London: Tavistock.

Yoffee, Norman, and G. Cowgill, eds. 1988. *The Collapse of Ancient States and Civilizations*. Tucson: University of Arizona Press.

Zaretsky, Eli. 1986. *Capitalism, the Family, and Personal Life*. Revised edition. New York: Perennial Library.

About the Contributors

Jean Bethke Elshtain is Centennial Professor of Political Science and Professor of Philosophy at Vanderbilt University, Nashville, TN.

Rebecca Grant is a member of the Political Science Department of the Rand Corporation of Santa Monica, CA.

Mona Harrington, a lawyer and political scientist, is a writer in Cambridge, MA.

V. Spike Peterson is Assistant Professor of Political Science at the University of Arizona in Tucson.

Anne Sisson Runyan is Associate Professor and Chair, Department of Political Science at Potsdam College of the State University of New York.

Christine Sylvester is Associate Professor of Political Science at Northern Arizona University in Flagstaff.

Mary Ann Tetreault is Professor of Political Science and Geography at Old Dominion University of Norfolk, VA.

J. Ann Tickner is Associate Professor of Political Science at the College of the Holy Cross, Worcester, MA.

R. B. J. (Rob) Walker teaches in the Department of Political Science and the Graduate Program in Contemporary Social and Political Thought at the University of Victoria, Victoria, B.C.

Index*

Addams, Jane, 87
Adultery, 35, 36
Africa, 46
AIDS, 71
Aliens: illegal, 71
Amazons, 88–89
American Civil War, 91
American Revolution, 91, 100, 101, 111
Anderson, Benedict, 148–149
Androcentrism, 6–7, 8, 15
Animism, 126
Anthropocentrism, 151
Anthropomorphism, 129, 130–131
Anti-militarists, 15
Arendt, Hannah, 144
Argentina, 147
Aristotle, 14, 33, 36, 37, 54, 85, 125
Armstrong, John A., 151–152
Aron, Raymond, 193
Ashcraft, Richard, 72
Ashley, Richard, 161, 188
Asquith government, 86
Association of American Foreign Service Wives, 165
Athens, 33, 35–38, 60(n29), 144
Atomism, 73, 109
Augustine, St., 197
Authority, 13, 23, 25–26(n27), 45, 111; in Athens, 35, 36; centralized, 5, 19, 34, 39; construction of, 40–41; patriarchal, 123, 186; public, 43–44

Autonomy, 54, 69, 108, 155, 177(n74), 196–197; and obligation, 156–157; relational, 172, 176(n66)

Bacon, Francis, 127
Balkan Wars, 169
Bananas, Bases, and Beaches: Making Feminist Sense of International Relations (Enloe), 159
Barber, Benjamin, 157
Benedict, Ruth: *The Chrysanthemum and the Sword*, 104
Bennett, Jane, 126, 135–136
Bilbo, Theodore, 70
Blacks, 79, 103, 170
Bodin, Jean, 127, 149
Borah, William, 70
Borders: integrity of, 79
Bradford, George, 130–131
Brittain, Vera: *Testament of Youth*, 145; *Chronicle of Youth*, 146
Brown, Peter, 100
Brown, Sarah, 165
Bruni, Leonardo, 112
Bryan, William Jennings, 70
Bull, Hedley, 155
Bush, George, 67, 90, 147
Business, 70, 76–77

Callicott, J. Baird, 130, 131, 132
Caritas, 146, 147, 152
Castro, Fidel, 147
Cawley, R. McGreggor, 123
Chaloupka, William, 123

*Index prepared by Linda Gregonis.

About the Book

While international relations (IR) theorists are increasingly critical of neorealist assumptions about the state and the international system, few have explored the gendered construction of the state and its implications for IR. Recognizing this, the authors of this innovative collection explore how core concepts of political and IR theory—the state, sovereignty, power—are reframed through feminist lenses.

Taking seriously the question "What difference *does* gender make?," the authors illuminate new directions in IR by highlighting the role of gender in constructing and maintaining the sovereign state system and its related notions of security, autonomy, and identity.